THE
# NEW YORK
# YANKEES
FANS'
# BUCKET LIST

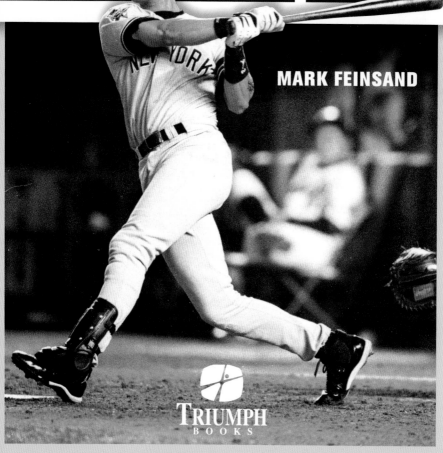

**MARK FEINSAND**

TRIUMPH
BOOKS

Library of Congress Cataloging-in-Publication Data available upon request

This book is available in quantity at special discounts for your group or organization. For further information, contact:

**Triumph Books LLC**
814 North Franklin Street
Chicago, Illinois 60610
(312) 337-0747
www.triumphbooks.com

Printed in U.S.A.
ISBN: 978-1-62937-339-3
Design by Andy Hansen
Page production by Patricia Frey

*To Dena, Ryan, and Zack: you inspire me every day.*
*Whatever is on our bucket list, I hope we do it together.*

*In memory of Jack Falla. Thanks for getting me into this*
*whole crazy business to begin with, my friend.*

# Contents

# *Foreword*

**M**any people associate the "bucket list" concept with those entering their later years, when time becomes something to treasure.

For a baseball player, your bucket list begins to formulate at a very young age.

Coming up through the minors, just making it to the big leagues was a huge deal. It took me five years. Toward the end, you would give anything just to say you made it to the majors for one day.

There comes a point in time where you just doubt everything, that you'll ever make it. Setting foot on the field at Kauffman Stadium for the first time the day of my major league debut was surreal. Running in from the bullpen, it felt like I was running underwater. Just to say I did it, that I made it, was my biggest bucket list moment.

But as you go through a baseball career, your bucket list items change. You get greedier the more you get. You keep upping the ante along the way.

First, it was getting to the big leagues. Then it was winning Rookie of the Year (which I did not), then winning a Cy Young and a World Series championship (both of which I did). It's amazing how you adjust your sights as you move up the ladder.

Growing up in the Midwest, one of my biggest goals was to pitch at Wrigley Field. During my rookie season in 1987, I finally got that opportunity.

I was so nervous the night before that start, I couldn't sleep. I tossed and turned all night and kept looking at the clock. It was a day game at Wrigley, so I said, "To hell with it," and went to the ballpark at about 6:00 AM.

I was the first one there. I sat up in the stands just looking around, trying to soak it all in. I ended up exhausting myself. It didn't go so well, but it was a bucket list moment nonetheless.

Pitching at Fenway Park—another iconic ballpark—was the same kind of thing for me. Growing up in Kansas City, we would play Wiffle ball in my backyard—it was "Coneway Park" if I was trying to be Luis Tiant or "Conedlestick Park" if I wanted to be Juan Marichal. Getting the chance to pitch in places like Fenway Park and Candlestick Park was a big deal to me.

You never really think about throwing a perfect game, so I can't say that was ever on my bucket list, though it remains one of the greatest accomplishments of my career.

When I had surgery to remove an aneurysm in May 1996, I had no idea whether I would ever pitch again. I didn't know what an aneurysm was, and even the doctors couldn't tell me if it was going to happen again if I pitched. There was no basis for comparison, so it was really breaking new ground.

At that point, the only thing on my baseball bucket list was throwing another meaningful pitch. I came back on September 2 and pitched seven no-hit innings against Oakland before Joe Torre pulled me. People ask me about the most emotional game I've ever pitched, and it was that comeback game over the perfect game or any World Series game.

I thought I was done. My dad was sitting over the dugout, and I can't ever remember another time that I pitched in a major league game and could make eye contact with my father, who was my coach in Little League. I felt like a little kid again.

Anytime I try to look back and say, "I wish I would have done a little more," I kind of shake myself and say, "I got way more than I ever thought I was going to get." I feel very thankful, very comfortable in my own skin as far as that goes.

As for Yankees fans, here are a few items you should all have on your own bucket lists:

**Sit in the bleachers.** I did it once and it was eye-opening for me to see it from that perspective. Everybody should sit with the Bleacher Creatures at some point in his or her life.

**Eat a postgame meal on Arthur Avenue.** After you take in a game at Yankee Stadium, head over to Arthur Avenue afterward for dinner at Dominick's or any of the great Italian restaurants over there.

**Attend Old Timers' Day.** I've become a fan of Old Timers' Day. I never thought I would, but now it's pretty fun. It's going to get more and more interesting the next few years if some of these guys start to come back.

**Attend a ticker-tape parade.** I never could have imagined what a ticker-tape parade would be like. The first one in 1996 was overwhelming. You can't prepare for anything like that. That many people, that kind of adulation coming your way. Even for a fan, it's one of the ultimate experiences.

The last one might not be as easy as the others, but if you can ever do it, you won't regret it: find the bar that David Wells hangs out at. I'll probably be there, so you can buy us a beer and hear some great stories. Going drinking with Boomer and Coney—that's a bucket list item, for sure!

—David Cone

# Acknowledgments

There are many people I would like to thank for their help on this book, most notably those who lent their time for interviews, both on the phone and in person: Jim Abbott, Marty Appel, Lindsay Berra, Aaron Boone, Bartolo Colon, Billy Crystal, Jack Curry, Bucky Dent, Brett Gardner, Michael Gibbons, Joe Girardi, Stacey Gotsulias, Didi Gregorius, Jeff Idelson, Reggie Jackson, David Kaplan, Michael Kay, Jim Leyritz, Bill Madden, Tom McGarry, Vinny Milano, Tony Morante, Paul O'Neill, Andy Pettitte, Brian Richards, Dave Righetti, Alex Rodriguez, CC Sabathia, Buck Showalter, Charley Steiner, John Sterling, Nick Swisher, Mark Teixeira, Chris Vollmer, Suzyn Waldman, David Wells, and Bernie Williams.

Special thanks to David Cone, not only for sitting down with me for a pair of interviews, but also for writing the foreword.

Given the time crunch baseball writers face throughout the season, special thanks to Peter Abraham, Kristie Ackert, Jordan Bastian, Jason Beck, Dan Connolly, Alyson Footer, Alden Gonzalez, Jane Lee, Andy McCullough, Scott Merkin, Doug Miller, La Velle Neal, Jack O'Connell, Jesse Sanchez, Susan Slusser, Justin Tasch, and Marc Topkin for assisting me in various ways.

Plenty of research went into this project, so thanks to Jason Zillo and Lauren Moran of the Yankees' media relations department, Jon Shestakofsky of the National Baseball Hall of Fame, Rick Vaughn, John Cirillo, and Steve Fortunato for their help along the way. I would also like to thank the folks at Baseball-Reference.com, a site I simply could not live without.

Some of my friends on the Yankees beat helped me with ideas as I began to put the book together during spring training, so many thanks to Pete Caldera, Bryan Hoch, Chad Jennings, and Sweeny Murti for being there as I embarked on this project. Also, thanks to my friend Josh Sipkin, who's always happy to serve as my second set of eyes.

Ariele Goldman Hecht took many wonderful photos of me, proving her genius as a photographer regardless of her subject.

A huge thank you to Filip Bondy for recommending me to Tom Bast of Triumph Books. And thanks, of course, to Tom, for trusting me not to screw this whole thing up. Also to Michelle Bruton, my wonderful editor.

Stacey Glick has been my sounding board on potential book ideas for several years, so thanks to her for putting up with me and helping guide me throughout this entire process. I couldn't have done this without you.

To Mom and George, Dad and Ellen, thanks for all your encouragement not only on this book, but for everything over the years.

Lastly, the biggest thank you goes to Dena, Ryan, and Zack, who not only left me alone to write this whole thing, but serve as my inspiration on a daily basis.

# Chapter 1

# Yankee Stadium

*This is where it all begins—*
*the cathedral of baseball.*

*Consider this chapter a guide to the Yankees'*
*palatial ballpark in the Bronx; a what-*
*where-when-why manual on getting the*
*most out of any trip to Yankee Stadium.*

Opened in 2009, the newest version of Yankee Stadium gives fans the feel and look of the old ballpark with all the bells and whistles of a new stadium. (Mark Feinsand)

# Attend a Game at Yankee Stadium

**WHERE:** Yankee Stadium

**WHEN:** 81 regular season games each season

**HOW TO DO IT:** Buy tickets at Yankees.com

**COST FACTOR:** Varies based on seats

**BUCKET RANK:** 🪣 🪣 🪣 🪣 🪣

No longer the "House that Ruth Built" since the move across 161st Street in 2009—many refer to it now as the "House that Jeter Built" or the "House the Boss Built"—Yankee Stadium remains among the most famous sports venues in the world.

For any Yankees fan, there's nothing like the experience of hopping on the subway (the B, D, and 4 lines all take you to the 161 Street–Yankee Stadium station) and heading to the ballpark to catch a game. The team's history is on display from nearly every angle, from the photos of all 27 championship teams that hover over concession stands to Monument Park to the legendary frieze that evokes memories of the old yard across the street.

There is plenty to see before you enter the stadium, starting with Babe Ruth Plaza, which lines 161st Street. The plaza recounts the Great Bambino's life through a series of porcelain images and storyboards, giving you a look at the most celebrated slugger of all time.

Look from the street at the architecture of the ballpark, which was designed to pay homage to the original Stadium that legends such as Ruth, Lou Gehrig, and Joe DiMaggio called home.

Inside the stadium, check out the Great Hall, a 31,000-square-foot space that features enormous double-sided banners of Yankees greats, a 24-foot-high, 36-foot-wide HD video board, and several concession and merchandise stands.

Both Monument Park and the Yankees Museum (more on these later) are must-see stops for any fan, offering a look at the team's retired numbers, plaques, and monuments, as well as a great collection of memorabilia from the most successful franchise in North American sports history.

While you're at the game, you're going to want to eat. Unlike the old stadium, the new place offers much more than hot dogs, sausages, and chicken fingers, giving fans a wide variety of options to choose from.

Among the most popular concessions are the steak sandwiches at Lobel's of New York (Sections 133 and 321), BBQ at Brother Jimmy's (Sections 133, 201, 214, and 320A), the meatball parm sandwich at Parm (Section 105), and the cheesesteak at Carl's Steak, which can be had with Cheez Whiz or white American cheese (Sections 107, 223, and 311). Melissa's Farmers Market (Section 121B) offers a variety of choices for those seeking healthy options.

If you're looking for a sit-down meal, both NYY Steak and the Hard Rock Cafe are good spots to dine before the game.

Sightlines are good from pretty much every seat in the ballpark, though if you're looking to spoil yourself, sink some dollars into tickets in the Legends Seats in the area behind home plate. The view from down low can't be beat, and tickets also include entrance into

*If you're heading to the Bronx, check out some of the great places to eat and drink before or after a Yankees game.* (Mark Feinsand)

*The old Yankee Stadium was home to hundreds of incredible players and many memorable moments.* (Mark Feinsand)

the club behind the seats, giving you a smorgasbord of dining options that will make you forget you're at a ballpark.

"It's hard to do, but a must-thing for any Yankees fan is to see a game in the Legends Seats," said Michael Kay, a longtime Yankees broadcaster. "It's pretty amazing. The amenities are great, the restaurant is incredible, and the food is never-ending. It's pretty neat."

For the true baseball fan, Kay also recommends a different view.

"When my kids are old enough to understand, I want them to sit in the upper deck in the last row," Kay said. "That's where I always used to sit; it gives you a whole perspective, seeing the entire field from above."

Some fans are quick to point out that the new stadium doesn't have the history or atmosphere that the old park did; they're right to some extent. Although you can no longer point to center field and say, "That's where Joe D. and the Mick stood," the Yankees have provided plenty of memorable moments during the early years in their new home.

From the World Series championship in the stadium's inaugural 2009 season to Mariano Rivera setting baseball's all-time saves record to Derek Jeter passing Lou Gehrig for the team's all-time hits mark or recording his 3,000th hit, fans have already been treated to their fair share of history.

As for the aura—and mystique, which Curt Schilling memorably pointed out during the Yankees' improbable Game 4 and 5 wins in the Bronx in the 2001 World Series—there is one important constant that moved from one stadium to the other: Yankees fans.

"There's an edge to the Bronx," said former Yankee and current YES Network broadcaster David Cone.

Yes, there are more corporate fans in the ballpark now than there used to be, but the true fans still remind visiting players where they are.

"The fans are loud and they're smart," said Alex Rodriguez, who played five years in the old stadium and eight seasons in the new one. "They know when to cheer, they know when to put pressure on the other team; they're always into the game. One thing you know playing there is that it doesn't matter who you're playing; it could be a Tuesday night in July, they're never going to let you get back on your heels and get comfortable. I always appreciated that.

"The stadiums are both great for different reasons. You'll never replace the feeling of nearly 60,000 people hanging all over you, but in 2009, we took that energy and brought it across the street. You see the history, you see the fans, the energy in the Stadium, who wouldn't want to be a part of that?"

# Join the "Bleacher Creatures" for Roll Call

**WHERE:** Yankee Stadium

**WHEN:** 81 regular season games each season

**HOW TO DO IT:** Buy tickets at Yankees.com

**COST FACTOR:** Varies based on seats

**BUCKET RANK:** 🪣 🪣 🪣 🪣 🪣

One of Yankee Stadium's greatest traditions came as a result of boredom.

It was May 1996 during an afternoon game against the Chicago White Sox that the Roll Call was born.

"People were bored; we said, 'Do you think we can get Tino [Martinez] to wave to us?'" said Vinny Milano, better known as "Bald Vinny" in the bleachers. "That's literally how it started. We started chanting Tino's name and he turned around and waved.

"We thought, 'Holy shit. They hear us.' Unheard of. You could scream all day long and never get a reaction. As soon as you get a reaction? It's on. It broke the wall between the fan and the players on the field. It was crazy to even think about it.

"We started moving around the field and calling every player's name. They talked about it after the game on MSG after our first Roll Call and that's how it was born. It became a tradition."

The "Bleacher Creatures," as the group of fans in the section is known, have been around since the mid-1980s, though they became a cult of sorts in New York after *Daily News* columnist Filip Bondy began writing about them during the '96 season.

Bernie Williams recalled being one of the first players involved in the Roll Call, noting the persistence of the fans in the bleachers.

"What really caught my attention the first couple of times was that they weren't taking no for an answer," Williams said. "I had to acknowledge them or they weren't going to stop. It started with me in center field, then left field, and then right field. Then it started trickling down to the infield. Once you got called, they wouldn't stop until you waved or tipped your cap.

"Whether we were struggling or doing well – and granted, we were doing well most of the time – they never changed. It became a staple of being at Yankee Stadium. I was proud to be a part of that whole thing."

The Roll Call, as it became to be known, begins with the center fielder, followed by the left fielder, right fielder, first baseman, second baseman, shortstop, and third baseman.

"You'd listen for your name," former right fielder Paul O'Neill said, "because you'd better salute them."

On rare occasions, the pitcher and catcher will also be included, though David Wells was the only pitcher that was a regular part of the Roll Call.

Joe Girardi, who caught for the Yankees from 1996 to '99 before later becoming the manager in 2008, was always jealous of his teammates' participation in the tradition.

"You're watching all these other guys do things and I'm thinking, 'I can't do anything—

I'm back here calling signs!'" Girardi said. "It's special to be part of that. When you talk about the Roll Call, it just says 'Yankee Stadium.'"

When Hideki Matsui played his first home game as a Yankee in 2003, the chant of "Mat-su-i!" went on for nearly two minutes as the left fielder had no idea he was supposed to acknowledge the crowd.

Matsui's ignorance was understood, as he had never seen or heard of such a thing playing in Japan. But third baseman Scott Brosius, a key cog on the Yankees' championship teams from 1998 to 2000, was known for taunting the Bleacher Creatures by making them wait for a response.

New Yankees would sometimes be caught off guard the first time they heard their names, while others took the field for the first time in the Bronx with anticipation of being part of the Roll Call.

"I love it," Alex Rodriguez said. "I thought it was one of the neatest things when I first came over from Texas."

Each Roll Call begins with the leader—Milano held that role for several years—shouting "Yo, Bernie!" (or whoever is playing center field that day) at the center fielder before making the rounds. That forged a special relationship between the Creatures and Williams, who manned center field for the first decade of the Roll Call's existence.

"We love Bernie forever," Milano said. "Roll Call used to center on Bernie and then everybody else. Bleacher Creatures have a special place for Bernie, and we feel he's been improperly left out of the whole Core Four thing. Andy [Pettitte] left and Bernie never did, even though he had a chance to."

One of Milano's favorite Roll Call moments centered around Williams, who showed a sense of humor few realized he had.

"It was Bernie bobblehead day," Milano said. "Instead of waving, he turned around and bobbled his head. It's one of my favorite things I've seen at the stadium."

In 2006, Williams had been taken out of center field and reduced to a designated hitter role to open the season. Batting ninth in the lineup, he began the home opener in the clubhouse, so he was unaware that the Bleacher Creatures were chanting his name—something they rarely did for a DH since he was not on the field.

Pitcher Shawn Chacon ran to the clubhouse to inform Williams.

"Shawn came into the clubhouse and said, 'They want you down there,'" Williams said after the game. "By the time I went down, it was already calm."

Right fielders always had a special bond with the Creatures, starting with O'Neill in 1996.

"You start to see guys, the regulars," O'Neill said. "You see them every day. Those are your true fans. Those are the guys that were there before it became cool to be there with the winning. There was nothing better than getting a big hit, hitting a home run, then running out to right field next inning to the Bleacher Creatures cheering."

For the past decade or so, outfielders have taken to creating custom responses to the Creatures. Nick Swisher stood at attention and saluted, while Brett Gardner flexes like a pro wrestler. According to Milano, Johnny Damon was the first to customize a Roll Call response back in 2006.

"Everybody used to just wave, but Johnny got down on one knee and did the double finger-point," Milano said. "He's the father of all the outfielders doing their own thing."

Swisher's salute became his signature during his four years in pinstripes.

"It was a match made in heaven; they appreciated me and I appreciated them for everything they did," Swisher said. "I came up with the salute in part because my grandfather was a military man, but also it was saluting the fans for the way they brought me in and the way they made me feel every time I took that field."

In this era of free agency, players move from team to team regularly. That doesn't stop the Bleacher Creatures from welcoming back their old friends in familiar fashion, giving some former Yankees the Roll Call treatment even while they wear another uniform.

When Jason Giambi left the Yankees after the 2008 season, he said the following season, "The biggest thing I miss is the Roll Call. There's no doubt about it; it's the best thing in baseball."

Not surprisingly, Giambi received a Roll Call chant when he returned to the Bronx as a member of the Oakland Athletics.

"I was honored and grateful to get that reception," Giambi said.

Other former players to receive such an honor from the Creatures include Alfonso Soriano, Wells, Damon, and Swisher.

"That doesn't happen very often," Swisher said. "I definitely had a special bond that will never be forgotten. Not many people get to experience that."

The Bleacher Creatures resided in sections 37 and 39 at the old Yankee Stadium, relocating to section 203 in the new stadium when it opened in 2009. The vibe isn't quite the same as it used to be, but for a first-timer who has never done it, sitting among the Creatures and chanting Roll Call is an experience not to be missed.

"It's weird how Roll Call is here now, thinking about how it was at the old stadium," Milano said. "We were just there to make noise, be as loud and obnoxious as humanly possible. It still happens every day. When the crowd is electric, it's still one of the best places in the world to sit. We have our own brand of fun. We try to keep it as alive as possible."

*If you've never been to Stan's Sports Bar before a Yankees game, you haven't had the full Bronx experience.* (Mark Feinsand)

# Party Pregame at Stan's Sports Bar

**WHERE:** 836 River Avenue, Bronx, NY

**WHEN:** Before or after every Yankees home game

**COST FACTOR:** No cover charge

**BUCKET RANK:** 🪣 🪣 🪣 🪣 🪣

. . . . . . . . . . . . . . . . . . . . . . . . . . . . . . . . . . . . . . . . . . . . . . .

**F**ootball stadiums have elaborate tailgating parties. Yankee Stadium has Stan's Sports Bar.

Think of it as the Bronx's very own version of Cheers, only instead of everybody knowing your name, they all speak the same language: Yankees baseball.

"It's like going to your old house," said Chris Vollmer, a former Yankees season-ticket holder and a fan since the mid-1980s. "Your father went there, your uncles went there; it's tradition. It's part of the tradition of going to Yankee Stadium.

"Every true Yankees fan goes there. You have that bond with everybody in the place. People are telling stories about some game they went to, some moment they saw."

Season-ticket holders use Stan's as a customary pregame meeting spot, while tourists make a point to stop in at the bar before their maiden voyage to Yankee Stadium.

"It's a tradition," said Tom McGarry, who has been a bartender at Stan's since 2007. "It's been here since 1979, so people have been coming here just as their parents did. People have met their wives here, met their husbands here. It's a tradition; if you go to Yankee Stadium, you go to Stan's first, you go to the game, then you go back to Stan's."

Structurally, the place is nothing special. Walk in from River Avenue and you see a long bar accessible from both sides, the bar top covered with 8x10 photos taking patrons through the Yankees' illustrious history in chronological order.

Starting with black-and-white pictures of Babe Ruth and Lou Gehrig, a walk around the bar takes you through a journey from Joe D. to Mickey to Reggie to Donnie to Derek. You can spend a half hour just looking at the photos, though it's unlikely you'll be able to see them all during pregame as beers and plates will surely be in your way.

The walls are adorned with old illustrations and murals of Yankees greats, photos, and more. On the top of the street-side wall, you'll find replicas of the Yankees' retired numbers. And if it looks like there's one too many, you're not wrong: Stan's has already put up a pinstriped No. 2 with the retired numbers despite the fact that the Yankees had not officially retired Derek Jeter's number as of 2016.

*Stan's Sports Bar is the ultimate pregame stop before any Yankees game in the Bronx.* (Mark Feinsand)

Jeter showed up at Stan's during his final season in 2014, making a pit stop in the legendary establishment while filming a farewell commercial for Gatorade.

"So this is Stan's," Jeter said as he walked through the doors like thousands of his fans had done before.

"It was crazy," McGarry said. "He kept introducing himself, 'Hi, I'm Derek.' We were like, 'Yeah, we know who you are.'"

Stan's is the pregame or postgame spot for Yankees fans, though fans of other teams are more than welcome. McGarry said fans promote "a friendly rivalry type of atmosphere," no matter what jersey or cap you may be wearing. Even Red Sox gear.

"We get a lot of out-of-towners, especially fans of teams that travel a lot like Detroit, Toronto, and Baltimore," McGarry said. "Everyone

# YANKEE TAVERN OFFERS AN ALTERNATIVE

Stan's Sports Bar is a River Avenue tradition, but some think of it as the fraternity house for Yankees fans.

For the more adult crowd—or those with children—the Yankee Tavern may be your speed.

Nearly as old as the original Yankee Stadium itself—open since 1925, Babe Ruth himself used to frequent the establishment—the tavern features walls and shelves filled with historic Yankees memorabilia including an autographed photo of Joe DiMaggio and a signed Yogi Berra bat. The tavern refers to itself as "the original sports bar."

The walls are covered with history, as dozens of framed Yankees photos hang throughout the establishment. A painted mural of the old Stadium is a reminder of the team's pre-2009 home.

"It's just a family atmosphere," said "Bald Vinny" Milano of Bleacher Creature fame. "Unlike Stan's, which has no seats, there's a big dining room area in the back and it's kid-friendly. Everybody knows you there. Stan's is the bro bar; Yankee Tavern is where you go if you want to sit and watch the game."

wears their team's stuff here. And there seems to be at least one Red Sox hat in the crowd every game no matter who we're playing. If you're funny about it, you can talk trash and get away with it."

All 12 televisions are usually set to some type of baseball programming, showing live games whenever they're on. Whether it's a game that impacts the Yankees—a Red Sox-Blue Jays game, for instance—or a Padres-Diamondbacks matchup that means very little to anybody in New York, baseball is always the focal point of the sports-centric saloon.

"Everyone here loves baseball; that's the common theme," McGarry said. "If there's a no-hitter going on, no matter if it's the Mets, Red Sox, or whoever, we'll put it on one of the televisions and everyone will pay attention to it because we all love baseball. It's a baseball bar and everyone loves baseball here."

For a typical night game, Stan's is packed by 6:00 PM as people make their way from work to the B, D, or 4 train, then straight to the bar beneath the elevated 4 train, just a stone's throw from the site of the old Stadium. By the third or fourth inning, it's a ghost town as virtually every patron has made their way into the game.

"Stan's is an underrated part of the Yankee Stadium experience," David Cone said. "I've been there a few times and it's a great meeting spot before or after a game."

For a big game—think Opening Day or the postseason—fans fill the bar all night, watching the Yankees on one of Stan's 12 televisions.

"If it's Opening Day or a big game, it's packed all day," McGarry said. "If you can't get a ticket, come to Stan's and hang out. You'll get at least half the experience."

And if the Yankees win that big game? The party can go on for hours, long after the stadium has emptied.

"The best experience I ever had at Stan's was after Aaron Boone hit his home run to win the 2003 pennant," Vollmer said. "River Avenue was so packed and that place was crazy. Every time they showed the replay of the home run on the TV, the entire place relived it. It was amazing."

# Take a Tour of Monument Park

**WHERE:** Yankee Stadium

**WHEN:** Opens when gates open; closes 45 minutes before first pitch

**COST:** Free with game ticket

**BUCKET RANK:** 🪣 🪣 🪣 🪣 🪣

Just about every ballpark in the majors honors the greats of its franchise's history in some form or fashion, but few have enough to create an area such as Yankee Stadium's Monument Park.

"Monument Park is the most exclusive part of not only Yankee Stadium, but any other sports arena," said Yankees historian Tony Morante. "There's no other like it."

In 1932, the Yankees dedicated their first monument in the original Yankee Stadium, honoring late manager Miller Huggins, who died suddenly in 1929. Huggins guided the Yankees to six American League pennants and three World Series championships in his 11-plus seasons at the helm, beginning a long line of legendary skippers in the Bronx.

Eight years later, the Yankees hung their first plaque on the center-field wall, honoring former owner Jacob Ruppert, who built Yankee Stadium and set the tone for the organization's winning tradition.

Two more monuments were added in the 1940s: Lou Gehrig received one in 1941, followed by Babe Ruth in 1949. Gehrig's monument was unveiled one month after his death, while Ruth's was erected in the year following his passing.

"In its origin, it was on the playing field and it wasn't even called Monument Park," said Marty Appel, author of *Pinstripe Empire* and a former Yankees public relations director. "It was three monuments and a bunch of plaques, but it was so iconic to Yankee Stadium."

The next plaques placed in center field honored general manager Ed Barrow in 1954, then Joe DiMaggio and Mickey Mantle in 1969.

Because the plaques were located approximately 10 feet in front of the center-field wall on the warning track, balls would occasionally be hit to the area and roll behind the monuments.

According to the book *The Gospel According to Casey*, an outfielder was once struggling to retrieve a ball that had rolled into the monuments when manager Casey Stengel shouted, "Ruth, Gehrig, Huggins, somebody get that ball back to the infield!"

When the Stadium was renovated in 1976, the plaques and monuments were moved into an enclosed area between the Yankees and visitors bullpens, creating what we now know as Monument Park.

"It was George Steinbrenner's appreciation of the history that made that happen," Appel said. "When he wrote that $10 million check [to purchase the team], it included the history. For all the negative things that surrounded his first dozen years as owner, his appreciation for the legacy was so strong and that was a positive thing.

"It became more of a destination. It became accepted that when you went to Yankee Stadium, you had to visit Monument Park."

In 1976, two more plaques were added to memorialize managers Stengel and Joe McCarthy. During the 1980s, the Yankees added 10 more plaques to Monument Park: Thurman Munson (1980), Elston Howard and Roger Maris (1984), Phil Rizzuto (1985), Billy Martin

(1986), Whitey Ford and Lefty Gomez (1987), Yogi Berra and Bill Dickey (1988), and Allie Reynolds (1989).

As of 1996, the only monuments built had been Huggins, Gehrig, and Ruth, each of them dedicated following their deaths. On August 25, 1996, one year after Mantle's death, his plaque was removed from Monument Park, replaced by a fourth monument. The Yankees did the same for DiMaggio on April 25, 1999, less than two months after his passing.

"Monument Park became a Mecca," Morante said. "It's part of the fabric of New York."

The original Mantle and DiMaggio plaques were donated to the Yogi Berra Museum & Learning Center in Montclair, New Jersey, where they remain on display today.

The organization has also dedicated plaques to a pair of non-uniformed Yankees legends, honoring longtime broadcaster and "Voice of the Yankees" Mel Allen in 1998, and Bob Sheppard, the longtime public address announcer known as the "Voice of Yankee Stadium," in 2000.

Over the years, other legendary players, coaches, and managers have been honored with plaques: Don Mattingly (1997), Reggie Jackson (2002), Ron Guidry (2003), Red Ruffing (2004), Tino Martinez, Rich "Goose" Gossage, Paul O'Neill, and Joe Torre (2014), Bernie Williams, Willie Randolph, Mel Stottlemyre, Jorge Posada, and Andy Pettitte (2015), and Mariano Rivera (2016).

The Yankees aren't the only ones recognized in Monument Park, however.

Plaques commemorating the visits of Pope Paul VI in 1965 and Pope John Paul II in 1979 were dedicated by the Knights of Columbus, while another was added in 2008 following the visit of Pope Benedict XVI. Nelson Mandela's 1990 visit to the Stadium was also commemorated by a plaque.

In a pregame ceremony on September 11, 2002, the Yankees dedicated a monument in remembrance of the victims and heroes of the 9/11 tragedy the previous year. It was the sixth monument dedicated at the Stadium, though the first to non-Yankees personnel.

Two months after George Steinbrenner died, the entire team joined the Steinbrenner family and some Yankees alumni to unveil a monument in the owner's honor.

"He resurrected a famed organization and brought it back into prominence," Morante said.

In all, there are seven monuments and 35 plaques in Monument Park, making it a must-see destination for any Yankees fan.

- - - - - - - - - - - - - - - - - - - - - - - - - - - - - - - - - -

# Buy a Pinstriped Jersey—with No Name on the Back!

There is no more classic uniform in baseball—or sports, for that matter—than the Yankees' home pinstripes. Even non-baseball fans immediately associate the look with baseball's most successful franchise.

The interlocking NY on the front-left chest, the crisp pinstripes, and the number on the back make for a simple, elegant jersey with no bells and whistles. So why do some people insist on buying jerseys with a player's name on the back? Those don't exist!

"The names on the jerseys are horrendous," said Vinny Milano, better known as "Bald Vinny" of Bleacher Creature fame.

# TEN COOLEST YANKEES JERSEYS TO OWN

O bviously buying a jersey of your favorite player is the way to go in most cases, but if you're struggling to decide which Yankees jersey to add to your collection, here are some to consider.

**No. 3:** You can't ever go wrong with the Great Bambino. Babe Ruth is the best player in the history of the game and his jersey will stand the test of time.

**No. 4:** Unlike every other between 1 and 68, this is the only one that was worn by exactly one player: Lou Gehrig. After the Iron Horse retired, nobody ever wore the digit again, making him the first and last man ever to wear it.

**No. 6:** Retired in 2014 for Hall of Fame manager Joe Torre, No. 6 has also been worn by Tony Lazzeri (1929–37), Joe Gordon (1938–46), and Roy White (1969–79), among others. Little known fact about No. 6: It was Mickey Mantle's first number when he came up in 1951.

**No. 8:** The only number retired for two different players: Yogi Berra and Bill Dickey.

**No. 9:** Just as Mantle wore No. 6 when he first came up, few people realize that Joe DiMaggio wore No. 9 in 1936 before switching to his legendary No. 5 the following year. Other notable No. 9s: Roger Maris, Graig Nettles, and Hank Bauer.

**No. 18:** Two different World Series MVPs have worn this digit: Scott Brosius (1998) and Don Larsen (1956). Other notables include Johnny Damon, Didi Gregorius, and Whitey Ford, who wore 18 in his rookie year of 1950.

**No. 24:** This one's had a rich history over the past 30 years: Rickey Henderson, Tino Martinez, Robinson Cano, and now, Gary Sanchez. Hopefully Sanchez won't follow in the footsteps of another notable 24: Kevin Maas.

**No. 30:** Several key players have worn 30 through the years: Eddie Lopat (1948–55), Willie Randolph (1976–88), and David Robertson (2008–14), but the biggest reason to wear 30 is Mel Stottlemyre, who wore it from 1964 to '74 while pitching for the Yankees.

**No. 42:** Sixteen players wore this number before 1995, and while Major League Baseball retired it in 1997 for Hall of Famer Jackie Robinson, it wasn't officially retired by the Yankees until the end of 2013, when legendary closer Mariano Rivera finally hung up his spikes and stopped wearing it.

**No. 54:** Two of the most intimidating relievers in history have worn this number with the Yankees—and we're not even talking about Mariano Rivera! Rich "Goose" Gossage formed part of his Hall of Fame résumé in this number, while Aroldis Chapman was unleashing 105-mph fastballs with No. 54 on his back in 2016.

The famous interlocking NY logo first showed up on the New York Highlanders uniform in 1909, though according to the Yankees, it was originally created in 1877 by Louis B. Tiffany for a medal given by the New York City Police Department to Officer John McDowell, the first NYC officer shot in the line of duty.

Speculation is that because one of the Highlanders' owners, Bill Devery, was a former NYC police chief, the team adopted the design to represent the club. It first appeared on the cap and the left sleeve of the jersey in 1909, though the famed pinstripes didn't appear for three more years.

The pinstripes didn't become permanent until 1915, a look that has not changed in more than a century. The Yankees used a few different cap designs between 1903 and 1922, when the current look—a solid navy cap with the interlocking NY logo—became permanent.

A separated "N" and "Y" had been on the left breast of the jersey until 1917, when the team removed the monogram and went with a plain, pinstripes-only look. It remained that way until 1936, when they reinstated the interlocking NY, a look the team still uses to this very day.

In 1929, the Yankees came up with the idea to make numbers a permanent part of the uniform, a concept the Cleveland Indians also adopted. The Yankees were rained out on Opening Day, making the Indians the first team to officially use numbers on their backs, though the idea originated in New York.

The numbers were assigned based on the batting order. Leadoff hitter Earle Combs wore No. 1, followed by No. 2 Mark Koenig, No. 3 Babe Ruth, No. 4 Lou Gehrig, No. 5 Bob Meusel, No. 6 Tony Lazzeri, No. 7 Leo Durocher, No. 8 Johnny Grabowski, No. 9 Benny Bengough, and No. 10 Bill Dickey, the final three sharing catching duties throughout the season.

At least, that was supposed to be the batting order. Manager Miller Huggins switched things up with the lineup at one point during the season, but the players did not switch numbers to match their new spots in the batting order.

"I saw a picture from a game in 1929 and you can see the scoreboard; they have Gehrig batting third and Ruth batting cleanup, so it says 1-2-4-3," said Yankees Museum curator Brian Richards. "It was supposed to be based on the batting order, but Gehrig wasn't hitting so they flipped them around."

Representing your favorite team by wearing their jersey to a game or your favorite sports bar is a big part of being a fan. But wear the actual jersey, with nothing more than a logo on the front (or *New York* if you're buying a road jersey) and a number on the back. The

Yankees don't put names on the back of their jerseys, so don't put one on yours.

The best part of going old school? In this age of free agency and frequent player movement, buying a jersey with a number and no name means you can still wear it with pride even if the player wearing that number leaves.

For instance, I'm sure plenty of people bought No. 24 jerseys when Tino Martinez was manning first base for the Yankees in the late 1990s, but in the 15 years since Martinez left New York, that jersey became a Robinson Cano jersey from 2006 to '13. Then in 2016, it became a Gary Sanchez jersey!

• • • • • • • • • • • • • • • • • • • • • • • • • • • • • • • • • • • •

# Relive the Past at Old Timers' Day

**"T**he right fielder, No. 21, Paul O'Neill."

He may have retired after the 2001 season, but if you're longing to hear "The Warrior" introduced for one of his meticulous at-bats, we've got the perfect answer: Old Timers' Day.

Every summer, the Yankees invite dozens of former players back to the Bronx for a trip down memory lane. Some played integral roles in championship seasons, while others may have had but a handful of at-bats, but on this day, they're all Yankees.

"Baseball is passed down from generation to generation," said longtime Yankees broadcaster Michael Kay, who has co-emceed the event for more than 20 years. "On Old Timers' Day, a grandfather, a father, and a kid can be sitting together and they can all identify with a player and tell the others about them. That's pretty cool. It's kind of like a passing of the torch and a passing of the memories."

O'Neill remembers the other side of Old Timers' Day, being an active player watching Hall of Famers take over his field for a couple hours on a sunny summer day.

"How often do you walk in a locker room and see Mickey Mantle and Joe DiMaggio?" O'Neill said. "Those names are almost fictitious names to everybody. You just don't put yourself in the same locker room as those people."

Current Yankees likely feel the same way when championship players such as O'Neill, David Cone, and Hideki Matsui take the field these days, evoking memories of the franchise's most recent championship teams.

"The first few times, it's a little embarrassing," O'Neill said. "You can't have Old Timers' Day in other cites because they don't have the traditions and the names."

"You get to put the uniform on again, though there are some lumpy bodies under there," Cone said. "It's not the prettiest sight in the locker room. There's still a lot of pride wearing those pinstripes."

The first Old Timers' Day took place in 1939, when the Yankees brought back many of Lou Gehrig's former teammates on the day he gave his "Luckiest Man" speech. The second didn't take place until 1947, which began the tradition as it's known today.

The 2016 edition included appearances by recent stars such as O'Neill, Matsui, Cone, Bernie Williams, John Wetteland, and Joe Girardi, but it's the players from previous eras that often draw equally loud cheers.

Bucky Dent, Ron Guidry, Rich "Goose" Gossage, Lou Piniella, Willie Randolph, and Roy White all took part in the festivities, evoking memories of the late-1970s title teams.

"I think it's a thrill; you get to see a bunch of your teammates, and there aren't a lot of settings where that happens and you can all get together," Girardi said. "You reminisce about a lot of good times. That's so special. Also, to see the guys that played before you—some of them 30 or 40 years before you—it's really amazing to watch them walk out. They're so beloved by the fans. Yankees fans don't forget. That's the amazing thing to me."

For more than 45 years, DiMaggio was the highlight of Old Timers' Day, drawing the biggest ovation as the final player introduced. The tradition of Hall of Famers at the event continues to this day; Whitey Ford, Gossage, Reggie Jackson, Rickey Henderson and Joe Torre all appeared in 2016, making Old Timers' Day one of the biggest gathering of Hall of Famers outside of Cooperstown.

The Yankees also recognize a handful of late legends, inviting their widows to the field to join many of their husbands' former teammates. In 2016, Arlene Howard (widow of Elston Howard), Helen Hunter (widow of Jim "Catfish" Hunter), Jill Martin (widow of Billy Martin), Diana Munson (widow of Thurman Munson), and Kay Murcer (widow of Bobby Murcer) all attended Old Timers' Day.

It's not only the stars that feel the love on Old Timers' Day. Fans will never forget Charlie Hayes catching the final out of the 1996 World Series, and they make sure he knows that when he's introduced. The same goes for left-handed reliever Graeme Lloyd, who got some huge outs during that same Fall Classic.

"It's nice to be remembered," Cone said. "It's nice to see the look on some of the real old timers' faces, guys like Hector Lopez, that come back. Even some of the lesser names, they're all so proud to have been a Yankee and to get an ovation from the crowd when they go out there. The sense of history, the sense of being remembered, it's tremendous."

The fans understand that history. For every player introduced to the crowd, there's likely a moment or two that fans immediately recall upon hearing their name.

"Some of these guys that may not have gotten more than a cup of coffee, they get to come back and relive a special time in their lives," Yankees historian Tony Morante said.

The "Bleacher Creatures" make sure every player on the field gets the red-carpet treatment, making for what "Bald Vinny" Milano calls "the longest day of the year."

"We Roll Call everybody," Milano said. "There's something cool about hearing your name chanted by fans, so we try to do it for as many people as possible. It is so hard because they don't really announce the lineups and I'm jotting names down on paper. It's always fun seeing guys that were heroes to you back on the field. There are a lot of special memories for a guy like Charlie Hayes."

After the Old Timers' Game—it typically lasts three innings, and while we're immediately reminded that these guys are no longer in baseball shape, there's usually a highlight or two, such as Matsui's 2016 home run against Cone—the current team takes the field for a game, giving fans a unique doubleheader experience.

"They have such a great history, they can bring back players that sport championship rings," Kay said. "A lot of organizations can't do that. To still be able to bring back guys that played and won in the 1950s and '60s, the Yankees are the team that can do that—and now it's extended to the teams from the 1990s. If you have a rich history and you're willing to spend the money like the Yankees are to bring them all together for a weekend, it means a lot to the fans."

# Play Hooky on Opening Day

**H**ope springs eternal. Never is this truer than on Opening Day, when the Yankees head home after seven weeks in sunny Florida.

Whether the Yankees open their season at home or on the road, Derek Jeter always said the season didn't really start until the Yankees played their home opener.

Each year, fans, players, and media alike descend upon Yankee Stadium for the first game in the Bronx, wishing each other "Happy New Year" as another season of Yankees baseball gets underway.

Fans play hooky from school and work to welcome the Yankees back to New York, getting their first look at that year's edition of the Bronx Bombers.

"It's like the first day of school," said "Bald Vinny" Milano. "You miss everybody all winter and then you come back and see all your old friends."

There are 81 home games every year, but there's nothing like Opening Day.

New players look to make a strong first impression on the home fans, especially those replacing fan favorites the way Tino Martinez did with Don Mattingly in 1996 or Didi Gregorius did with Derek Jeter in 2015.

For Paul O'Neill, Opening Day was always a special day, though he recalled his first opener in the Bronx in 1993 and remembered being more anxious than usual.

"I remember being nervous for my first Opening Day at Yankee Stadium," O'Neill said. "Opening Day every year, there are butterflies. Yankee Stadium only added to it, because you want to get off to a good start at home."

In years following a World Series championship, the home opener is a chance to reflect on the previous year's success, closing the book on another memorable season.

"Opening Day after you won the World Series and you're raising flags is the best," O'Neill said. "Spring training always felt one day too long. You couldn't wait to get going."

Here's a look at 10 memorable Opening Day games in the Bronx:

### 1. April 18, 1923
The Yankees open their new ballpark with a 4–1 win over the Red Sox. Babe Ruth delivers the big blow, a three-run home run in the third inning against his former team.

### 2. April 17, 1951
Joe DiMaggio starts on his final Opening Day, driving in a run in a 5–0 win against the rival Red Sox. Also knocking in a run that day: a 19-year-old rookie named Mickey Mantle.

### 3. April 13, 1955
The biggest Opening Day rout in Yankees history sees them beat the Senators 19–1. Mickey Mantle, Yogi Berra, and Moose Skowron all go deep in the win, while Whitey Ford pitches a complete game. Ford even has three hits and four RBI in the win.

### 4. April 13, 1978
In his first home game after his legendary three-homer night in Game 6 of the 1977 World Series, Reggie Jackson belts a three-run home run in the first inning of a 4–2 win over the White Sox. The game is delayed when fans shower the field with "Reggie" candy bars.

### 5. April 9, 1996
Andy Pettitte pitches 6⅓ innings on a snowy day in the Bronx, beating the Royals 7–3. A rookie shortstop named Derek Jeter goes 1-for-3 with a run scored while batting ninth in his first home opener.

### 6. April 10, 1998
The 1998 Yankees would go on to win 114 games, an American League regular season record at the time. They show what kind of offense they could be in the home opener, outlasting Oakland 17–13 as Tino Martinez homers and drives in five runs.

### 7. April 11, 2006
The Yankees trail 7–4 after seven innings, but Derek Jeter's three-run home run caps a five-run eighth to lift the Bombers to victory against the Royals. Mariano Rivera puts the tying runs on base in the ninth before locking down the win.

### 8. April 1, 2008
In the final home opener at the old Stadium, Chien-Ming Wang—a 19-game winner in 2006 and '07—outduels Toronto's Roy Halladay in Joe Girardi's first game as Yankees manager.

### 9. April 13, 2010
The Yankees receive their 2009 World Series rings during a pregame ceremony, as does Angels designated hitter Hideki Matsui, the World Series MVP, who joins his old teammates at the end of the ceremony. Prior to the ceremony, Joe Girardi and Derek Jeter bring George Steinbrenner his seventh—and final—World Series ring.

### 10. April 7, 2014
Derek Jeter plays his final Opening Day, going 1-for-4 with a double and run scored in a 4–2 win over the Orioles and manager Buck Showalter, Jeter's first-ever big-league manager.

# October Is Where Yankees Are Made: Go to a Playoff Game

**A** chill in the air. It might not be ideal baseball weather for many fans, but when it comes to October in the Bronx, there's nothing better.

The Yankees played in the postseason 52 times in their first 114 years, easily the most of any team in the majors. Their 27 World Series championships and 40 league pennants make them the most successful franchise in North American sports—and Yankee Stadium has been the site of some of the greatest moments in baseball history.

"The energy is literally indescribable," said Andy Pettitte, who won championships in both the old and new Yankee Stadium. "I don't know why it is the way it is, but night games, the playoffs, the feel is just completely different. For a player—and it has to be the same way for a fan—it's just a drastic change from the regular season."

The sellout crowd holds its collective breath as every pitch is delivered to the plate, the fans aware of the enormous stakes. The momentum can change in an instant, but for Yankees players, the fans give them an extra boost that provides a huge home-field advantage.

"Especially toward the end of my career, the confidence that I brought to the field, the comfort level that I had in the playoffs, and the surroundings with the fans and the energy that they brought, I felt like we would be able to get the big hit or the big out when we needed one," said Pettitte, who won the clinching game in all three rounds of the 2009 postseason including the ALCS and World Series at home. "The fans were a huge part of that for me. As a player, you feed off of that. I was able to dial in my focus even more in the games in October. There's no way to describe it because I've never had a feeling like that before. It's an amazing feeling."

Before the Yankees moved to their new ballpark, players often described the fans as "being on top of you," something that was lost in the move across 161st Street. But don't let the hype fool you; being part of a postseason crowd at the stadium remains a fan experience not to be missed.

Don't take my word for it. Take it from a couple of die-hard fans who have been part of those crowds over the past two decades as much as anybody.

"There's always an electricity," said "Bald Vinny" Milano. "There's always a buzz on River Avenue; the bars are packed. Everybody wants to see those memorable moments. That's why you come to the games. They're memories."

"People talk about the new stadium not being as loud as the old stadium, but that's because of the acoustics," said Stacey Gotsulias, a longtime season-ticket holder. "The old stadium, the upper deck hung over everything and there were a lot more people up there than there are now. But in 2009, those games were loud. It felt like the old stadium. When the Yankees are doing well and good things are happening, it's just as loud."

In Seattle, the Seahawks refer to the home crowd as the "12th Man," relying on the noise to disrupt their opponents' flow during the game. It's not as easy for a baseball crowd to affect the game to that extent, but the fans at Yankee Stadium give it their best effort, attempting to intimidate opposing players, many of whom have never seen or heard anything like a playoff crowd in the Bronx.

"In 2009, it was loud, but the thing that shocked me was the 2015 wild-card game against the Astros," said longtime Yankees broadcaster Michael Kay. "I thought it was deafening; the crowd was so into it. The acoustics in the new park aren't the same as the old one, because there the fans were on top of you. It's the fans, though.

"The history of the fans is passed on from generation to generation. When it's a big moment, they know it's time to get loud and that they're a part of the action on the field. They can spur on what happens."

For the Yankees, the regular season has always been a means to get to the postseason; October is where true Yankees are made. Seasons are defined by championships, not wins. For a fan, there is no better feeling than singing "New York, New York" as the Yankees shake hands—or, if you're lucky, pile up on the mound—to celebrate a postseason victory.

"It's the mecca," Alex Rodriguez said. "It's the capital of baseball. Everyone who loves baseball like we do, you think about playoff baseball, October baseball – the Bronx is where it belongs."

· · · · · · · · · · · · · · · · · · · · · · · · · · · · · · · ·

# Argue Yankee Stadium's Top 10 Postseason Moments

The House that Ruth Built was known as the cathedral of baseball, the home of more memorable moments than any other ballpark in the majors.

Many of those highlights took place between April and September, but those that happened during the month of October represented the best the sport had to offer.

Paring the list down to 10 was a challenge, as I could write an entire book based on these moments alone (something to consider, I suppose). Actually, it was so difficult I'm giving you 11, and while others' choices may differ, there's no arguing the impact these had on the celebrated history of the world's most famous baseball team. Create your own top 10 list (or 11, in my case) and try to convince your friends you're right.

### 1. Yankees vs. Red Sox: Game 7, 2003 ALCS

It's odd to think that my No. 1 moment would come in a non-championship year, but that's the magnitude that Aaron Boone's 11th-inning walk-off home run against Boston's Tim Wakefield had on not only the rivalry, but the sport as a whole.

Boone's home run was the exclamation point on what remains one of the most memorable games in recent memory. Game 7, the American League pennant on the line, Grady Little, Pedro Martinez, Jorge Posada, Hideki Matsui, Jason Giambi...all of it led up to the first-pitch knuckleball that Boone sent into the left-field seats, adding his name to an exclusive list that had previously included only Bucky Dent in Yankees–Red Sox lore.

### 2. Yankees vs. Dodgers: Game 5, 1956 World Series

To throw a perfect game on any day is a magnificent feat. To do it in the World Series? That's legendary.

Don Larsen retired all 27 Dodgers batters in Game 5 of the 1956 World Series, giving the Yankees a 3–2 lead in a series they would ultimately win in seven games. Mickey Mantle's fourth-inning home run off Sal Maglie would be all the support Larsen needed as he struck out seven. Larsen threw only 97 pitches to complete his masterpiece, getting to a three-ball count against only one batter all night—and that was Pee Wee Reese in the first inning.

Although Roy Halladay of the Phillies twirled a no-hitter in Game 1 of the 2010 NLDS, Larsen's perfecto remains the only no-hitter in World Series history.

### 3. Yankees vs. Pirates: Game 4, 1927 World Series

The 1927 Yankees were a regular season juggernaut that went 110–44, but only a World Series would validate the greatness of that team. Babe

Ruth hit .400 with two homers in the series, including one in each of the two games at the Stadium en route to a four-game sweep. His two-run blast in the fifth gave the Yankees a lead over the Pirates, though it took a two-out wild pitch—after the Babe had been intentionally walked to load the bases for Tony Lazzeri—to clinch the title. It was the first of 10 World Series clinchers in the Bronx for the Yankees.

**4. Yankees vs. Braves: Game 6, 1996 World Series**
After falling behind 2–0 with a pair of losses in the Bronx, the Yankees won three straight in Atlanta's Fulton County Stadium, giving them a chance to win their first World Series title since 1978 back at home in Game 6.

Joe Girardi's RBI triple sparked a three-run third inning against future Hall of Famer Greg Maddux, while Jimmy Key and four relievers hung on for a 3–2 win and a wild party throughout the city.

**5. Yankees vs. Dodgers: Game 1, 1949 World Series**
Tommy Henrich's game-winning home run off Don Newcombe in the ninth inning lifted Allie Reynolds and the Yankees to a 1–0 victory, a series the Yankees would capture in five games after winning three straight at Ebbets Field. It was the first of five straight World Series championships for the Yankees, the first time a team accomplished that feat.

**6. Yankees vs. Royals: Game 5, 1976 ALCS**
Tied 6–6 entering the ninth inning of the decisive Game 5, Chris Chambliss launched the Yankees to their first World Series in 12 years, belting a walk-off home run off Kansas City's Mark Littell.

Like Boone's pennant-winning homer 27 years later, Chambliss' home run got the Yankees as far as they would go that fall as they lost the World Series to the Reds in a four-game sweep.

**7. Yankees vs. Dodgers: Game 6, 1977 World Series**
Reggie Jackson hit three home runs on his only three swings of the night, guiding the Yankees to a six-game World Series victory over

the Dodgers. It was the Yankees' first championship since 1962, ending a 15-year drought.

### 8. Yankees vs. Mariners: Game 2, 1995 ALDS
The Yankees were stuck in another lengthy drought, missing the playoffs for 12 straight seasons beginning in 1982. They finally returned as the American League's first-ever wild-card team in 1995, providing fans with a memorable night in Game 2 as Jim Leyritz hit a two-run, walk-off home run against Tim Belcher in the 15th inning, ending a five-hour, 12-minute marathon that concluded shortly before 1:30 AM.

### 9. Yankees vs. Padres: Game 1, 1998 World Series
Following their 114-win season, the Yankees had survived a difficult ALCS against the Indians, leaving them only four wins from their second title in three years. They trailed 5–2 in the seventh when the offense busted out for seven runs, getting a three-run homer by Chuck Knoblauch and a grand slam by Tino Martinez. The Yankees would sweep the series, winning a total of 125 games during that historic season.

### 10. Yankees vs. Red Sox: Game 1, 1999 ALCS
In the first-ever postseason meeting between the two hated rivals, the Red Sox took a 3–2 lead into the seventh before Derek Jeter tied the game with an RBI single. Three innings later, Bernie Williams crushed a walk-off home run, sending the Bronx into hysteria. The Yankees would win the series in five games before capturing their second of three straight championships.

### 11. Yankees vs. Diamondbacks: Games 4 & 5, 2001 World Series
Okay, so I'm giving you 11 moments. Consider it a free bonus. How could any list of great postseason moments in the Bronx be complete without the unlikely, incredibly timely, game-tying ninth-inning home runs by Tino Martinez and Scott Brosius against Arizona closer Byung-Hyun Kim?

The two homers led to two victories as Derek Jeter homered in the 10th against Kim in Game 4 (spawning the "Mr. November" nickname) and Alfonso Soriano won Game 5 with a 12th-inning RBI single. The Yankees went back to the desert needing only one win, but they dropped both games, including a heart-breaking Game 7 that saw Mariano Rivera blow a lead in the ninth.

# Visit the New York Yankees Museum Presented by Bank of America

**WHERE:** New York Yankees Museum Presented by Bank of America (inside Yankee Stadium)

**WHEN:** Open during every Yankees home game; also part of the Yankee Stadium tour

**COST FACTOR:** Free during games

**BUCKET RANK:**

Tucked away past the right-field foul pole at Yankee Stadium is the New York Yankees Museum Presented by Bank of America, a shrine to the most historic franchise in American sports.

With plenty of material to work with, the museum features a number of rotating exhibits highlighting key players and moments in Yankees history. A featured exhibit in 2016 looked at "Five Great Teams" in Yankees history, showing off memorabilia from the 1927, 1939, 1961, 1977, and 1998 championship seasons.

"You have the biggest names in here," said Brian Richards, the museum's curator since the project was conceived in 2008 for the 2009 Stadium opening. "As a curator, you want people to stop, look, read, think, discuss, repeat. Reality dictates it doesn't always work that way; with this exhibit, it works."

Other exhibits in the museum include one on Yogi Berra and Elston Howard and another on Joe Torre, though Richards tries to change them up every two or three years. Past exhibits have included Mickey Mantle, Babe Ruth and Lou Gehrig, the Subway Series, and George Steinbrenner.

Most memorabilia is borrowed from private collections at no cost, which serves the fans well as there is no admission fee to enter the museum during game days.

Replicas of all 27 Yankees championship rings are on display—well, 26 rings and one pocket watch, which was given out instead of a ring after the team won the 1923 World Series. Balfour created reproductions of the rings specifically for the museum, making a majority of them from the original molds.

Perhaps the most attention-grabbing display in the museum is the "Ball Wall," which stands in the middle of the museum. The exhibit has 870 baseballs signed by Yankees players, coaches, managers, and broadcasters through the years. On one side of the wall is a statue of Don Larsen in his delivery, while a statue of a crouching Yogi Berra sits on the other side, awaiting the final pitch of Larsen's perfect game in the 1956 World Series.

"People love this display," Richards said. "It's a unique concept. It's pretty special."

The two statues are 60 feet 6 inches apart and the top of the wall follows the curve of the pitch from Larsen's hand to Berra's glove. Players from Derek Jeter to Scott Proctor have signed balls in the exhibit, though the museum's goal is to have every player, coach,

# PUT YOUR HANDS ON HISTORY

**W**alking through the Yankees Museum gives you a good look at the team's history. For those that want more, the museum offers you a chance to put your hands on history—literally.

The "Hands on History" experience offers an opportunity for guests to touch historic Yankees artifacts, including game-used bats, jerseys, baseballs, World Series rings, and more from the team's past and present players.

Each session—led by museum curator Brian Richards—begins approximately 90 minutes before gates open to the public. Richards will share entertaining stories while guests handle 15 to 20 artifacts each during their detailed tour of the museum. And don't worry; photography is welcomed and encouraged during the program.

Among the featured artifacts (subject to availability) are Babe Ruth's bat from 1922–23, Derek Jeter's jersey from his 3,000th-hit game in 2011, Mickey Mantle's 1963 outfielder's glove, home plate from the final game at the old Stadium and first game from the new ballpark, World Series rings from 2000 and 2009, Ichiro Suzuki's bat and batting helmet from 2012, and the Yankees' seven World Series trophies of the Steinbrenner era.

For more information on the "Hands on History" program, call (646) 977-8687 or email tours@yankees.com. "Hands on History" sessions may also be scheduled for private and corporate events.

manager, and broadcaster in franchise history sign a ball for the display.

"There are guys that played one or two games and there are players that played 20 years in Derek's case," Richards said. "Our goal is to get them all."

A 15-minute highlight film of the franchise's greatest moments runs on a loop, while all seven of the Yankees' World Series trophies from the Steinbrenner era are on display: 1977, '78, '96, '98, '99, 2000, and 2009.

A model of the new Yankee Stadium that once sat in George Steinbrenner's office is also on display, complete with lights that turn on during games. Babe Ruth's bats also draw plenty of attention, but the sentimental heart of the museum is Thurman Munson's locker from the old Stadium, honoring the late captain.

The locker had been unused in the clubhouse at the old ballpark following Munson's tragic death in 1979, but the team moved it across the street to the museum when the new Stadium debuted.

Inside the locker, which is covered in Plexiglas, is a bat from Munson's 1976 American League Most Valuable Player season along with a jersey from his rookie year of 1970. Munson's name is even misspelled inside the collar, labeled "Munsen."

"The perils of being a rookie," Richards said.

Diana Munson, Thurman's widow, has visited the museum a few times, once standing by the locker with her late husband's friend and teammate, Ron Guidry. The two stood together and talked, tears running down their cheeks as they remembered Thurman.

"It was powerful," Richards said.

Even those that never met Munson have been emotional when they see the locker.

"I couldn't believe I was there," Yankees manager Joe Girardi said, thinking back to the first time he saw Munson's locker inside the home clubhouse at the old Stadium. "I remember seeing it the first time and thinking, 'This is where Thurman was.' I was in awe."

· · · · · · · · · · · · · · · · · · · · · · · · · · · · · · · · · · ·

# Listen to Lou Gehrig's "Luckiest Man" Speech

"Today, I consider myself the luckiest man on the face of the earth."

Possibly the most famous and emotional line in the most celebrated speech in baseball history, Lou Gehrig bid farewell to the Yankee Stadium fans on July 4, 1939—two weeks after retiring as a player and more than nine weeks after playing his final game on April 30.

Having been diagnosed with ALS—a disease that would later bear his name—Gehrig was honored at Yankee Stadium on "Lou Gehrig Appreciation Day," with a ceremony taking place between games of a doubleheader between the Yankees and the Washington Senators.

"The fact that it's called 'Baseball's Gettysburg Address' enhances its importance," said Marty Appel, author of the fabulous book *Pinstripe Empire* and a former Yankees public relations director. "The importance of the event has grown over the years. It wasn't immediately apparent that day."

In his book, Appel wrote: "In a way, Lou Gehrig Appreciation Day had been every day for baseball fans. Now one would take its place in the pantheon of historic Yankee moments."

All of Gehrig's living teammates from the 1927 team—including Babe Ruth himself—were invited back for the celebration, lining up on the field across from the 1939 team. Ruth and Gehrig had not spoken in years following an incident involving their wives, but Ruth showed up for the event, anyway.

The ceremony, which lasted approximately 40 minutes, included gifts for Gehrig along with speeches by sports writer Sid Mercer, New York City Mayor Fiorello LaGuardia, and others. The Yankees announced that Gehrig's No. 4 would be retired, the first time a team had ever honored a player in that fashion.

Gehrig stepped up to the microphone to address the crowd, which was silent as the hometown hero spoke.

"You see the reels over and over and it's so touching every time," Yankees historian Tony Morante said.

While no formal transcript of the speech exists—Gehrig did not use notes to deliver it—the following is the entire transcript as printed in *Pinstripe Empire*:

> *Fans, for the past two weeks you have been reading about a bad break I got. Yet today I consider myself the luckiest man on the face of the earth. I have been in ballparks for seventeen years and I have never received anything but kindness and encouragement from you fans.*
>
> *Look at these grand men. Which of you wouldn't consider it the highlight of his career just to associate with them for even one day? Sure I'm lucky. Who wouldn't consider it an honor to have known Jacob Ruppert? Also, the builder of baseball's greatest empire, Ed Barrow? To have spent six years with that wonderful little fellow, Miller Huggins? Then to have spent the next nine years with the outstanding leader, that smart student of psychology, the best manager in baseball today, Joe McCarthy? Sure, I'm lucky.*
>
> *When the New York Giants, a team you would give your right arm to beat, and vice versa, sends you a gift, that's something. When*

*everybody down to the groundskeepers and those boys in white coats remember you with trophies, that's something. When you have a wonderful mother-in-law who takes sides with you in squabbles with her own daughter, that's something. When you have a father and mother who work all their lives so that you can have an education and build your body, it's a blessing. When you have a wife who has been a tower of strength and shown more courage than you dreamed existed, that's the finest I know.*

*So I close in saying that I might have had a bad break, but I have an awful lot to live for. Thank you.*

Two people in attendance that day told Appel that the most memorable part of the speech was not the one you would have expected.

"Both of them told me—independent of each other—that the most memorable part of the speech to those who were there that day wasn't the 'luckiest man on the face of the Earth,' but rather 'that I've been given a bad break,'" Appel said. "The crowd had not yet fully understood what was wrong with Lou. Nobody knew he was dying; they just knew he had some kind of illness that he wasn't going to be able to play anymore. The 'bad break' part seemed to register with people."

Gehrig watched the 1939 Yankees win 106 games and their fourth straight World Series title. He was inducted into the Baseball Hall of Fame that December in a special election.

"Without Ruth, he'd be in the conversation for greatest player ever," Appel said. "But there was Ruth. Gehrig's strength of character also played a big part in who he was and how everybody looked up to him."

Gehrig's historic speech plays on a loop on the 200 level at the stadium across from the New Era store, a pair of speakers surrounding a wall-sized photo of the Iron Horse on that memorable day.

# Chapter 2

# Around the Majors

Catching a game at Yankee Stadium should be the first item on any Yankees fan's bucket list, but there's something about seeing your favorite team play away from home that gets the baseball blood pumping.

New York may be the greatest city in the world (I was born and raised there, so clearly I'm biased), but Major League Baseball fills ballparks around North America every year, offering plenty of opportunities for fans to explore other cities while catching the Bronx Bombers in their classic road gray uniforms.

Below is a list of some of the top baseball destinations to target. Taking an annual road trip to see the Yankees play has become something of a tradition for many fans, knocking a ballpark or two off their list every year.

I'll stick mostly to spring training and American League cities, since the Yankees make annual visits to each of these locations. I would also recommend trips to Chicago's Wrigley Field, San Francisco's AT&T Park, Pittsburgh's PNC Park, and Los Angeles' Dodger Stadium if the Yankees are making an Interleague trip to any of those parks, as they're some of the best in the majors.

*The Yankees' spring home had its name changed from Legends Field to George M. Steinbrenner Field in 2008, while this statue was erected in 2011 after his death the previous year.* (Mark Feinsand)

# Soak Up the Sun at Spring Training

**WHERE:** George M. Steinbrenner Field

**WHEN:** Every February and March

**HOW TO DO IT:** Buy tickets at Yankees.com

**COST FACTOR:** Early-spring workouts are free; game tickets run $21–37

**BUCKET RANK:** 🪣 🪣 🪣 🪣 🪣

***P****itchers and catchers*. To the casual fan, those are simply positions on a baseball field. To the die-hards, they're three of the best words in the English language.

During the second or third week of February each year, the Yankees travel about 1,100 miles south to Tampa's George M. Steinbrenner Field, their spring home since 1996. (It was originally known as Legends Field when it opened, but was renamed for the Yankees' longtime owner in 2008.)

There are two phases of spring training, so consider what you're looking for when you plan your trip. The first two weeks consist of daily workouts at the ballpark's four fields, giving fans a close look at how major leaguers prepare for a season. Workouts tend to start between 9 and 10 AM and last into the early afternoon.

While hitters take batting practice on one field, pitchers perform fielding drills on a diamond in the back of the complex and catchers engage in blocking drills in a bullpen area. All fields are visible to fans, though all but the main stadium field are separated by chain-link fences. Even with the fences, the access to practices is excellent. The back field has a set of bleachers on each side for fans to sit and watch the Yankees work out.

The best part of attending a spring training workout? It's free! You can even park in the stadium's main lot at no cost. Spring rosters are sold on the concourse, a must-have given the 70-something players who start each spring in camp.

It's not uncommon for players to stop and sign autographs down the foul lines in the main ballpark, though the area behind Field 2 can also be a good signing spot. Early workouts don't tend to draw enormous crowds, giving fans a chance to sit up close and get a good look at their favorite players.

While you're at the ballpark, don't miss the garden of retired numbers in front of the stadium. Think of it as a mini-Monument Park, with each retired number represented along with a plaque listing each

*If you can't make it to Monument Park in the Bronx, the mini version outside of George M. Steinbrenner Field is the next best thing.* (Mark Feinsand)

honoree's career highlights. It's not the same as the real thing, but it's a good alternative if you can't make it to the Bronx—and the photo opportunities are terrific.

There's also a 9/11 memorial featuring steel from the World Trade Center, as well as a bronze statue of Steinbrenner, installed in 2011 following the owner's death the previous year.

If you're flying into Tampa, you'll probably get a look at the stadium—lovingly nicknamed "the Boss" by many locals and Yankees fans—on your final approach into the airport, which sits only a few miles from the ballpark. (It's also across the street from the much larger Raymond James Stadium, home of the NFL's Buccaneers.)

In April 2016, Hillsborough County commissioners approved a new lease agreement with the Yankees that will keep them training at Steinbrenner Field through 2046. The deal featured $40 million in renovations including the addition of areas providing fans a 360-degree view of the field via new outfield concourses as well as group and social gathering areas and additional shaded areas. There will also be improvements made to the ballpark's entrance to make for easier fan access, so your experience will be even better than it's been during the first 20 years.

Once the games start, the Yankees play half of their spring slate in Tampa, typically about 15 or 16 games. With a capacity of 11,026, Steinbrenner Field is the largest ballpark in the Grapefruit League, and the sightlines are good from pretty much every seat in the place.

For the pure baseball fan—or those hoping to get a look at the team's distant future—the Yankees' low-level minor leaguers work out at the team's complex on Himes Avenue, located about a mile from Steinbrenner Field. Fans may park beyond the outfield wall and there is no cost to attend a workout, though it can be difficult to pick out any player there by name on most days.

The big-name minor leaguers are typically with the team in big-league camp until the final couple weeks of spring training, though you can occasionally catch a major leaguer playing in a minor league game at the Himes complex if they're trying to get in extra work—or avoid a lengthy bus ride for a game across the state.

If you're looking to check out more than one game, the Yankees' spring home is in close proximity to those of the Phillies (Clearwater), Blue Jays (Dunedin), Tigers (Lakeland), Pirates (Bradenton), Orioles (Sarasota), and Braves (Disney World), so you can create a spring itinerary filled with ballparks within an hour drive from Tampa.

Once you're finished at the ballpark, Tampa offers a wide array of excellent restaurants, from chains to local favorites.

Whether you're looking for casual or high-end, pretty much every chain you can think of is located within 10 minutes of the ballpark: The Cheesecake Factory, P.F. Chang's, Seasons 52, Fleming's, Roy's, Ruth's Chris, Mitchell's Fish Market, Capital Grille, Bar Louie, Brio, and Ocean Prime.

**Bern's Steakhouse** is a Tampa destination not to be missed; from its dry-aged steaks to its enormous wine list to its legendary dessert room, Bern's describes itself as a "gastronomic adventure" you'll surely remember for quite some time.

Another steakhouse to check out—and Tampa has so many of them, you'd think you were back in New York—is **Malio's Prime Steakhouse** in downtown Tampa. A favorite of George Steinbrenner, the Boss often held court with players and executives at Malio's, even completing several player signings right in the restaurant. The steaks and seafood are incredible, the wine list is superb, and the service is impeccable.

For a casual meal, **Lee Roy Selmon's**, founded by the late Buccaneers Hall of Famer, is a great place to catch some NCAA hoops (or whatever else is on) while enjoying solid burgers, BBQ, or other southern favorites.

Any trip to the Tampa Bay area should include more than just a spring game or two. The beaches in St. Petersburg are beautiful, while Tampa's **Ybor City** (known as Tampa's National Historic Landmark District) offers tours of old cigar factories and endless dining and nightlife options. Other attractions of note include the **Lowry Park Zoo** and **Busch Gardens**, a phenomenal amusement park.

*No matter which side of the Yankees–Red Sox rivalry you're on, there's nothing quite like a New York–Boston game at Fenway Park.* (Mark Feinsand)

# Catch Baseball's Best Rivalry at Boston's Fenway Park

**WHERE:** Fenway Park

**WHEN:** Nine times every regular season

**HOW TO DO IT:** Buy tickets for games and the Fenway Tour at redsox.com

**COST FACTOR:** $20–$180 per ticket

**BUCKET RANK:** 🪣 🪣 🪣 🪣 🪣

**W**ith the explosion of new ballparks around the majors, Fenway Park and Wrigley Field are the only two historic gems still standing. Chicago is great, but the Yankees only play at Wrigley once every six years or so, leaving fans at the mercy of the schedule makers when it comes to planning a road trip.

That's not the case in Boston, where the Yankees play three series every season as part of baseball's greatest rivalry.

From Bucky Dent's legendary home run to former Red Sox Wade Boggs, Roger Clemens, Johnny Damon, or Jacoby Ellsbury returning to Fenway after jumping from Boston to New York, the Yankees and Red Sox always provide drama when they get together on Yawkey Way.

"It's great; the tradition, the rivalry, the intensity," Joe Girardi said of his trips to Boston. "I remember being a player, a lot of days you wouldn't go out because senses were heightened. Everybody was talking about the game. The passion of the fans is what makes it so special."

The ballpark itself, the oldest in the majors, is pretty special, too.

*Pregame at Fenway Park is at its best on Yawkey Way, where it feels more like a street fair than a tailgate party.* (Mark Feinsand)

# TOP 5 RIVALRY MOMENTS AT FENWAY

**Bucky F'n Dent**

The Yankees and Red Sox matched up in a one-game playoff for the 1978 American League East title, a game highlighted by Bucky Dent's home run over the Green Monster. One of the biggest home runs in Yankees history forever earned Dent a profane nickname in New England.

**2004 ALCS Games 4 & 5**

Yankees fans have tried to block these out, but they remain two classic contests. Trailing 3–0 in the series, Dave Roberts' stolen base in the ninth helped tie the game against Mariano Rivera before David Ortiz launched a walk-off homer in the 12th to win Game 4. The next day, the Red Sox got to Rivera again before Ortiz delivered another game-winning hit in the 12th, sending the series back to the Bronx where the Red Sox finished their historic comeback.

**Fisk and Munson Brawl**

The two catchers didn't care for each other, but when Thurman Munson barreled into Carlton Fisk at the plate in the ninth inning of a tied game on August 1, 1973—Fisk held on to the ball for the out—the two wound up in a fight that defined the heated rivalry.

**Zimmer vs. Pedro**

Speaking of brawls, the rivalry between the two teams came to a head in 2003 during the American League Championship Series. After Pedro Martinez fired a pitch toward Karim Garcia's head in the fourth inning, clipping his helmet, Roger Clemens threw one up and in to Manny Ramirez in the bottom of the inning, clearing the benches. But while most bench-clearing brawls are much ado about nothing, we'll never forget the sight of Pedro throwing 72-year-old

Don Zimmer to the ground after the bench coach charged at him. A bizarre moment in a legendary rivalry.

### A-Rod Sparks the Sox
Sensing a theme here? In July 2004, Alex Rodriguez and catcher Jason Varitek engaged in a shoving match after A-Rod was plunked by Bronson Arroyo. The violent brawl seemed to ignite the Red Sox, who came back to win the game to begin a second-half run that ended with Boston's first World Series title since 1918.

Whether you've been to a game at Fenway or not, the ballpark tour ($18 for adults, $12 for kids) is a must-see. You'll get to visit the press box, getting a bird's-eye view of the field from behind home plate. (You may even run into a baseball writer or two, which is always a plus. We're a friendly group.)

The **Ted Williams Seat** in the right-field bleachers—Section 42, Row 37, Seat 21, to be exact—marks the landing spot of the longest home run ever hit at Fenway Park, a 502-foot moon shot the Hall of Famer hit in 1946. Legend has it that the ball broke through a straw hat being worn by a fan, Joseph Boucher, who told the *Boston Globe*, "How far must one sit to be safe in this park?"

Weather permitting, you'll get to walk the warning track on the tour, getting close enough to the famed **Green Monster** wall in left field to touch it. The wall, which was made of wood when the ballpark opened in 1912, was covered in tin and concrete in 1934 and painted green in 1947. Although the wall is only 315 feet from home plate, at 37 feet high, it takes a blast for a hitter to clear the Monster.

Above the big wall are seats installed in 2003, which you'll also get to test out for a view from one of the most popular resting places for home runs in the yard.

Right field features its own unique characteristic in **Pesky's Pole**, the right-field foul pole named for Johnny Pesky, a popular, light-hitting shortstop who took advantage of the short dimensions—the

# TOP 5 PLAYERS WHO PLAYED FOR BOTH THE YANKEES AND RED SOX

**M**ore than 300 players have suited up for both the Yankees and Red Sox, but only a handful have left their mark on both New York and Boston. Here are the five best:

**Babe Ruth**

This one is obvious. The Great Bambino may be the most prolific hitter of all time, but his time in Boston was known more for his work on the mound, where he went 89–46 with a 2.19 ERA while hitting only 49 home runs from 1914 to '19. Ruth pitched a 14-inning complete game to help the Red Sox win the 1916 World Series, then won two games during Boston's 1918 World Series victory.

Ruth was traded to the Yankees after the 1919 season, dooming Boston to the 86-year title drought—it would be known as the "Curse of the Bambino"—while he hit 659 home runs for the Yankees and won four championships.

**Roger Clemens**

"The Rocket" was a Boston legend during his 13 seasons, winning 192 games and three Cy Young Awards while pitching for the Red Sox. A two-year stint in Toronto—and two more Cy Young Awards— predated a trade to New York, where he helped the Yankees to two World Series titles and two other AL pennants, and in 2001, won the sixth of his seven career Cy Young Awards.

**Wade Boggs**

Boggs was one of the most hated players in New York during his 11 seasons with the Red Sox, especially when a hamstring injury forced him out of the final four games of the 1986 season, helping him beat out Don Mattingly for the AL batting title. Boggs switched sides in the rivalry in 1993 after signing with the Yankees as a free agent, batting .313 for the Bombers (he hit .338 for the Sox) while helping them end an 18-year title drought in 1996.

**Johnny Damon**
Damon was a nomad throughout his career, playing for seven teams over 18 seasons. But he's one of the rare players to own championship rings from both teams, playing instrumental roles on both the 2004 Red Sox and the 2009 Yankees, spending four years with each club.

**Red Ruffing**
Ruffing never realized his potential during his first six-plus seasons with the Red Sox, going 39–96 with a 4.61 ERA while leading the league in losses in 1928 and '29. But after the Sox dealt him to the Yankees in May 1930, the right-hander went 231–124 with a 3.47 ERA over 15 seasons, making six All-Star teams while helping New York win six World Series titles.

pole is only 302 feet from home plate—to hit a handful of his six career Fenway homers. Despite the short distance, players rarely take advantage of Pesky's Pole as the outfield fence curves sharply from the pole to lengthen the distance.

Pesky's Pole was officially dedicated to the former player on his 87th birthday in 2006. He died six years later.

Many stadiums are considered extremely hostile territory for visiting fans, and while the Yankees–Red Sox rivalry continues to be one of the fiercest in baseball, the attitude of the fans in Boston has changed significantly ever since the Red Sox broke the curse in 2004 and got a taste of winning with championships in 2004, '07, and '13.

"Boston's not as hostile as people think," said "Bald Vinny" Milano of the Bleacher Creatures. "It was worse when the Yankees were constantly winning. Once the Sox started winning and that upper hand got taken away, it relaxed a bit."

The ballpark's signature concession is the Fenway Frank, its homage to the staple of any stadium. The Lobster Roll, a New England tradition, is another fan favorite.

On game days, **Yawkey Way** is closed to the public and turned into a Red Sox–themed block party. There are many culinary options to choose from there, most notably the **Fenway Fish Shack** and **El Tiante**, the latter named for former All-Star pitcher Luis Tiant, who pitched for both the Red Sox and Yankees. The Luis Tiant Cuban Sandwich is the signature item.

While a Yankees–Red Sox game would surely be the highlight of any trip, the city offers a multitude of sightseeing options including—but certainly not limited to—the **Freedom Trail**, the **USS Constitution Museum**, the original **"Cheers,"** a **Duck Tour**, **Faneuil Hall**, and the **New England Aquarium**.

# Head to Baltimore for a Game at "Yankee Stadium South"

**WHERE:** Oriole Park at Camden Yards

**WHEN:** Nine times every regular season

**HOW TO DO IT:** Buy tickets for games and the ballpark tour at orioles.com

**COST FACTOR:** $15–$72 per ticket

**BUCKET RANK:** 🪣 🪣 🪣 🪣 🪣

*The glut of Yankees fans at Camden Yards every year make the ballpark feel like Yankee Stadium South.* (Mark Feinsand)

The gold standard of ballparks that spawned an entire generation of throwback stadiums, Oriole Park at Camden Yards is as good as it gets when it comes to a baseball experience away from home.

"It's the first of the new parks, but it still has that old-school charm to it," said former Yankees first baseman Mark Teixeira, who grew up in the nearby suburb of Severna Park. "That was deliberate; they told us for years, 'We're building a new park, but don't worry, it's going to feel like one of the old parks.' They nailed it. Whoever designed it and built that stadium absolutely nailed it with the warehouse, the brick, the colors. They did a great job."

The best part of Camden Yards for a Yankees fan? When the Bombers play in Baltimore, many refer to the ballpark as "Yankee Stadium South," as fans routinely make the trek from New York to Baltimore to catch the Yankees in enemy territory.

# MIKE MUSSINA—THE BEST PLAYER TO PLAY FOR BOTH TEAMS

**R**eggie Jackson is the most successful player to ever suit up for both the Yankees and Orioles during his career, though with only one season in Baltimore (1976), very few people think of the Orioles when they talk about Mr. October.

When it comes to success in both New York and Baltimore, nobody can compare to what Mike Mussina accomplished for the two AL East rivals, playing his entire career with the two historic franchises.

Mussina pitched the first 10 seasons of his career with the Birds, compiling a 147–81 record and a 3.53 ERA in 288 starts, making five All-Star teams between 1991 and 2000.

Mussina pitched more than 2,000 innings for the Orioles, ranking third on the club's all-time list in wins and second in win percentage, strikeouts, and WAR. He is considered by many to be the second-best pitcher in the team's history behind only Hall of Famer Jim Palmer.

He helped the Orioles to the playoffs in 1996 and '97, producing a marvelous postseason in 1997. Mussina went 2–0 with a 1.93 ERA in an AL Division Series win over the Mariners, then struck out 15 Indians in seven innings in Game 3 of the ALCS and 10 more over eight shutout innings in Game 6.

Following the 2000 season, Mussina signed a six-year, $88.5 million contract with the Yankees, joining the three-time defending World Series champions.

Mussina went 123–72 with a 3.88 ERA during eight years in pinstripes, helping the Yankees reach the postseason in the first seven of those seasons. He had double-digit wins in all eight seasons with the Yankees, winning at least 15 games five times.

In 2001, Mussina reached the World Series for the first time in his career, pitching to a 2.62 ERA in his four postseason starts. He twirled seven shutout innings in Game 3 of the ALDS in Oakland, though his effort wound up being forgotten as Derek Jeter made his legendary "Flip Play" in the 1–0 victory that kept the Yankees' season alive.

The biggest knock against Mussina for years was his lack of a World Series ring, a Cy Young Award, and a 20-win season. His Yankees lost the World Series in both 2001 and '03, though he produced stellar outings in two of his three Fall Classic starts.

In 2008, Mussina finally posted his first 20-win season, earning win No. 20 in his last start of the season at Fenway Park. It turned out to be the final start of Mussina's career, as he retired less than two months later with a total of 270 career victories.

Will Mussina be remembered most as an Oriole or a Yankee?

"I think I made a name for myself in Baltimore, but I had a lot more exposure and opportunities in New York," Mussina said after announcing his retirement. "We had seven trips to the postseason, a couple of trips to the World Series.

"You're on a bigger stage pitching for the Yankees. I played my last game as a Yankee. I loved playing in both places, but when retirement came around, I was still a Yankee."

"Every time we go to a road stadium and we can hear our fans cheering us on, that's huge," Teixeira said. "Baltimore is one of those places."

Located in the heart of Baltimore's Inner Harbor, Camden Yards—which opened in 1992—is set in the middle of an active area on game days. It doesn't have the block-party atmosphere that Fenway Park offers, but there are plenty of bars and restaurants to hit in the area before and after the game. **Pickles**, located across the street from the stadium, is a pregame favorite for the drinking crowd. A couple blocks down, stop in at the **Pratt Street Ale House** for a wide beer selection and a good pregame meal.

Take in **Eutaw Street**, just beyond the right-center-field fence. It's like a contained tailgate party in front of the historic B&O Warehouse, which you may recognize from Ken Griffey's 1993 Home Run Derby performance (there's a plaque there to commemorate the only blast to ever hit the warehouse building) or Cal Ripken's 1995 pursuit of Lou Gehrig's consecutive-game streak, where Ripken's tally was updated daily.

Make sure to look down by your feet as you walk along the **Flag Court** behind right field, where 88 brass baseballs (and counting) mark the spots of the home runs that have landed on the walkway.

Orioles.com keeps an updated chart of every home run that has landed on Eutaw Street—with video of each homer!—so look to see if your favorite player has made the cut. Among the Yankees that have deposited home runs on Eutaw Street are Jason Giambi (three times), Curtis Granderson (twice), Johnny Damon, Paul O'Neill, Robinson Cano, and Nick Swisher.

For those looking to add to their autograph collection, the Orioles Alumni Autograph Series sends former Orioles to sign for fans on Eutaw Street during every Monday and Thursday home game.

The highlight of Eutaw Street, of course, is the famed **Boog's BBQ**, the signature concession of Camden Yards. It's not Kansas City or

Texas BBQ, but the smoked beef, pork, and turkey are all worth the trip. Boog himself—four-time All-Star Boog Powell—can often be found hanging out at his own place, giving an extra touch to the experience of getting a pit beef sandwich.

"You see that smoke coming from right field all game long," Teixeira said.

Also on Eutaw Street is **Dempsey's Brew Pub**, named for former Orioles catcher Rick Dempsey, the 1983 World Series MVP. If you're in town on a non-game day, Dempsey's is open year round.

Other notable concessions include Chesapeake waffle fries (with crab, naturally) and the "Crab Chipper," which is a tray of chips covered in lump crabmeat, cheese sauce, and Old Bay seasoning, a Baltimore favorite.

Beyond center field, there's **Orioles Legends Park** (consider it Baltimore's version of Monument Park) where you can check out six larger-than-life bronze statues of Orioles legends Eddie Murray, Jim Palmer, Ripken, Brooks Robinson, Frank Robinson, and Earl Weaver commemorated in one of their signature poses. All six are in the Hall of Fame.

The statues, created by Maryland sculptor Antonio Tobias "Toby" Mendez and cast into bronze by Baltimore's New Arts Foundry, range from seven to eight feet in scale and weigh between 600 and 1,500 pounds each according to the Orioles.

There are also statues of the retired numbers for those six Orioles greats, as well as a statue of Babe Ruth, a Baltimore native who did a thing or two in the majors himself.

From left field, you can get a good look at both bullpens, where that day's starters will be warming up before the game.

The ballpark opens to the public two hours before the game, giving Yankees fans plenty of time to catch the Bombers taking batting practice.

# TOP 5 YANKEES–ORIOLES MOMENTS AT CAMDEN YARDS

**The Yankees Clinch the Pennant**

The Yankees hadn't won the American League pennant in 15 years, but that streak came to an end on Baltimore's home turf on October 13, 1996, in Game 5 of the ALCS. Andy Pettitte allowed two runs over eight innings, while the Yankees capitalized on a Roberto Alomar error to spark a six-run third inning as Cecil Fielder, Jim Leyritz, and Darryl Strawberry all went deep in the frame.

**Jack Cust's Fatal Flop**

Mariano Rivera suffered a rare blown save against Baltimore (he successfully converted 79 of 88 opportunities against the Orioles, blowing only nine saves against them during his 17 years as a closer) on August 16, 2003, serving up Luis Matos' game-tying homer in the ninth.

But the game will always be remembered for its ending in the 12th inning, as Cust—a little-known 24-year-old—fell down as he rounded third and got caught in a rundown. He somehow found himself heading home without anybody covering the plate when he inexplicably stumbled and hit the deck, allowing Aaron Boone to tag him out to end the game.

**The Birds Get to Mariano**

In another rare hiccup against the Orioles, Rivera allowed three runs in the ninth on Jay Payton's two-out, game-tying triple on September 28, 2007. Melvin Mora completed the comeback with a two-out, bases-loaded bunt single in the 10th to win the game, but the Yankees had the last laugh—they won 94 games to reach the postseason for a 13th straight season while the Orioles finished 69–93.

**Orioles Go Deep Again and Again**

This game on September 6, 2012, was one-sided for most of the night as the Orioles took a 6–1 lead into the eighth inning. The Yankees rallied for five runs in the top of the eighth to tie the game, but David Robertson gave up home runs by Adam Jones and Mark Reynolds in the bottom of the inning, then Chris Davis took Boone Logan deep, capping the four-run inning as the Orioles hit six homers in the win.

**End of an Era**

Cal Ripken did the impossible and ended Lou Gehrig's consecutive-game streak in 1995 with No. 2,131, but the streak lasted three more years. After playing in his 2,632nd straight game, Ripken decided it was time to take a day off—and it happened to be against the Yankees on September 20, 1998. There was no press conference or major announcement by the Orioles, and in the days before lineups were announced on Twitter, fans routinely didn't know who was playing that night. Rookie Ryan Minor replaced Ripken at third base, though Ripken got a bigger ovation than anybody at Camden Yards that day in the Yankees' 5–4 win. Even the Yankees gave Ripken a standing ovation from their dugout.

Virtually every seat at Camden Yards is a good one, so don't feel the need to spend excessively for tickets.

"Every seat is a good seat," said Teixeira, who attended about a half-dozen games each year as a youngster. "You can get the top bleacher seats and still feel like you're a part of the game, which is neat."

Ballpark tours are also available, taking fans inside the Orioles dugout, the press box, and the scoreboard control room while offering a historical perspective of area attractions including the Inner Harbor, the B&O Railroad, and the city's most famous native, the Great Bambino himself.

As a bonus, fans under 14 years old are invited to run the bases after every Sunday home game, giving youngsters a chance to follow the footsteps of their favorite players.

While the game-day experience can take anywhere from three to five hours, there are plenty of great sites to visit in the area including the **National Aquarium**, the **Maryland Science Center**, and the **B&O Railroad Museum**, all of which are located within a mile of the ballpark.

• • • • • • • • • • • • • • • • • • • • • • • • • • • • • • • • • • •

# O Canada! Take a Trip to Toronto

**WHERE:** Rogers Centre

**WHEN:** Nine times every regular season

**HOW TO DO IT:** Buy tickets for games and the ballpark tour at bluejays.com

**COST FACTOR:** $30–$299 (Canadian) per ticket

**BUCKET RANK:** 🗑 🗑 🗑 🗑

• • • • • • • • • • • • • • • • • • • • • • • • • • • • • • • • • • •

Retractable-roof ballparks are a dime a dozen these days (okay, not really; there are only six in the majors and four more in the NFL), but Toronto's Rogers Centre was the first major league stadium to feature a fully operational roof when it opened in 1989.

*The CN Tower stands above Rogers Centre, where the Yankees play three series every season.* (Mark Feinsand)

The roof itself is 339,343 square feet and weighs almost 11,000 tons, yet it takes only 20 minutes to open or close the lid, so a sudden change in the weather won't cause extended delays during games.

The roof isn't the only technological wonder at Rogers Centre; the video board above center field is 110 feet long and is capable of projecting 4.3 trillion colors. Who knew that many colors even existed? The biggest Crayola box I ever had was only 128! It consists of more than 400,000 light bulbs.

All seats at Rogers Centre have clear views of the field; there are no sections with limited sightlines. But like most ballparks, some seating areas offer better views than others.

The Renaissance Hotel is located inside the ballpark, offering a unique opportunity to watch a game from the comfort of your hotel room. The views aren't as good as a seat in the yard—some rooms overlook the outfield—but you can't beat the commute. Only 70 of the 348 rooms overlook the field, so make your reservations well in advance if you want to experience this unique vantage point.

Another terrific—and pricey—view comes from the "Action" seats, which allow fans to sit in foul territory in front of the wall that separates the field from the stands.

Rogers Centre is one of only two ballparks left in the majors with an artificial turf field (Tampa Bay's Tropicana Field is the other), though the Blue Jays transformed the base paths to all-dirt in 2016. Previously, only small squares around the bases consisted of dirt, while turf covered the rest of the infield.

There is a lot of chatter about Rogers Centre installing a natural grass field in 2018 now that the Argonauts of the Canadian Football League have left the stadium for nearby BMO Field.

For an inside look at the ballpark, take the **Rogers Centre Tour Experience**. The tour offers a newly renovated museum area, memorabilia from the stadium's events, a trip to the press box, and more. The one-hour tour runs Monday through Friday at 11:00 AM, 1:00 PM, and 3:00 PM and costs $16 for adults, $12 for seniors and ages 12 to 17, and $10 for children ages 5 to 11.

Once you're inside the ballpark, there are several solid concession options to fulfill your appetite.

The **Muddy York Market**, located by Section 109, is my personal favorite. The porchetta sandwich is outstanding, as is the house-smoked roast beef dip. Any first-time visitor should also try the poutine, which is french fries with gravy and cheese curds.

**T.O. Street Eats** by Section 135 has a local flair with features such as brisket poutine, sausage poutine, buffalo cauliflower poutine (vegetarian), and chicken and waffles on a stick.

The **Budweiser King Club**, located behind home plate at Section 122, offers a variety of carved sandwiches—the top sirloin is a local favorite—with an assortment of beers.

**Corktown Fresh Burger Co.** (Section 117) has you covered if you're craving a burger, while the **Garrison Creek Flat Grill** (located on both the 100 and 200 levels) features the ballpark's signature Foot Long Hot Dog with grilled peppers and onions.

Lastly, there's the **12 Kitchen** by section 215, created to honor Roberto Alomar, the first player inducted into the Baseball Hall of Fame as a member of the Blue Jays. Menu items are inspired by Puerto Rican tastes in honor of the Puerto Rico native and Toronto fan favorite. The similarly named **12 Bar** is in the same area, showing off memorabilia from the second baseman's career.

There are some good nearby spots to hit before or after games, the first being **Wayne Gretzky's**, a sports bar that hosts the Great One's personal memorabilia collection and is open late every night. The food is excellent, the walls are adorned with Gretzky's greatest moments, and the bar area features 40 HDTV screens showing every

# FIVE BEST PLAYERS TO PLAY FOR BOTH THE YANKEES AND BLUE JAYS

### Dave Winfield

The Hall of Famer hit 205 of his 465 career home runs and 1,300 of his 3,110 hits in pinstripes, playing for the Yankees from 1981 to '90 before being traded to the Angels. He played only one year with the Blue Jays, but helped Toronto to the first of its two straight World Series championships, hitting 26 homers with 108 RBI in the last great season of a great career.

### David Cone

Like Winfield, Cone enjoyed more success with the Yankees than the Blue Jays, winning 64 regular season games and four World Series rings in the Bronx. But Cone was dealt to the Blue Jays in August 1992, going 4–3 with a 2.55 ERA in eight starts before making four postseason starts to help Toronto win its first-ever World Series title.

### Roger Clemens

The Rocket had his biggest years with the Red Sox, but he made significant contributions with both New York and Toronto. Clemens won 41 games and two Cy Young Awards in his two years with the Blue Jays (1997–98) before being traded to the Yankees. The right-hander won 77 games from 1999 to 2003 with the Yankees, winning the 2001 Cy Young and World Series titles in 1999 and 2000.

### David Wells

Wells began his career as a reliever in Toronto before having his first 15-win season with the Jays in 1991 and contributing to the 1992 World Series title team. He played for the Yankees in 1997–98, throwing a perfect game and going 18–4 for the '98 team, considered by many to be the greatest of all time. After being traded back to the Jays for Clemens in 1999, Wells returned to New York in 2002, winning 34 games over two more seasons.

**Russell Martin**

Martin was a gritty player during his two seasons in New York, honoring the Yankees' rich tradition behind the plate. The Canadian native left as a free agent after the 2012 season, ultimately signing a big contract with the Blue Jays before the 2015 season, returning home to play in front of family and friends while helping return Toronto to baseball relevance.

event you could want to watch. From May to October, you can also enjoy a seat on the rooftop patio.

If you're looking for a pregame beer, make sure to stop into the **Loose Moose**, which features more than 50 draft taps including 30 local craft beers. Be sure to try one of the rotating selections from the **Left Field Brewery**, a local baseball-themed brewery. Among their beers are the Maris Pale Ale, 6-4-3 Double IPA, and Wrigley Oat Pale Ale.

There are plenty of non-baseball attractions to take in while you're in Toronto, including the CN Tower and the Hockey Hall of Fame.

The **CN Tower**, an 1,800-foot-tall structure that stands next to the ballpark, offers a "Tower Experience" that includes a view from the LookOut Level more than 1,100 feet in the air and a walk on the famous Glass Floor. For an additional price, you can make your way up to the SkyPod, one of the highest observation platforms in the world. At more than 1,400 feet high, the SkyPod gives you a 360-degree perspective looking down on Toronto, Lake Ontario, and beyond. On a clear day, you can even see all the way to Niagara Falls and the state of New York.

The **Hockey Hall of Fame** is about a 15-minute walk from the ballpark, and although it's located in a mall and not a quaint village like Cooperstown, the museum is spectacular and a must-see for any hockey fan. (Admission is $18 for adults, $14 for seniors, and $12 for children ages 4–13.)

The **Great Hall** is a beautiful room that serves as the centerpiece of the Hall of Fame, featuring plaques with portraits of every Hall of Famer. Every National Hockey League trophy is on display, with the names of the annual winners engraved on each one. At the center of the room is the hallowed Stanley Cup, situated so fans can take a closer look and pose for photos with the old silver mug.

In addition to the multiple exhibits highlighting the history of the game with amazing memorabilia, the hall also features a number of interactive activities including the NHLPA Game Time area, where fans can test their talents in the "Shoot Out" and "Shut Out" games, even sharing their videos on social media. Aspiring sportscasters can show their skills at the TSN/RDS Broadcast Zone.

Catching a Yankees–Blue Jays game is a great way to spend a day or night in Toronto, but let's face it: it will always be a hockey town.

# Head to Sunny St. Petersburg and Take In Some Indoor Baseball

**WHERE:** Tropicana Field

**WHEN:** Nine times every regular season

**HOW TO DO IT:** Buy tickets for games and the ballpark tour at rays.mlb.com

**COST FACTOR:** $26–$130 per ticket

**BUCKET RANK:** 🗑️ 🗑️ 🗑️ 🗑️

*Tropicana Field may not have the same feel of a vintage old park, but on the plus side—no rain delays!* (Mark Feinsand)

It's not Yankee Stadium by any means, but if you're looking for a fun, inexpensive weekend road trip to watch the Bombers, Tampa Bay is a great option.

Tropicana Field, opened in 1990 under its original name, the Florida Suncoast Dome (and later the ThunderDome), has been the home of the Rays (who removed the "Devil" from their name in 2008) since the team's inception in 1998.

The ballpark is viewed by many as antiseptic and characterless, but since the Rays broke through as a contender in 2008, the crowds can be lively and tend to be younger than you'd think given the changing demographics in the area. It is extremely family-friendly, so kids will have a great time taking in the ballgame while partaking in the many other peripheral activities.

The roof—a massive, white dome—lends a unique feel for both players and fans. Baseballs can blend into the roof easily, making it difficult at times for fans—and fielders—to track pop-ups or fly balls.

The advantage, of course, comes with the lack of weather-related delays, which would be routine given Florida's somewhat steady rain. It also guarantees a game-time temperature of 72 degrees, which is typically 20-plus degrees cooler than the weather outside, which can be oppressive during the summer months.

"Ideally, the Rays would have—or someday soon will have—a stadium with a retractable roof and glass side panels to see outside, like they do in Miami and Houston," said Marc Topkin, who has covered the Rays for the *Tampa Bay Times* (formerly the *St. Petersburg Times*) since they entered the league. "But until then, the idea of playing under the Trop roof is much better than playing without one."

The field is made of artificial turf, though the base paths are all dirt.

Among the unique features of the Trop is the **Rays Touch Tank**, located in center field. Fans can get a close-up look at a collection of actual rays in the 35-foot, 10,000-gallon tank, which was created in a partnership with the Florida Aquarium, marking the first such exhibit at a major league ballpark. Fans are encouraged to touch the rays, and while there is no cost to visit the tank, you may purchase food for the rays for $5, with the proceeds going to the Florida Aquarium and the Rays Baseball Foundation.

Once you've fed the rays, it's time to feed yourself. The Trop's concessions are pretty good for ballpark fare, featuring much more than hot dogs. **Pipo's Café** features Cuban sandwiches, empanadas, and fried plantains, while the Rays also have their own craft beer called 2-Seam Blonde Ale, sold exclusively at the ballpark.

"Tropicana Field gets a bad rap; seriously, I should know. I've been covering 70-plus games a year there for 19 years," Topkin said. "Sure, it looks weird from the outside with the tilted roof. And it's got the

*One of the highlights of any visit to Tropicana Field: the Rays' touch tank.*
(Steven Kovich/Tampa Bay Rays)

catwalks, which are a major design flaw, cramped concourses, and those blue multipurpose-looking seats. But it's really not a bad place to watch a game."

The team has done a good job of renovating the building during the past decade, making for a positive experience for fans of all ages. The Rays also offer a **Summer Concert Series** each year, bringing acts to play in the outfield following select games. In 2016, concerts included the Fray, Bret Michaels, and Hunter Hayes.

During summer Sundays, the Rays offer **Family Fun Days**, which offer a number of fun activities for children including face painting, air brush tattoos, magicians, jugglers, and balloon artists. Complimentary concourse activities such as Grand Slam Alley, Strike 'Em Out Home Run Derby, Raymond's Art Studio (Raymond is the Rays' mascot), and Topps Make Your Own Baseball Card are also

# TOP FIVE YANKEES– RAYS MOMENTS

**Game 162**

Considering the lopsided nature of the history between the Yankees and Rays, it's ironic that the most memorable game ever played between these two teams saw the Rays come out on top in one of the most dramatic finishes we've ever seen.

It was the final day of the 2011 season, and although the Yankees had the AL East title all wrapped up, the Rays were still battling for a wild-card berth. The Yankees jumped out to a 7–0 lead while using eight pitchers to get through seven shutout innings.

Although Joe Girardi vowed to rest his two top relievers, Mariano Rivera and David Robertson, he turned to three other dependable arms to finish the final two innings. But Boone Logan, Luis Ayala, and Cory Wade gave up seven runs as the Rays tied the game on Dan Johnson's ninth-inning home run.

The teams played into the 12th inning before Evan Longoria blasted a walk-off home run against Scott Proctor, depositing the ball inside the left-field foul pole to a spot now known as "162 Landing" at the Trop.

**DJ3K**

Derek Jeter certainly didn't need another memorable moment to bolster his Hall of Fame résumé, but the Captain stamped his ticket to Cooperstown on July 9, 2011, drilling a home run against Rays ace David Price at Yankee Stadium for his 3,000th career hit.

Jeter became only the second player to hit a home run for his 3,000th hit, joining his former teammate Wade Boggs, who collected his milestone as a member of the Rays in 1998 and is the only player to have his number retired by Tampa Bay.

## Spring Slugfest

Bench-clearing brawls have become a rarity in the majors, but they're even more uncommon in spring training. That didn't stop the Yankees and Rays from going at it in March 2008, engaging in a pair of incidents four days apart. On March 8, Rays infielder Elliot Johnson collided violently with Francisco Cervelli at the plate, breaking the Yankees catcher's wrist and infuriating manager Joe Girardi. Four days later, Yankees outfielder Shelley Duncan slid into Rays second baseman Akinori Iwamura with his spikes up, prompting Jonny Gomes to sprint in from right field and take out Duncan, sparking a bench-clearing melee.

## Around the World

The Yankees and Rays opened the 2004 season with a pair of games at the Tokyo Dome in Japan, the only games either franchise has ever played outside North America. Hideki Matsui, playing his second year with New York, was the star of the show, though the series also marked the Yankees debut of Alex Rodriguez. Former Yankee Tino Martinez homered in the opener, an 8–3 Rays win, while Jorge Posada hit two home runs and Matsui wowed the fans with one of his own in a 12–1 win in the finale as 55,000 fans packed the building for both games.

## A-Rod Announces His Return

Nobody was sure what to expect from Alex Rodriguez when he returned from a one-year performance-enhancing-drug suspension in 2015, but A-Rod put on a show at the Trop on April 17, reminding us why he was considered the best player in baseball since the turn of the century. Rodriguez went 3-for-4 with two home runs—one of which traveled a jaw-dropping 471 feet—for his first multiple-homer game since May 2012.

offered. After the game, kids can head down to the field and run the bases.

Oh, and as a bonus, parking is free on these days for cars with four or more passengers.

"Sure, the Rays are looking for a new park," Topkin said. "But that's more because not nearly enough people are coming to the Trop, located in downtown St. Pete, a haul from the population center and growth areas of Tampa, not because it's that bad a place."

For Yankees fans, the Trop can often feel like home. The Yankees have called Tampa their spring training home since 1996 (their minor league complex is also across the street from George M. Steinbrenner Field), so there are plenty of Yankees fans in the area. Each time the Yankees visit, a high percentage of fans in the stands will be sporting New York colors, making games feel as homey for the Bombers as any ballpark other than Baltimore's Camden Yards.

Although Tampa Bay remains a relatively new major league town, the Trop also features one of the coolest features of any yard in the league: The **Ted Williams Museum & Hitters Hall of Fame**.

Williams, the Red Sox Hall of Famer, had no direct connection to the area aside from retiring to Florida in his later years. Originally opened in 1994 in Citrus County (about 100 miles from the ballpark), it was moved to the Trop in 2006 after the original facility went bankrupt.

In 2007, the museum was expanded with a new 7,000-square-foot wing that now features exhibits on Williams' career and his time in the Marines during World War II and the Korean War. Other exhibits include nods to the Negro Leagues, the All-American Girls Baseball League (as seen in one of my favorite movies, *A League of Their Own*), the Triple Crown, and a "Pitching Wall of Great Achievement" giving some of the game's great pitchers their due.

*Fans of all ages seem to enjoy touching the live rays at Tropicana Field—then watching the Yankees try to beat their namesakes.* (Steven Kovich/Tampa Bay Rays)

Several players with Yankees ties have been inducted into the Ted Williams Hitters Hall of Fame including Tino Martinez, Lou Piniella, Cecil Fielder and Joe DiMaggio. Admission to the museum, which is located to the right of the rotunda, is free. Autograph signings are also common, so make sure to check the website before you go.

The Rays also offer a tour of Tropicana Field, and while it doesn't have the history that Fenway Park offers, the tour takes you to a number of areas in the ballpark including the Gate 1 Rotunda, which is modeled after Ebbets Field; the Rays dugout; the visitor clubhouse (where the Yankees and every other visiting team prepares for games); the press box; the Rays Touch Tank; 162 Landing, where Evan Longoria's game-winning home run landed to clinch a postseason berth on the final day of the 2011 season; the Raysvision Control Room; and the Ted Williams Museum & Hitters Hall of Fame. Tours are $9 for adults, $8 for seniors, and $7 for children ages 3–14 (the tour is free for children ages 2 and under).

# Take the 7 Train to the Subway Series

**WHERE:** Citi Field

**WHEN:** One series each regular season

**HOW TO DO IT:** Buy tickets for games and the ballpark tour at mets.com

**COST FACTOR:** $19–$505 per ticket

**BUCKET RANK:** 🗑 🗑 🗑 🗑 🗑

The reports of the demise of the Subway Series in recent years have been greatly exaggerated.

Whether the Mets and Yankees are contenders or pretenders, this annual Interleague series remains one of the highlights in New York sports.

When Major League Baseball introduced Interleague play in 1997, the Yankees–Mets rivalry instantly became one of the centerpieces along with the Cubs and White Sox, another intracity matchup.

Prior to 1997, the Subway Series consisted of either exhibition games—the Mayor's Trophy Game was an annual tradition between the Yankees and Dodgers, then later the Yankees and Mets, who played 19 times—or World Series matchups between the Yankees and either the Dodgers or Giants before the two teams headed to California in 1958.

Once the Yankees and Mets began playing during the regular season in 1997, those annual meetings turned New York into a divided city. You were either for the Yankees or the Mets, or you weren't part of the hottest conversation in town.

The rivalry in the stands was fiercer than it was on the field, though the teams certainly fed off the energy in the stands.

"It was like the World Series," said Joe Girardi, who was catching for the Yankees when Interleague play debuted. "That's how intense those games were. They're still a big deal, but like anything, the first time is going to be a lot more hyped. People really got into it."

The Mets won the first-ever meeting, with right-hander Dave Mlicki throwing a shutout at Yankee Stadium against the defending World Series champions. The Yankees went on to win the next two, capturing the first meaningful series between the crosstown rivals.

# TOP 5 SUBWAY SERIES MOMENTS

**Clemens Beans Piazza (July 8, 2000)**

The crosstown rivalry was never more heated than this night at the old Stadium, when Roger Clemens drilled Mike Piazza in the head with a pitch during the nightcap of the first two-stadium doubleheader. Clemens became Public Enemy No. 1 with all Mets fans, a title that was ramped up even more when he threw a piece of a broken bat at Piazza during Game 2 of the World Series later that fall.

**Mlicki's Gem Gets the Series Started (June 16, 1997)**

Dave Mlicki had a largely forgettable career, going 66–80 for five teams over a 10-year career. But he pitched a shutout at Yankee Stadium in the first-ever regular season meeting between the Yankees and Mets, possibly the most hyped nonplayoff game in recent memory.

**Castillo Drops the Ball (June 12, 2009)**

The Mets first visit to the new Yankee Stadium looked like it would be a successful one when Alex Rodriguez hit a pop-up to second baseman Luis Castillo with two out in the ninth. But Castillo inexplicably dropped the ball, allowing Derek Jeter and Mark Teixeira to hustle around the bases from second and first, respectively, lifting the Yankees to an improbable 9–8 victory.

**Mariano Suffers a Rare Meltdown (July 10, 1999)**

The Yankees took a one-run lead into the ninth inning at Shea, handing the ball to Mariano Rivera, their unbeatable closer. The Mets put runners at second and third with two out, prompting Joe Torre to order an intentional walk of Mike Piazza to load the bases. Pinch-hitter extraordinaire Matt Franco delivered a two-out, two-strike single against Rivera, lifting the Mets to a 9–8 win while snapping the Yankees' streak of 124 straight wins when leading after eight innings.

> **Rivera Does It All in Milestone Save (June 28, 2009)**
> Mariano Rivera entered the game in the eighth inning, striking out
> Omir Santos with the tying run at third base to protect a one-run
> lead. The future Hall of Fame closer gave himself an insurance run
> by drawing a bases-loaded walk against Francisco Rodriguez for his
> first career RBI, then pitched a scoreless ninth for the 500th save of his
> career.

The Yankees won the three-game series the next season at Shea
Stadium, but the two teams began playing six games each year in
1999, with each club hosting three games.

In 2000, the June 11 game at Yankee Stadium was rained out, setting
up a day–night, two-stadium doubleheader the following month. Doc
Gooden beat his former team in the afternoon game at Shea, while
Roger Clemens won the nightcap in the Bronx, a game known mostly
for his beaning of Mike Piazza.

Only three months later, the Subway Series reached a new level of
importance as the Yankees and Mets faced off in the World Series for
the first time. The Yankees won in five games, capturing their third
straight championship.

Through the first 20 years of Interleague, the Yankees owned the
Subway Series, going 62–46 against the Mets. The series has been
played in four stadiums (the Yankees moved to their new stadium in
2009, the same year the Mets moved from Shea to Citi Field) and has
featured three two-stadium doubleheaders.

For a Yankees fan, attending a Subway Series game in the Bronx is
obviously a comfortable experience. But Citi Field is a great place
to catch a game, so why not head to Queens when the Yankees are
making the trip across the city?

Before you enter the ballpark, check out the parking lot to get a
taste of Shea Stadium. The four bases and the pitcher's rubber are

# TOP 5 PLAYERS TO PLAY FOR BOTH NEW YORK TEAMS

### David Cone

Cone went 81–51 with a 3.13 ERA for the Mets from 1987 to '92 before being traded to the Blue Jays, going 20–3 in 1988 to break out as a major star during the Mets' NL East title season. Following stops in Toronto, Kansas City, and Toronto again, Cone was traded to the Yankees in 1995, going 64–40 with a 3.91 ERA from '95 to 2000. He won four rings with the Yankees from 1996 to 2000, pitching some huge postseason games during the run.

### Doc Gooden

Gooden made his name with the Mets, winning the NL Rookie of the Year award in 1984 and the 1985 Cy Young Award with a 24–4 record and 1.53 ERA in his second season before helping the Mets to the 1986 World Series title. Following a drug suspension that cost him the 1995 season, Gooden resurfaced with the Yankees in 1996, throwing his first career no-hitter while filling in for Cone, who was out following surgery for an aneurysm. Gooden went 24–14 with a 4.67 ERA in parts of three seasons (1996–97, 2000) with the Yankees.

### Darryl Strawberry

Like Gooden, Strawberry became a star in Queens, bashing 252 home runs from 1983 to '90 with the Mets. He was a key cog in the 1986 World Series title team and after winning Rookie of the Year honors in 1983, the right fielder made seven straight All-Star teams beginning in 1984. Following three seasons with the Dodgers and a short stint with the Giants, Strawberry signed with the Yankees as a free agent in June 1995 and remained in the Bronx until he retired at the end of 1999, serving as a role player on three championship teams.

### Carlos Beltran

Beltran wanted to sign with the Yankees as a free agent in 2005, but with Bernie Williams already occupying center field in the Bronx, he signed a seven-year, $119 million deal with the Mets. Beltran hit 149 homers with the Mets—more than he hit with any team during his career—before being traded to the Giants prior to the 2011 trade deadline. Beltran eventually signed a three-year, $45 million pact with the Yankees before the 2014 season, posting solid numbers before being dealt to Texas at the 2016 deadline.

### Rickey Henderson

The Hall of Famer will always be remembered for his days in Oakland, but he stole 326 bases over five seasons with the Yankees and made four All-Star teams during their good-but-not-good-enough years in the late 1980s. Henderson played only one full season with the Mets, but he hit .315 with a .423 on-base percentage and stole 37 bases in 121 games—at age 40.

all marked in their original spots, while the "Home Run Apple" that used to rise every time a Mets player hit a home run sits between the 7 train exit and the main entrance to the ballpark.

As you approach Citi Field, you'll notice the similarities between the ballpark and Ebbets Field, the old Brooklyn ballpark the Dodgers called home before moving to Los Angeles. Enter through the **Jackie Robinson Rotunda**, which honors the life and career of the Hall of Famer. No, he never played for the Mets, but he did play in New York and made a bigger impact on the game than any other player in history. The eight-foot sculpture of Robinson's No. 42—which was retired by MLB in 1997—is quite a sight.

Adjacent to the Rotunda on the first-base side is the **Mets Hall of Fame and Museum**, a 3,700-foot space dedicated to the team's history featuring several interactive displays and highlight videos. Open only on game days, fans can check out the team's 1969 and 1986 World Series trophies along with plaques for each member of the team's Hall of Fame. Admission is free as long as you have a ticket to the game.

If you want a better look at the ballpark, take a one-hour Citi Field tour that brings you to the clubhouse, the field, the dugout, the press box, the scoreboard control room, the suite level, and the Mets Hall of Fame and Museum. Tours cost $13 for adults and $9 for seniors 60 or older and children 12 and under. Active military personnel are given complimentary tour tickets.

Here's the biggest tip I can give you about taking a trip to Citi Field: don't eat before you head to the ballpark. Citi Field features some of the best concessions in the majors, including **Shake Shack**, one of New York's favorite burger chains. The lines are always long, but don't fret—there are plenty of other options.

The **World's Fare Market** features **El Verano Taqueria** (tacos), **Daruma** (sushi), and **Mama's of Corona**, which has terrific Italian hero sandwiches and a tremendous turkey and mozzarella hero. (There's a second Mama's stand located on the upper level, which typically has much shorter lines.)

Out in left field, stop by **Keith's Grill**, named for former Mets first baseman Keith Hernandez, which serves a solid burger. If you're looking for barbeque, **Blue Smoke** has locations in center field and behind home plate on the Promenade level. For the seafood aficionado, **Catch of the Day** offers a fried flounder sandwich, a lobster roll, and clam and corn chowder. **Pat LaFrieda's** filet mignon sandwich is also a popular item.

Take the kids out to the **Good Humor Fan Fest** on the field level in center field to check out **Mr. Met's Kiddie Field**, a scale version of Citi Field, a batting cage, dunk tank, video game kiosks, and more. The area opens when the gates open and closes at the seventh-inning stretch.

While the Yankees have "YMCA" and "Cotton Eye Joe," the Mets have their traditions to watch for, too. The team takes the field to the classic "Meet the Mets" tune, while fans dance to "Lazy Mary" during the seventh-inning stretch.

Most seats offer a good view of the game, though Mets fans recommend not sitting too far down either baseline on the main level or in fair territory in left field or you might as well bring a radio to listen to the game for updates.

As for super fans, the Mets have a group called "The 7 Line Army" that rivals the Bronx's Bleacher Creatures. They sit in center field, just to the right of the current "Home Run Apple," making their voices heard throughout the game.

The best value—if you're up for it—might very well be to purchase a cheap ticket and find a good standing-room spot in the infield. Ushers will allow you to stand there for the entire game, giving you a great view of the field at a bargain price. Warning: Early in the season, these standing-room areas can be extremely windy and cold.

The Subway Series is as New York as it gets. It's one of the rare times that baseball takes center stage in both stadiums, with the crowd bringing back the feelings of both classic ballparks. If you've never been to a Yankees–Mets game, it's a must for any fan's bucket list.

*It might not have the history of Wrigley Field, but Chicago's newly named Guaranteed Rate Field makes for a fun weekend road trip to catch the Yankees away from the Bronx each season.* (Mark Feinsand)

# Tour the Rest of the American League One City at a Time

### Chicago: Guaranteed Rate Field

**Why to go:** The ballpark on the South Side doesn't have the same charm as Wrigley Field, but the White Sox do a good job of celebrating their history with more than a half-dozen statues located in the **White Sox Legends Sculpture Plaza** on the outfield concourse including Paul Konerko, Frank Thomas, Harold Baines, Nellie Fox, Carlton Fisk, and Minnie Minoso.

**What to see:** Young fans can check out the **Fundamentals Deck** high above the left-field bullpen, a 15,000-square-foot area providing children with a chance to learn the game's fundamentals from White Sox Training Academy coaches. There's a youth-sized Wiffle ball diamond, batting and pitching cages, and more. Also be sure to check out the **Plumbers Union Local 130 UA Shower** near Section 160, which was brought over from the old Comiskey Park.

**What to eat:** Elotes (also known as Corn off the Cob) is the most popular concession at the ballpark: fresh corn topped with various ingredients including butter, spices and cheese. The **Xfinity Zone Carvery** offers excellent sandwiches including pastrami, corned beef, and turkey, while the **Home Plate Club** and **Stadium Club** both have several solid options. For the truly gluttonous, grab some friends and several spoons and give the three-pound banana split a try.

**What else to do:** It's Chicago, so there's no shortage of things to do. The **Magnificent Mile** is a tourist trap (think Chicago's version of Times Square), but on a gorgeous summer day, there are few places I'd rather take a walk. Get some deep-dish pizza at **Giordano's**, then walk it off with a stroll through **Millennium Park**. Or do one of the other million things the Windy City has to offer.

## *Kansas City: Kauffman Stadium*
**Why to go:** The ballpark underwent a $250 million renovation before the 2009 season, making it one of the nicest facilities in the majors at which to catch a game. Among the activities at the **Outfield Experience** are a five-hole baseball-themed mini-golf course, playground, carousel, base-running area, batting cage, and pitcher's mound complete with radar gun.

**What to see:** The **Royals Hall of Fame Museum** is included in the cost of your ticket and is open through the top of the eighth. Watch a 15-minute film narrated by Buck O'Neil in a dugout-style theater, learn about the Hall of Famers in Cooperstown with K.C. connections, and check out the No. 5 made up of 3,154 baseballs, one for each of George Brett's career hits.

*Renovated before the 2009 season, Kauffman Stadium is one of the most beautiful ballparks in the American League.* (Mark Feinsand)

**What to eat:** By Section 249, check out **Andrew Zimmern's Canteen Skewers**, brought to you by the creator of Travel Channel's *Bizarre Foods*. He also has a hot dog stand in the ballpark. Kansas City's favorite local beer can be found at **Boulevard Brewing Co.'s** locations in Sections 206 and 252.

**What else to do:** The **Negro Leagues Baseball Museum** is located in the historic 18th and Vine district, just east of downtown. The **American Jazz Museum** is also nearby. While you're in town, make a point to stop at **Joe's Kansas City** for the best BBQ you'll ever have. Yes, it's in a gas station, and yes, the line is well worth the wait. Try a half-rack of ribs and take a Z-Man sandwich to go.

*Located in the heart of downtown Cleveland, Progressive Field is a great place to catch the Yankees on the road.* (Mark Feinsand)

### Cleveland: Progressive Field

**Why to go:** Cleveland might be the butt of many jokes, but Progressive Field is a great place to watch a game, complete with a nice view of downtown beyond the recently renovated center-field entrance. There's a two-story bar, **The Corner**, with a rooftop, while families can enjoy a two-story **Kids Clubhouse**, complete with games, toys, and interactive elements.

**What to see:** Like other teams, the Indians honor their franchise greats with statues of Bob Feller, Larry Doby, and Jim Thome beyond the center-field gate. Other Indians icons are honored in **Heritage Park** in center field, while the Bob Feller exhibit—complete with items from the Hall of Famer's life and career—can be found in the stadium's Terrace Club. Atop the bleachers, you'll find longtime Tribe fan John Adams, who attends every home game and bangs his drum, providing a sound that has become a signature at Indians games.

**What to eat:** The Indians have teamed with multiple popular local eateries for a long list of unique concession options. **Great Lakes Brewing Co.**, **Barrio**, **Melted Bar**, and **Grilled and Happy Dog** are among the fan favorites.

**What else to do:** A stop at the **Rock and Roll Hall of Fame** is a must during any trip to Cleveland, but leave yourself some time: there's so much to see there, it can take up most of your day. The East 4th Street and West 6th Street areas downtown have a variety of shops and eateries and are a short walk from the ballpark.

## Minnesota: Target Field

**Why to go:** Simply put, it's one of the nicest ballparks in the league and as fan friendly as it gets. Built in 2010, Target Field is set in the heart of downtown Minneapolis, giving you a huge variety of restaurants and bars to choose from before and after games. The gates are numbered after Twins greats Kirby Puckett (34), Harmon Killebrew (3), Tony Oliva (6), Rod Carew (29), and Kent Hrbek (14). Statues of all five players, former owners Calvin Griffith and Carl & Eloise Pohlad, and a giant Gold Glove are great photo opportunities, though my favorite is the statue of team mascot T.C. Bear.

**What to see:** The **Town Ball Tavern** is located on the third-base side of the park, honoring the tradition of amateur baseball in Minnesota. Be sure to look down at the floor, part of which is made of wood from the old Minneapolis Auditorium court that Minneapolis Lakers Hall of Famer George Mikan played on from 1948 to '56.

**What to eat:** Grab a polish sausage at **Kramarczuk's** and you'll fit in with most locals, or give **Red Cow**'s 60/40 burger a try—that's a burger with bacon ground right into the patty, then topped with cheese and more bacon. And of course, **State Fair Classics** by

Section 133 offers corn dogs, deep-fried pickle chips, a pork chop on a stick, and much more.

**What else to do:** Take a walk or bike ride along the Mississippi River, or check out the trendy Uptown area. Relax with a cocktail at **Seven Ultra Lounge** a couple blocks from the ballpark and enjoy great views of downtown. Or take the light rail to the **Mall of America** and **Nickelodeon Universe**, a theme park right inside the mall. Bonus shopping tip: there's no tax on clothing in Minnesota!

## *Detroit: Comerica Park*

**Why to go:** Where else can you catch a big-league game *and* ride a carousel and Ferris wheel in the same building? Not to mention the carousel has tigers instead of horses and the Ferris wheel cars are baseballs. The rest of the ballpark is pretty nice, too.

**What to see:** Before you enter the park, check out the 15-foot Tiger sculpture for a good photo op. Once you're inside, stop at the statue of Ernie Harwell and remember one of the great baseball voices of all time. There are also statues of Tigers greats Ty Cobb, Hank Greenberg, Charlie Gehringer, Hal Newhouser, Al Kaline, and Willie Horton beyond center and right field.

**What to eat: Big Cat Court** features a food court with everything from Mexican food to Greek food, with the gyro widely considered a fan favorite. There's a wide array of hot dog options, including the "Mac Daddy Dog" topped with mac and cheese. The **Michigan State Fair** stand offers corn dogs, deep fried Oreos, and a "Brat Pop," which is exactly what it sounds like: deep-fried bratwurst.

**What else to do:** The **Motown Museum** is a must-see, as fans can stand in the very place that legendary acts such as the Temptations, Four Tops, and Supremes recorded their hits. You can even sing a few bars of your own in Motown's Studio A. The **Henry Ford Museum** in Dearborn is also a terrific way to spend a day. For the gambling types, there are three casinos in downtown Detroit. If you can't get

*Comerica Park in Detroit is one of the many great new ballparks built in the past 20 years.* (Mark Feinsand)

enough baseball, head to the **Detroit Public Library** to see the Ernie Harwell Sports Collection of baseball artifacts.

### Anaheim: Angel Stadium

**Why to go:** Two words: **Rally Monkey**. The Angels' unofficial mascot first appeared in 2000 and became a fan favorite during the team's 2002 World Series season. The monkey, which only shows up in the seventh inning or later when the Angels trail by four or fewer runs, dances to House of Pain's "Jump Around" while holding a sign that says either RALLY TIME!!! or BELIEVE IN THE POWER OF THE RALLY MONKEY!!! The primate is also often spliced into some iconic movie scenes for dramatic effect. Oh, and the weather in Anaheim is usually perfect, making for a great day at the ballpark.

**What to see:** Opened in 1964, Angel Stadium is actually the fourth-oldest ballpark in the majors behind Fenway Park, Wrigley Field, and Dodger Stadium, but it feels much newer than that. A pair of giant hats—size 649½, to be exact—sit outside the home plate entrance, making for a great photo opportunity. The rock pile in left-center field was added as part of a late-1990s renovation, complete with fountains and fireworks.

**What to eat:** By Section 211, check out **The Big Cheese**, which features a short rib grilled cheese sandwich considered by many to be the best item in the ballpark. **Chronic Tacos**, a very popular Orange County chain, offers "The Nacho Daddy," a head-sized helmet piled high with all the fixings.

**What else to do: Disneyland** is only minutes away from the ballpark, and as long as you're fine with long lines and spending money, there are few places more family-friendly. Orange County also features some of the most beautiful beaches and gorgeous views you'll ever see.

## Seattle: Safeco Field

**Why to go:** First, it's my favorite ballpark in the majors. The retractable roof guarantees you'll see a game, and the summer weather in Seattle is usually gorgeous. Opened in 1999, there have been some pretty memorable moments at Safeco, including Felix Hernandez's 2012 perfect game and the Mariners' 116-win season in 2001 that featured Ichiro Suzuki's dazzling debut campaign.

**What to see:** The **Mariners Hall of Fame** features exhibits dedicated to franchise greats including Ken Griffey Jr., Edgar Martinez, Randy Johnson, and Jay Buhner. You'll also learn about the history of baseball in the Pacific Northwest dating back to 1877. Make sure not to miss the statue of late Mariners Hall of Fame broadcaster Dave Niehaus on the concourse overlooking center field.

*One of the best ballparks in the majors, Seattle's Safeco Field is a must-see for any baseball fan.* (Mark Feinsand)

**What to eat:** **Ivar's** is a great local seafood joint with a location inside Safeco that features Pacific Northwest clam chowder in a bread bowl and a salmon Caesar salad, among other offerings. **Edgar's Cantina**, named after Martinez, has a wide variety of Mexican-themed offerings, while **Intentional Wok** has excellent Thai food.

**What else to do:** The **Space Needle** provides incredible views of Mount Rainier, the entire Puget Sound, the Olympic Mountains, the Cascades, and every bit of the Emerald City from its observation deck. **Pike Place Market** isn't just a tourist destination, but also a real, working market with fresh fruits and vegetables from nearby farms and, of course, fish galore. You can watch the fishmongers as they pick the fresh catch off the ice and toss it for packaging, a long local tradition. The original **Starbucks** location is also a block away, though lines tend to be lengthy.

## Texas: Globe Life Park

**Why to go:** For starters, it won't be around much longer, so you have a limited time to check it off your list; the team and the City of Arlington are building a new, retractable-roof ballpark scheduled to open by 2021.

**What to see:** Be sure to check out the statue of Hall of Famer Nolan Ryan in the area behind center field, while the home run porch in right field is modeled after the old Tiger Stadium.

**What to eat:** Many concessions here are big; after all, they do everything big in Texas. The "Boomstick" is a two-foot-long hot dog with chili and cheese, named after Nelson "Boomstick" Cruz, while the "Choomongous" (named for Shin-Soo Choo) is a two-foot beef teriyaki sandwich. Also popular are the **State Fare** and **Just Bacon** stands.

**What else to do:** The **Six Flags Over Texas** amusement park is only minutes from the ballpark, as is **AT&T Stadium** if you want to try catching a Cowboys game. The **Sixth Floor Museum** at Dealey Plaza in Dallas is a quick 20-minute drive from Arlington and a must-visit for any JFK or American history buff.

## Houston: Minute Maid Park

**Why to go:** A very comfortable ballpark experience, thanks in part to the retractable roof that remains closed for much of the steamy summer. (The roof is often open in April and May, as well as part of September, when the weather is quite lovely.) As the Astros fans showed in 2015, the place can be electric when the team contends, making for a very exciting atmosphere.

**What to see:** Look for the train that travels from left field to center field whenever the Astros score or hit a home run. The train runs near Union Station, located adjacent to the ballpark, which served as a main train station in the early 19th century and helped Houston become a prominent southwestern city. Tal's Hill—a hill in fair territory deep center field—was another notable feature, but it was scheduled to be razed following the 2016 season. Outside the ballpark, take a photo with statues of Craig Biggio and Jeff Bagwell.

**What to eat:** You can't go to Texas and not have some BBQ, right? **Texas Smoke**—from celebrity chef Bryan Caswell—offers brisket and chopped beef sandwiches, though the baked potato loaded with chopped brisket is a local favorite. Caswell's **El Real** is another great option, featuring Tex-Mex such as beef and chicken fajitas, house-fried corn chips, and house-made salsa.

**What else to do: Space Center Houston**, the official visitor center of the Lyndon B. Johnson NASA Space Center, features more than 400 space artifacts along with several permanent and traveling exhibits. If you're fortunate to be in Houston when it's not oppressively hot, check out **Discovery Green**, a public urban park that offers food, activities, and more.

### Oakland: Oakland Coliseum

**Why to go:** Although the Coliseum lacks the charm it once did before "Mount Davis" was added on for the Raiders, it still offers an affordable night of entertainment for families, and the Athletics are usually competitive despite their financial constraints. The Coliseum is one of the few remaining ballparks that allows tailgating, giving it a football-like feeling with better weather.

**What to see:** According to beat writer Susan Slusser of the *San Francisco Chronicle*, sitting in the right-field seats with the die-hards "is a treat no serious baseball fan should miss." Fans there bring banners, they chant, and they'll even bring some drums from time to time, often interacting with the right fielders on both teams. "As fun a bunch of fans as you'll find anywhere," Slusser said.

**What to eat:** The Coliseum doesn't have the quality concessions that many newer ballparks offer, but there are a few standouts: **Kinder's**

**BBQ** has a signature Famous Ball Tip steak sandwich; **Ribs and Things** has excellent BBQ ribs, while **Saag's Club Level** offers several varieties of sausages. The best idea, however, is to stop at **In-N-Out** for an animal-style double-double before or after the game; it's one exit from the ballpark.

**What else to do:** We'll stick to the Oakland area, though keep in mind San Francisco is a short 20- to 30-minute drive away. The **USS Hornet** in Alameda (10 minutes from Oakland) is among the top historical ships in the United States, while **Jack London Square** is a popular Oakland entertainment, shopping, and dining destination. Downtown Oakland also has several of the area's best restaurants.

# Chapter 3

# Yankees Legends

*If you're reading this book, then chances are you never had an opportunity to watch Babe Ruth play baseball.*

*Perhaps you were able to see Yogi Berra or Thurman Munson in action, though. Depending on your age, you probably watched most if not all of Derek Jeter and Mariano Rivera's careers.*

*Sure, you've listened to Michael Kay, John Sterling, and Suzyn Waldman, but do the names Mel Allen, Red Barber, or Frank Messer mean anything to you?*

*It's one thing to know everything there is to know about the current team, but knowing the legendary figures in Yankees history— players, managers, broadcasters, and more— is just as important for any die-hard fan.*

*The Babe Ruth Birthplace and Museum includes reproductions of several rooms from the original home.* (Babe Ruth Birthplace Foundation, Inc.)

# Visit the Babe Ruth Birthplace and Museum

**WHERE:** 216 Emory Street, Baltimore, Maryland

**WHEN:** April–September: Monday through Sunday, 10 AM–5 PM; open until 7 PM for Orioles night games. October–March: Tuesday through Sunday, 10 AM–5 PM

**HOW TO DO IT:** For information, visit baberuthmuseum.org

**COST FACTOR:** Adults $10; Seniors/Military $8; Children 5–16 $5

**BUCKET RANK:** 🗑️ 🗑️ 🗑️ 🗑️

. . . . . . . . . . . . . . . . . . . . . . . . . . . . . . . . . . . . . . . . .

**W**hen the Yankees visit the Orioles in Baltimore, their fans come out in full force, turning Camden Yards into Yankee Stadium South.

But how should a Yankees fan spend the hours in the Inner Harbor before he or she heads to the ballpark?

What better way than to visit the birthplace of the most iconic Yankee—and baseball player—who ever lived?

Only blocks away from the ballpark, the Babe Ruth Birthplace and Museum is one-stop shopping for any fan looking to learn about the Great Bambino.

"In my opinion, that historic house is hallowed ground," said Michael Gibbons, the museum's executive director. "Aside from ballparks for baseball, there are very few buildings people would say are hallowed ground. The Babe Ruth Birthplace is one of them."

Follow the 60 baseballs painted on the sidewalk starting at the Ruth statue by Oriole Park and enter the quaint recreation of the home in which one of America's greatest icons was born on February 6, 1895.

The museum includes reproductions of several rooms from the original home. Ruth's widow, Claire, his two daughters, Dorothy and Julia, and his sister, Mamie, who was also born in the house, assisted in the design, assuring the recreations were as close to reality as possible.

The property was leased by Ruth's maternal grandfather, Pius Schamberger. The site was scheduled for demolition in the late 1960s, but a member of Baltimore Mayor Theodore McKeldin's staff launched a campaign to save and restore the site, which opened to the public as a national shrine in 1974.

In addition to the recreated rooms, there's enough Ruth memorabilia to make you think you were in Cooperstown.

*Among the many artifacts at the Babe Ruth Birthplace and Museum are the Bambino's bat and several balls from the 500 Home Run Club.*
(Babe Ruth Birthplace Foundation, Inc.)

Among the highlights:

- Ruth's hymnal from his days at St. Mary's Industrial School inscribed with the words "World's worst singer, world's best pitcher" and a crucifix he made at the school. The hymnal was found during construction of Cardinal Gibbons High School after St. Mary's closed.

- Bats used by both Ruth and Shoeless Joe Jackson

- A ball signed by the 1932 Yankees

- A lineup card from Ruth's first professional game with the Orioles vs. Buffalo

- A Ruth rookie baseball card worth an estimated $1 million

- A bat from Ruth's 1927 season with seven notches carved into it. What did the notches represent? "Hot dogs, home runs, women," Gibbons said. "Who knows?"

- The "Sportsman of the Century" award for baseball presented to Ruth's family by *Sports Illustrated*

- Family photos and home movies from Ruth's childhood in Baltimore

An exhibit titled "Playing the Babe" looks at Ruth's history on the silver screen and on television, including John Goodman's 1992 portrayal of the Bambino in the film *The Babe*.

*Called Shot Theater* features footage of Ruth's famed called home run against the Cubs in Game 3 of the 1932 World Series at Wrigley Field. The film is the property of Kirk Kandle, whose great-grandfather, Matt Kandle, shot from his seat about 15–20 rows behind third base.

The museum has exclusive rights to show the film, which Gibbons had merged with an old MovieTone piece and narrated exclusively for the exhibit by Hall of Fame broadcaster Jon Miller.

A "500 Home Run Club" exhibit features Ruth's fellow members of the exclusive club, including Eddie Murray, the Hall of Fame Oriole who donated his 500th home run ball to the museum.

In the "Babe Ruth Theater" is a marvelous film titled *O' Say Can You See: The Star Spangled Banner in Sports*, created by the Babe Ruth Birthplace Foundation in 2013 for Baltimore's citywide effort to celebrate the 200th anniversary of our national anthem.

The film looks at the origin of the anthem's place in sports, which dates back to the 1918 World Series, when Ruth pitched the Red Sox to a championship. It features some of the greatest anthem performances in baseball history, lacing them together in a memorable rendition of the song.

It takes about an hour to get through the museum, though the city features other notable Ruthian sites including his parents' grave sites, the site of St. Mary's Industrial School where Ruth played his high school baseball, and the house Ruth called home during his youth.

# Visit the National Baseball Hall of Fame and Museum

**WHERE:** 25 Main Street, Cooperstown, New York

**WHEN:** Late May through Labor Day (9 AM–9 PM); Labor Day through Memorial Day (9AM–5PM)

**HOW TO DO IT:** For information, visit baseballhall.org

**COST FACTOR:** Adults $23; Seniors $15; Veterans/Children $12

**BUCKET RANK:** 🪣 🪣 🪣 🪣 🪣

The National Baseball Hall of Fame and Museum honors the history of the game, but once you walk into the building in Cooperstown, New York, it doesn't take long to realize that the Yankees are the most prominent team represented in the building.

It makes sense. No team has won as many championships or boasts as many Hall of Famers as the Bronx Bombers, something that becomes evident as you make your way through the hallowed halls of this must-see museum.

"Given the Yankees' history, their legendary players, managers, and executives that have made the Hall of Fame, as well as all of the indelible moments and dynasty teams they have had, I would think that after going to a Yankees game, the Hall of Fame would be second on the 'bucket list' of any Yankees fan," said Jeff Idelson, president of the National Baseball Hall of Fame and Museum.

"The Yankees have an incredible amount of real estate in the Baseball Hall of Fame; not because we play favorites, but because of how they've contributed to baseball's vast history."

As of 2016, there were 312 elected members of the Hall of Fame, consisting of 217 former major league players, 28 executives, 35 Negro leaguers, 22 managers, and 10 umpires.

Of that group, 52 had ties to the Yankees, including 28 that spent more time with the franchise than any other team. Twenty Hall of Famers have a Yankees logo on their cap (or, in Yogi Berra's case, pinstripes on his uniform, as his plaque features a profile view of the catcher).

Although the 1927 and 1998 Yankees are considered two of the greatest teams of all time, it's the 1931–33 Yankees—they won the World Series in 1932, finishing second in the other two seasons— that has more Hall of Fame representation than any other in history. Six of their eight everyday players—a whopping 75 percent!—were inducted, along with three pitchers and manager Joe McCarthy.

Fans of the most recent Yankees dynasty will have a field day at the Hall of Fame, where manager Joe Torre became the first member of that team inducted back in 2014.

These numbers should grow in the coming years as Mariano Rivera and Derek Jeter—both near certainties to be first-ballot inductees— become eligible for the Hall of Fame.

"Any time that a player from the organization gets elected, it helps fans further engage the Hall of Fame because all of a sudden their favorite guy is now in Cooperstown," Idelson said. "Many fans have been there, for some it's a bucket list item, but when your favorite player earns election, fans tend to come out to salute them. Some of the Yankees in the voting pipeline, that bodes well for Cooperstown because of the relationship they had with the fans."

Although Torre is currently the lone Hall of Famer from the Yankees most recent era, the museum features a number of artifacts from the past 20 years of great Yankees for your viewing pleasure.

Among them are Jeter's 1996 World Series jersey and his batting gloves from his 3,000th hit, the bat Hideki Matsui used during the six-RBI Game 6 that helped him win 2009 World Series MVP honors, the glove Andy Pettitte used to set the Yankees' strikeout record in 2013, Rivera's cap from the 2013 All-Star Game (his final Midsummer Classic), and the bat Aaron Boone used to hit his pennant-winning home run against the Red Sox in 2003.

As great as the Yankees were in the late 1990s and early 2000s, a trip to the Hall of Fame will remind you what real greatness was.

Ruth is considered to be the greatest slugger in the game's storied history, making him worthy of his own room in the museum.

"When fans come to the Baseball Hall of Fame, they invariably want to ask about players that they're familiar with, which are usually players from recent history," Idelson said. "There are two players that transcend time for their impact on the game: Jackie Robinson and Babe Ruth. Jackie covers not only being a great player, but his cultural contribution. With Ruth, there's also a lot of culture with him, but he's recognized for all of the accolades that he achieved."

Ruth's career is chronicled in the hall, which features the silver crown he received to commemorate his 59-homer season in 1921, the bat he used to hit three home runs in Game 4 of 1926 World Series, his bat from his 60th home run in 1927, and the bat he used to hit his 714th and final home run in 1935.

The 1927 bat is notable not only for what Ruth did with it, but also for what Ruth did to it.

"Marking equipment was more allowable, so every time he homered, he would carve a notch around the bat's trademark," Idelson said. "There are 28 notches around this bat, which is unique because of what he did, but also because he had 60 home runs that year, more than any other American League team."

Ruth may have his own room, but nearly every exhibit in the Hall of Fame has some association with the Yankees.

"The Yankees show up in our Women in Baseball exhibit with Suzyn Waldman's pioneering ways as a viable woman sportscaster who calls games," Idelson said. "The 'Core Four' and A-Rod are part of our 'Whole New Ballgame' exhibit, which is the most recent part of baseball history. We have Lou Gehrig's locker, Joe DiMaggio's locker, Mickey Mantle's locker. They're everywhere. Even in our broadcasting exhibit, you've got Mel Allen."

An exhibit called "Autumn Glory" highlights the World Series, and given the Yankees' 40 American League pennants and 27 World Series titles, they are front and center. Twenty-seven televisions show highlights from Yankees World Series seasons, while an authentic replica of the 1996 World Series trophy is also on display.

Among the other Yankees artifacts on display at the Hall:

- Yogi Berra's 1951 MVP Award

- Joe DiMaggio's glove, bat, and shoes

- Lou Gehrig's home and away jerseys from his final season in 1939

- Ron Guidry's jersey and cap from his historic 1978 season

- Miller Huggins' Yankees sweater from 1925

- Don Larsen's cap from his 1956 World Series perfect game

- Mickey Mantle's bat from his 1956 Triple Crown season

- Mantle's bat from his 500th career home run

- Don Mattingly's bat from his major league–record eight-game home run streak

- Allie Reynolds' bronzed glove used in two no-hitters in 1951

- Roger Maris' 61st home run baseball from 1961

- The microphone used by longtime PA announcer Bob Sheppard

"The Yankees have had such an enormous influence on baseball that they show up all over the museum," Idelson said. "They're everywhere."

. . . . . . . . . . . . . . . . . . . . . . . . . . . . . . . . . .

# Learn the Yankees' Retired Numbers

No team has the rich history that the Yankees do, and nowhere is that more evident than on the wall in left field, where 21 numbers hang in honor of the men that made the Bronx Bombers great.

The Yankees' 20 retired numbers—for 21 players and managers, as Yogi Berra and Bill Dickey both wore No. 8—are by far the most of any team. The Cardinals are second with 13, followed by the Reds, Dodgers, White Sox, and Braves with 10 each.

"Getting your number retired with the Yankees was extremely special for me," said Hall of Famer Reggie Jackson, who played with the Yankees from 1977 to '81. "I was already in the Hall of Fame when that happened. It was an extremely special moment because you start getting compared with some of the greatest players in baseball history.

"When you're included in that fraternity, it really does validate your career. It's something you know is very special because you're included with one of the great franchises in history. For any player

*Babe Ruth isn't just the greatest Yankee of all time; he's widely considered the best baseball player ever.* (Babe Ruth Birthplace Foundation, Inc.)

that played with the Yankees to be singled out as a special player is great."

Lou Gehrig's No. 4 was retired on January 6, 1940, though general manager Ed Barrow simply made an announcement rather than the club holding a ceremony. It was the first number ever retired by a major league team.

On April 15, 1997, Major League Baseball retired No. 42 throughout the entire game to honor Jackie Robinson, though players who had the number at the time were permitted to continue wearing it.

Mariano Rivera was one of those players, keeping the number he would wear until his retirement in 2013, when he became the last player to ever claim 42 as his own. Although the Yankees had retired 42 in Dodgers colors like every other team, Rivera's 42 was officially retired by the club during a special celebration of the closer's career on September 22, 2013. A pinstriped 42 was hung with the rest of the Yankees' retired numbers.

Joe DiMaggio had his No. 5 retired at the Yankees' home opener in 1952, while Berra, Dickey, Roger Maris, Whitey Ford, Elston Howard, and Casey Stengel all had theirs retired during an Old Timers' Day at the Stadium.

While some teams only retire numbers for players that make it into the Hall of Fame, being a legend in the sport and being a legend in the Bronx are two different things.

Don Mattingly was the face of the franchise through much of the 1980s and the first half of the 1990s, while Ron Guidry was one of the most dominant pitchers in Yankees history, playing a huge role in the 1977–78 World Series titles.

Bernie Williams was the heart of the Yankees' championship run in the late 1990s, and although his numbers weren't quite enough to get him into Cooperstown, his impact in the Bronx made it a no-brainer to hang No. 51 at Yankee Stadium.

"It is an unbelievable honor," said Williams, whose number was retired on May 24, 2015. "It's the culmination of not only the work that I put in from the time that I was eight years old—I never envisioned myself being a Yankee, even less having my number retired—but it has more significance than that.

"It wasn't only about myself, but also everybody else that helped put me in that position. It was my parents, first and foremost, my family, my friends, my teammates, coaches, and everybody else that gave me great vibes and great thoughts and wanted me to do well. My generation, even beyond my generation, when I pass on, people are still going to see that number and know about me."

Williams is one of five players from those late-1990s/early-2000s teams to have his number retired, joined by Rivera, Andy Pettitte, Jorge Posada, and manager Joe Torre. Derek Jeter's No. 2 is scheduled to be retired in May 2017, as the Yankees officially retire their final single digit.

"I consider that a great honor, knowing how many people have played for that team and how many people were part of all those great championship teams," Williams said. "There was a group of us that were lucky enough and blessed enough to be considered to have our numbers retired by this great organization. I have no words to describe what a big honor that is."

Pettitte's No. 46 was retired on August 23, 2015, the day after the Yankees honored his longtime batterymate, Posada, by hanging up No. 20. For Pettitte, seeing his number out there along with those of Babe Ruth, DiMaggio, and Mickey Mantle was an incredibly humbling experience.

"When I see who's out there, that's what really gets me; I feel like there's no way I should be out there with those guys," Pettitte said. "Coming up as through the minor leagues as a young player, having the opportunity to be around Yogi and at a very young age in the big leagues to meet Joe DiMaggio, to know that I'm out there and that no one else is going to wear my uniform number, it's surreal.

"I really can't believe it because I guess I don't think that much of myself as a player. I know I had a great career and a special career, what I was able to accomplish. I just look at it that I had so many wonderful people around me, my teammates, to help me do what I did. Extremely blessed and honored to have had my number retired by them."

Here is the complete list of the Yankees' retired numbers and a little bit about the men who wore them:

**No. 1: Billy Martin (Number retired August 10, 1986)**
Martin was most well-known for his five managerial stints with the Yankees and his on-again, off-again relationship with owner George Steinbrenner throughout the 1970s and 1980s. But he was a key contributor to four championship teams (1951, '52, '53 and '56), hitting .333 in 28 career World Series games, while managing the 1977 championship club.

**No. 3: Babe Ruth (Number retired June 13, 1948)**
Considered by many to be the greatest player—and one of the most colorful—in the game's history, Ruth was sold to the Yankees by the Red Sox in 1920 before becoming the most prolific slugger ever. A part of four World Series champions, Ruth was a member of the Hall of Fame's inaugural class in 1936.

**No. 4: Lou Gehrig (Number retired January 6, 1940)**
Gehrig's streak of 2,130 consecutive games was the gold standard until Cal Ripken Jr. broke his record in 1995, but the "Iron Horse" didn't just play every day—he produced like few players ever. Gehrig drove in at least 100 runs in 13 straight seasons and holds the American League's RBI record with 184 in 1931. A two-time AL MVP, Gehrig also won the league's Triple Crown in 1934.

## No. 5: Joe DiMaggio (Number retired April 18, 1952)

One of the greatest all-around players in history, the man known as the "Yankee Clipper" blended the ability to hit for average and power with phenomenal center field skills and a strong, accurate arm. A two-time batting champion and three-time AL MVP, DiMaggio had a .325 career average and won nine World Series rings despite losing three years of his career to military service. His record 56-game hitting streak in 1941 hasn't been—and may never be—broken.

## No. 6: Joe Torre (Number retired August 23, 2014)

Although the *Daily News* shouted CLUELESS JOE on its back page the day after he became manager, Torre clearly knew what he was doing. The Brooklyn native guided the Yankees to six AL pennants and four World Series titles, reaching the postseason during all 12 of his seasons in the Bronx. His 1,173 wins are second only to Joe McCarthy in team history.

## No. 7: Mickey Mantle (Number retired June 8, 1969)

In his first 14 seasons with the Yankees (1951–64), Mantle led the Yankees to 12 AL pennants and seven World Series titles, setting Fall Classic records for home runs, RBI, runs scored, and walks that still stand today. The three-time MVP won the Triple Crown in 1956 with a .343 average, 52 home runs, and 130 RBI, considered by many to be one of the greatest seasons in history.

## No. 8: Yogi Berra (Number retired July 22, 1972)

Berra never led the league in a single offensive category, yet he is one of only 10 players with three league MVP awards and was considered the foundation of the Yankees' dominant teams from the end of World War II through the early 1960s.

## No. 8: Bill Dickey (Number retired July 22, 1972)

Dickey caught more than 100 games per year for 13 straight seasons from 1929 to '41, an American League record. His streak of 125 games behind the plate without allowing a passed ball has also never been matched in the AL. Dickey won seven World Series titles in pinstripes, batting .300 or better in 10 of his first 11 seasons.

### No. 9: Roger Maris (Number retired July 21, 1984)

Maris' 1961 season remains one of the greatest ever, as he slugged it out with teammate Mickey Mantle all summer before eventually catching and passing Babe Ruth for a then–major league record 61 home runs. His record stood until 1998, though it remains the most home runs ever hit by a player in the AL. A two-time AL MVP, Maris was also considered to be one of the best defensive right fielders in Yankees history.

### No. 10: Phil Rizzuto (Number retired August 4, 1985)

In his 13 years with the Yankees, Rizzuto—the beloved "Scooter"—played in nine World Series and won seven titles. Known for his slick fielding, Rizzuto won the 1950 AL MVP award with a .324 average, 200 hits, and 125 runs scored, then hit .320 in the 1951 World Series to earn MVP honors. He went on to a second career as one of the most popular broadcasters in team history from 1957 to '96.

### No. 15: Thurman Munson (Number retired August 3, 1979)

The leader of the Yankees' late-1970s championship teams, Munson was a rock behind the plate and a force with the bat. He won three consecutive Gold Gloves (1973–75) and hit .300 with at least 100 RBI in each season from 1975–77. He also hit the first home run in the remodeled Yankee Stadium. The Captain's life was tragically cut short by a plane crash on August 2, 1979.

### No. 16: Whitey Ford (Number retired August 3, 1974)

The greatest starting pitcher in Yankees history, Ford's 236–106 career record marks the best winning percentage (.690) of any $20^{th}$ century pitcher. Ford, nicknamed the "Chairman of the Board," led the AL in wins three times, also leading in ERA and shutouts twice. The 1961 Cy Young Award winner also pitched in 11 World Series (he won six, including MVP honors in 1961), setting various records including 10 victories, 33 consecutive scoreless innings, and 94 strikeouts.

### No. 20: Jorge Posada (Number retired August 22, 2015)

A member of the Core Four, Posada played all 17 of his seasons with the Yankees, hitting 275 home runs with 1,065 RBI while making five All-Star teams. Posada is one of only six catchers all-time to have at least 11 seasons of at least 17 homers, playing for four World Series winners.

### No. 23: Don Mattingly (Number retired August 31, 1997)

A nine-time Gold Glove winner and the 1985 AL MVP, Mattingly—nicknamed "Donnie Baseball"—was named the 10th captain in Yankees history. The popular Mattingly never won a championship, reaching his lone postseason in 1995 before retiring at the end of that season, but he was the face of the franchise through most of his career before passing the baton to Derek Jeter.

### No. 32: Elston Howard (Number retired July 21, 1984)

The first African-American player in Yankees history, Howard won two Gold Gloves behind the plate while helping the Yankees to nine AL pennants and four World Series championships. Howard won the 1963 AL MVP award and made nine straight All-Star teams from 1957 to '65.

### No. 37: Casey Stengel (Number retired August 8, 1970)

One of the most successful managers in history, Stengel guided the Yankees to 10 AL pennants and seven World Series titles in a 12-year span. With 1,905 wins with four franchises over 25 seasons, Stengel was elected to the Hall of Fame in 1966.

### No. 42: Mariano Rivera (Number retired September 22, 2013)

Quite simply, the greatest of all time. No reliever had the success Rivera enjoyed, his cut fastball shattering bats and hitters' confidence throughout his 19-year career. The all-time saves leader with 652, Rivera—a Core Four member—took his game to the next level in October, establishing postseason records with 96 games, 42 saves, and a 0.70 ERA, winning five World Series titles and the 1999 World Series MVP award.

### No. 44: Reggie Jackson (Number retired August 14, 1993)

"Mr. October" put on one of the most memorable displays in World Series history in 1977, hitting three home runs—all on the first pitch—in the Game 6 clincher. Jackson was an All-Star in all five of his seasons with the Yankees, hitting 144 of his 563 career home runs. Jackson—who was inducted into the Hall of Fame in 1993—still works with the Yankees as a special advisor.

### No. 46: Andy Pettitte (Number retired August 23, 2015)

Pettitte holds the Yankees' franchise record for strikeouts with 2,020 and his 219 wins with the club trail only Whitey Ford and Red Ruffing. The left-hander pitched 15 seasons (1995–2003, 2007–10, 2012–13) for New York, making three All-Star teams while becoming the only player drafted by the Yankees to win 200 big-league games. Pettitte won 18 games in the postseason, including the clinchers in all three rounds of the 2009 title run.

### No. 49: Ron Guidry (Number retired August 23, 2003)

A four-time All-Star, three-time 20-game winner, two-time World Series champion, and former co-captain, Guidry posted one of the most dominant seasons in history in 1978. Guidry—who became known as "Louisiana Lightning"—went 25–3 with a 1.74 ERA, striking out a club record 248 batters while throwing nine shutouts and winning the AL Cy Young Award. His 18-strikeout game against the Angels remains the franchise standard.

### No. 51: Bernie Williams (Number retired May 24, 2015)

The first homegrown cog in what became a dynasty in the late 1990s and early 2000s, Williams played his entire 16-year career (1991–2006) in pinstripes. Williams made five All-Star teams, and won four Gold Gloves and the 1998 AL batting title, helping the Yankees to four World Series titles between 1996 and 2000. The 1996 ALCS MVP, Williams is the Yankees' all-time postseason leader in home runs (22) and RBI (80).

# Crunch the Numbers: Know the Yankees' Records

**N**o sport treasures its statistics the way baseball does, with numbers such as .406, 762, and 4,256 immediately conjuring images of Ted Williams, Barry Bonds, and Pete Rose.

Yankees players have reached their share of milestones through the years, the franchise's all-time lists looking like a who's who of baseball greats. Here are a few numbers to know:

**3,465:** Derek Jeter's career hit total is the most of any Yankee in history, having passed Lou Gehrig's previous franchise record of 2,721 on September 11, 2009. Jeter became the only Yankee to record 3,000 hits on July 9, 2011, reaching the milestone with a home run against Tampa Bay's David Price.

**56:** Joe DiMaggio's major league–record hitting streak, a mark that has never been seriously challenged since he set it in 1941. In fact, Hal Chase's 33-game streak in 1907 is the only other time a Yankee even hit in 30 straight games.

**61:** Roger Maris' single-season Yankees home run record stood as baseball's gold standard for more than 35 years before Mark McGwire (70) and Sammy Sosa (66) broke it in 1998, only to see Barry Bonds set a new mark (73) in 2001. Maris, Babe Ruth, Mickey Mantle, and Alex Rodriguez are the only Yankees ever to hit 50 or more homers in a season.

**659:** Babe Ruth hit 714 home runs in his career, a mark that stood until Hank Aaron passed him in 1974. The Great Bambino hit 659 of those in a Yankees uniform, the most any player has ever hit with the club. Mickey Mantle (536) is the only other Yankee to hit 500 homers in pinstripes.

**1,993:** Lou Gehrig hit 166 fewer home runs for the Yankees than Ruth did, yet the Iron Horse's 1,993 RBI remain the franchise record as do his 184 RBI in a single season (1931). Gehrig also holds the Yankees' consecutive games played mark at 2,130, a streak surpassed only by Cal Ripken Jr. in major league history.

**.349:** Ruth's .349 batting average is the highest in Yankees history (minimum 2,500 plate appearances), besting Gehrig's .340.

**.484:** Ruth posted an incredible .484 on-base percentage with the Yankees, making him one of six players to have an OBP of .400 or higher with the club (Gehrig, Mantle, Charlie Keller, Jason Giambi, and George Selkirk).

**236:** Whitey Ford's 236 victories are the most by any Yankees pitcher, while only two others—Red Ruffing (231) and Andy Pettitte (219)—won as many as 200 games for the team. Four members of baseball's 300-win club have pitched for the Yankees, though neither Roger Clemens (83), Randy Johnson (34), Phil Niekro (32) nor Gaylord Perry (4) even reached triple digits in wins with New York.

**2,020:** Andy Pettitte holds the Yankees' career strikeout record, the only pitcher in team history to collect more than 2,000 Ks.

**248:** Ron Guidry holds the Yankees' single-season strikeout record with 248, which came during his epic 1978 season. Guidry's 1.74 ERA that season is also the lowest any Yankees left-hander has ever had, though righty Spud Chandler's 1.64 in 1943 remains the team record.

**652:** Mariano Rivera's 652 career saves are not only a Yankees record, but they're more than anybody has ever had in baseball history. Rivera recorded nine seasons of 40 or more saves, topping the 50-save mark twice.

**22:** The Yankees have won 22 American League MVP awards, with Joe DiMaggio, Yogi Berra, and Mickey Mantle winning three times each. Lou Gehrig, Roger Maris, and Alex Rodriguez each won twice as a Yankee, while Spud Chandler is the only Yankees pitcher to ever capture the award.

. . . . . . . . . . . . . . . . . . . . . . . . . . . . . . .

# Debate the Yankees' Mount Rushmore

It's one of the great bar-stool arguments in sports: Who is your Mount Rushmore of (fill in the blank)?

The real Mount Rushmore, located in Keystone, South Dakota, honors four U.S. presidents: George Washington, Thomas Jefferson, Theodore Roosevelt, and Abraham Lincoln.

The sports version of the famous mountain can work with any team, league, or sport. Just pick the four most influential people in the organization's history and that's your Mount Rushmore.

Of course, choosing those four is a completely subjective exercise, leaving plenty of room for spirited debate.

"I love these arguments," Hall of Famer Reggie Jackson said. "That's one of the great things about baseball. It's part of the game."

In 2015, Major League Baseball held a fan vote for every team's "Franchise Four," a clear nod to the Mount Rushmore concept. The results, announced at the All-Star Game in Cincinnati, revealed the following four for the Yankees:

Babe Ruth, Lou Gehrig, Joe DiMaggio, and Mickey Mantle.

The other four finalists were Yogi Berra, Whitey Ford, Derek Jeter, and Mariano Rivera.

It's difficult to argue with these selections. Four legendary Hall of Famers considered to be on the short list of the greatest baseball players of all time. Ruth, Gehrig, DiMaggio, and Mantle seem like the obvious choices, but is there an argument to be made for anybody else?

"If you're limiting it to four, then I don't see an argument," said Marty Appel, author of *Pinstripe Empire* and a longtime Yankees public relations employee.

But if nobody had an argument, this wouldn't be a debate.

*Lou Gehrig, Babe Ruth, Joe DiMaggio, and Mickey Mantle are all definite candidates for a Yankees Mount Rushmore.* (AP Images)

# TOP 10 MOUNT RUSHMORE CANDIDATES

**Babe Ruth:** The Great Bambino hit 659 of his 714 home runs with the Yankees, starting the franchise's winning tradition with seven trips to the World Series and four championships.

**Lou Gehrig:** The Iron Horse spent his entire 17-year career in the Bronx, hitting 493 home runs before his disease forced him to retire at 36—and deliver the most famous speech in baseball history.

**Red Ruffing:** The Hall of Famer won 231 games during 15 seasons with the Yankees, pitching in seven World Series while winning six titles.

**Joe DiMaggio:** Perhaps the greatest all-around player in team history, DiMaggio hit .325 with 389 home runs and 1,537 RBI in 13 seasons, missing three years in his prime to serve in the Army.

**Mickey Mantle:** A 16-time All-Star, the Hall of Famer hit 536 home runs and played in a dozen World Series, winning seven titles. Mantle is considered the greatest switch-hitter in baseball history.

**Yogi Berra:** A lifelong Yankee who won three MVP awards during his 19-year career, Berra made 15 consecutive All-Star teams and is one of the most beloved Yankees of all time.

**Whitey Ford:** The "Chairman of the Board" holds the team record with 236 career wins, while he also won the 1961 Cy Young Award and World Series MVP honors. Ford pitched in 11 World Series, taking home six rings.

**Don Mattingly:** For a six-year stretch in the 1980s, Mattingly was the best player in the game and the face of the Yankees franchise. The respected and popular captain made six All-Star teams, but never played in the World Series.

**Derek Jeter:** The only Yankee with 3,000 hits, Jeter was a steady constant during the late-1990s/early-2000s dynasty, winning another title in 2009 after the Yankees opened their new ballpark.

**Mariano Rivera:** The greatest closer of all time, Rivera helped lock down five World Series titles and provided incredible stability in the back-end of the bullpen. His 652 saves are a major league record.

"There are about 10 guys you can pick and you're not going to go wrong with any of them," said Brian Richards, curator of the New York Yankees Museum Presented by Bank of America.

Richards and Yankees historian Tony Morante chose Ruth, DiMaggio, Berra, and Jeter as their Mount Rushmore in the Bronx.

"That's not to take anything away from Mickey or Lou," Richards said. "Yogi, I think, is underrated. What he did as a catcher, he was the heart of those teams in the early '50s. His bat, he was an RBI machine in the middle of the lineup, he knew how to call a game and get the most out of those starting pitchers.

"Casey (Stengel) was platooning all these guys; that's why nobody has huge stats from the early '50s. The only regulars were Mickey, (Phil) Rizzuto, and Yogi. Everyone else was platooning and being moved around. Yogi was the heart of those teams, offensively and defensively. He was the bridge between DiMaggio's later years and the prime of Mickey's career. Mickey was there, but he was so green and so raw, he just wasn't ready until 1956 when he set the world on fire. Yogi was really the link from DiMaggio to Mantle."

As for Jeter, Richards believes his legacy will only grow as the years pass.

"Derek is in the position now where Yogi was in the late '60s," Richards said. "He had an awesome career, but he wasn't on the level of these guys. Twenty or 30 years from now, I think you'll see Derek's name mentioned alongside these guys. He wasn't a home run hitter, but his overall play, his offensive contributions year after year after year, you're going to see more and more with time how great he was."

Jack Curry, a longtime baseball writer for the *New York Times* who now works for the YES Network, believes the fans got the vote right with the big four.

"I can't mess around with the main four: Ruth, Gehrig, Mantle, DiMaggio," Curry said. "If you look at the numbers, it's not difficult. There might be people who want to talk about Jeter with the number of hits that he accumulated, but I look at those guys as being on a slightly higher level.

"If you let me go to a fifth or sixth, Jeter and Rivera would be in contention, but how do you leave Yogi Berra and his 10 World Series rings off? You'd have to have an unbelievable argument to convince me that Ruth, Gehrig, Mantle, and DiMaggio aren't the guys."

Limiting the list to four players is the fun of the debate, though some people have far too much trouble reducing their list to a foursome.

"It's hard to limit it to four people," Joe Girardi said. "Do I have to answer this one? It's too hard. I think I'd have eight. I think I'd put a front and a back side of the mountain."

Jackson, who was inducted into the Hall of Fame in 1993, said he needed six spots for his personal Mount Rushmore.

"You have to have Ruth and Gehrig, and I think the next guy would be Mantle," Jackson said. "I couldn't do four. I think the next greatest Yankee is Yogi Berra. Yogi's accomplishments, he might be up with Mickey. He finished second or third six times in the MVP award—and he won three."

"Then you have Whitey and DiMaggio. You can put those last three in any order. I have no problem saying that my Mount Rushmore is six. You're talking about the greatest Yankees of all time. I wouldn't name four; I would build a bigger mountain."

# Holy Cow! Listen to Yankees Broadcasters through the Years

**B**aseball broadcasters can sometimes feel like members of your family.

For six-plus months per year, their voices fill your home or car, bringing you all the Yankees action from the Bronx or wherever the team happens to be playing.

For more than two decades, Mel Allen was the voice of the Yankees, an Alabama native who was as much a part of the fabric of New York as any of the players whose home runs he called.

"When I was a little girl, my brother and I would take the streetcar to Fenway Park to watch the Yankees get off the bus," said Yankees broadcaster Suzyn Waldman, who grew up in the Boston area. "The Yankees always won, and Mel Allen always came with a topcoat and a hat. I had a really deep connection to this team, because growing up in Boston, they were like the cousin who was always better than you because the Red Sox never won and the Yankees always did."

In Allen's final years calling Yankees games, he worked with Red Barber and Phil Rizzuto, the popular former shortstop who went on to become one of the most beloved broadcasters in team history.

"The guy I think is underappreciated as a broadcaster is Rizzuto," current Yankees broadcaster Michael Kay said. "You listen to some of his calls, they were awesome. People think of him in his later years when he was trying to get to the George Washington Bridge, but when there was a big moment in a game, he stepped up and was a really good broadcaster and communicator."

The Yankees fired Allen after the 1964 season, never giving a reason for the decision. Rizzuto worked with Jerry Coleman and others over the next five years, including Frank Messer, who joined Rizzuto and Coleman in the booth in 1968.

By 1971, Rizzuto and Messer were joined by Bill White, a trio that would call Yankees games together into the mid-1980s.

"Growing up, I had a sister, and there were four male voices in my house: my dad, Phil Rizzuto, Bill White, and Frank Messer," Kay said. "I listened to them every single day. That was it for me. Bill White was awesome; really underappreciated. Frank Messer was a really good nuts-and-bolts guy; his voice told you it was the Yankees."

Messer left the booth after 1984, while White continued broadcasting games until he was elected to replace Bart Giamatti as the president of the National League in 1989.

Rizzuto continued to call games until 1996, when he called Derek Jeter's first career home run. He retired that year, having broadcast Yankees games for 40 seasons, the longest tenure of anyone in the franchise's history.

Rizzuto helped break in another former Yankee, Bobby Murcer, who became a beloved member of the broadcast team during his two-plus decades in the booth. Murcer had been a popular player during his 13 years in pinstripes (1965–66, '69–74, and '79–83), making him a fan favorite in the booth, too.

"As wonderful a player as he was, he was a better person," Waldman said. "Fans got that. He was the connection to Mickey Mantle; he was the only one left of that group, which is why people loved him so much."

While the Yankees' television broadcast featured a number of different voices through the 1990s, the primary radio play-by-play seat was filled in 1989 by John Sterling, who had worked in New York in the 1970s calling Islanders and Nets games before heading to

Atlanta in the 1980s to do Hawks and Braves games.

Sterling—a New York City native who grew up rooting for the Yankees—had his dream job.

"It meant a whole lot more to me than it would have with another team because I grew up a Yankees fan listening to Mel Allen," Sterling said. "You couldn't listen more than I did. Not only did I listen because I was fan, but also because I knew as a young boy that this was what I was going to do for a living. It's a great kick that I followed Mel and Scooter and people like that.

"To think that a New York kid grows up a Yankees fan, wants to get into broadcasting and actually gets the Yankees job? Luck, timing, kismet. Just amazing."

In 1992, Sterling was joined by Kay, a former *New York Post* and *Daily News* Yankees beat writer.

"Since I was nine years old, all I wanted to be was the Yankees announcer,"

## Michael Kay's Top 5 Yankees Memories

**David Cone's perfect game:** "Although everybody in the media is supposed to be objective, everybody wanted David Cone to get that perfect game. I also remember going to a great Springsteen concert at Giants Stadium that night."

**The 1998 season:** "I don't think we'll ever see a team that good again. That team was shocked every time they lost. They should have won way more than 125 games, but they went into a slump in September."

**Mariano Rivera's final game:** "Mariano being taken out by Jeter and Pettitte was very emotional. We ended up winning an Emmy for that game at YES, but I just shut up. I would have cried. I was all choked up to see a man like that, stoic, lose it like that. It was really special."

**The 2001 World Series:** "The thing that will always resonate with me was George W. Bush throwing out the first pitch to Todd Greene. There was such tension and electricity, but joylessness in the ballpark. I'll always remember that. After 9/11, it seemed preordained for them to win it, which is why it was so shocking that they lost."

**The ticker-tape parades:** "Hosting those parades was amazing. The Yankees allowed me and John to be in a car, and to see those people, to see the love and emotion, the first one in 1996 was the best. It had been so long, they hadn't won since 1978, people were so into it. You just felt that love."

# IT IS HIGH! IT IS FAR! IT IS...GONE!

If you've listened to Yankees games on the radio—or highlights on ESPN, MLB Network or anywhere else—you have undoubtedly heard John Sterling's home run call.

"It is high! It is far! It is gone!"

So how did Sterling come up with his signature call? It all started long before he ever stepped foot in the Yankees broadcast booth.

"In Atlanta, I was on TV one day and Dwight Gooden was facing Dale Murphy," Sterling said. "He threw a breaking ball and Murphy hit it well. I said, 'Hit in the air to deep left field; it is high! It is far! It is gone!' I don't know why I said that. It just came to me."

Over the next few days, Sterling began hearing fans recite the call back to him—a sure sign that it was being received well by the listening public.

"When you start hearing calls come back to you, whether it's, 'Theeeee Yankees win!' or the home run calls, you know you have something," Sterling said. "I'm a big reader and I've read all the Bob Hope books. He said he would throw lines out, and if he heard them come back during the week, they knew they were on to something. I'm very lucky that they caught on."

Sterling eventually added in a personal call for every Yankees player, starting in the mid-1990s with Bernie Williams.

"I had done nicknames before, especially in basketball with Bernard King and Dominique Wilkins," Sterling said. "With the Yankees, the first nickname was 'Bern Baby Bern' and it just took off from there."

Sterling used to come up with his player calls on the spot, but he acknowledges that he thinks ahead when a new player joins the team.

"Now I have to have one for every person; you can't just come up with one for Ronald Torreyes on the spot," Sterling said. "The 'A-bomb from A-Rod' just happened. Some of them just come to me. They all can't be great. Sometimes you have to search a little bit."

Sterling had trouble picking his favorite home run call, though one that stood out to him was Russell Martin, who played for the Yankees in 2011–12.

"I have a good memory, especially for unimportant things," Sterling said. "I read in *Sports Illustrated* a long time ago when the Canadiens were great that the fans in the Forum would chant, 'Les Canadiens, sont la!' Translated, it means 'The Canadiens are there,' but it didn't mean that at all. It was idiomatic and it meant 'The Canadiens are on top' or they're the best.

"Russell Martin speaks French, so I went to him and said, 'I can't say sont la; I have to say est la, the singular,' and he agreed. So when he hit a home run I would say, 'Russell has muscle!' and then I would say, 'Monsieur Martin, est la!' People had no idea what I was doing, but I kind of liked it."

Kay said. "To be able to do that, it's pretty darn special. It's pretty amazing. I never fail to appreciate how lucky I am, because these jobs don't come around very often."

Sterling and Kay manned the radio booth together for a decade, also serving as the voices for events such as Old Timers' Day and ticker-tape parades.

"When I first started doing it, I was announcing Joe DiMaggio and Mickey Mantle; you just feel like you're living in a fairy tale," Kay said. "For a kid growing up 10 minutes from Yankee Stadium, that's all I ever wanted to do.

In 2002, the YES Network became the television home of the Yankees. Kay moved from the radio team to become the lead TV voice, a position he's held for the past 15 seasons.

"I still feel unbelievably lucky every time I walk into the booth, even for an August game that doesn't mean much," Kay said.

Charley Steiner, a popular anchor on ESPN, replaced Kay in the radio booth. Like Sterling and Kay, Steiner had grown up in the New York area—Brooklyn, then Long Island, to be exact—so becoming one of the voices of the Yankees was a childhood dream come true.

"It was staggering," Steiner said. "My first memory after being hired was my parking space right outside the players' entrance. They pointed me in the right direction and it was spot No. 61. I thought, 'I've made it to the big-time.'"

The first time Steiner walked into the radio booth at the old Stadium, he was taken aback by his new workplace.

"I walked into the booth and it hit me; Mel Allen, Red Barber, Phil Rizzuto, Tony Kubek, Bill White, and all those guys worked there, and now I was part of that lineage," Steiner said. "That was one of those moments when you just pinch yourself and say, 'Please don't wake me up. I'm actually here.' It was one of those things you couldn't help but treasure.

"To be able to come home and do this job in this place for this team, it was…I don't even know how to finish the sentence. It was pretty cool."

Steiner called Yankees games from 2002 to '04, after which Waldman took over as Sterling's radio partner. Like many before her, Waldman had received advice from Allen when she broke into the business, covering the Yankees and Knicks for WFAN radio beginning in 1987.

### John Sterling's Top 5 Yankees Moments

**1996 AL Division Series, Game 3:** "The Yankees were down 2–1 to the Rangers going into the ninth inning. Tim Raines missed two bunt attempts, then lined a single that keyed the winning rally before Mariano Duncan delivered the go-ahead hit. That game took all the pressure off that team."

**1996 World Series, Game 4:** "The Yankees were down 6–0 in the sixth. Jim Leyritz hits the huge home run in the eighth, Wade Boggs wins it in the 10th. Joe Torre used his roster brilliantly. Mel Stottlemyre said it was the best-managed game he had ever witnessed. It's probably the best overall game I've seen."

**May 1, 1996, Yankees at Baltimore:** "Tino Martinez hit a grand slam in the 15th inning to win the game and became a 'True Yankee' with that home run. The Yankees took over first place and they never relinquished it on their way to winning the World Series."

**David Cone's perfect game:** "I had called a perfect game the year before with David Wells, but I was such good friends with David Cone, I was rooting for him so hard to achieve that—and he did. Cone said he kept going into the clubhouse every half inning and he heard Michael and I mentioning that he was perfect about 100 times. He didn't believe in any jinxes."

**1996 World Series, Game 6:** "It was just thrilling. The second-to-last pitch was popped up near the Atlanta dugout and Charlie Hayes couldn't make the catch and almost fell into the dugout. The very next pitch, Mark Lemke popped up the same ball, but that one ended the series. Amazing."

# SUZYN WALDMAN'S TOP 5 YANKEES MOMENTS

**1996 World Series, Game 6:** "That was the year I went through breast cancer treatments. I was standing with George [Steinbrenner] when the team won and I felt like I had won something, too. That year was very difficult for so many people."

**Jim Abbott's no-hitter:** "That was something I knew was special because he was so special. It's something we'll never see again. Expectations are limits for people; he had just exceeded every single limit that was ever put in front of him."

**1995 AL Division Series, Game 1:** "When they started to announce the team, starting with Buck Showalter and ending with Don Mattingly, I'd never heard anything like that. The whole place shook. I had never heard ovations like that. By the time it got around to Mattingly, I was sure the whole press box was coming down."

**Yogi Berra Day/David Cone's perfect game:** "I remember standing in the dugout while Yogi was going around in the little car, tears coming down my eyes, thinking, 'I did that.' Then the idea that he got to watch—with his buddy Don Larsen—a perfect game, it was too much. It was something that only happens in Yankee Stadium."

**Derek Jeter's 3,000th hit:** "That was one of the first times I ever saw Derek Jeter in public with the smile that is reserved for his family. It was just a beautiful day, and what he did and the way he did it, he pointed up to his mom and dad and that smile, you only saw it when he was talking to his parents. He had a different smile for us, but that day, I saw it."

"Mel introduced himself to me and he said, 'Don't let anybody ever stop you because you have an intrinsic love of this game,'" Waldman said. "I became really good friends with him and I sang at his funeral and at his memorial service at St. Patrick's Cathedral. I think of Mel all the time."

Waldman had done plenty of radio and television work during her career, but becoming a part of the team's official radio broadcast provided her with a new perspective.

"It was really freeing, because on radio, you paint a picture," Waldman said. "I've always thought that you have to tell the fans something they don't know by watching on television or reading in the paper. I'm very aware that I'm a female and that I'm not an ex-player, so what I have to do is something different. Somebody once said to me that when you're on television, you're putting a caption on a picture. I don't have to do that; I draw my own picture. I love to talk and I'm very dramatic. I know to whom I'm speaking, which is a big thing."

While some broadcasters struggle to choose one moment that defines their tenure in the booth, Steiner has no such problem selecting his signature call: Game 7 of the 2003 ALCS between the Yankees and Red Sox.

"During the playoffs, they always stick in extra commercial time; it's the bottom of the 11th and the commercial is still going as Aaron Boone is leaving the on-deck circle," Steiner said. "I'm thinking, 'Oh shit, we've got a Heidi Bowl here.' As Boone steps into the batter's box, John says something really quick and throws it to me and then, bang!

"There was no time to think, no time to set anything up. The ball goes out, the place goes crazy, Boone has his hands in the air and you have no safety blanket. I was caught up in the moment. When he crossed the plate and I could lay out for a few seconds, I pumped my fist under the desk and thought to myself, 'Yes! I didn't fuck it up.'"

Steiner's call of Boone's pennant-winning home run is replayed constantly, reminding fans of one of the Yankees' greatest home runs—and of Steiner's brief contribution to the long line of voices that have called their games.

"It was one of those singular, dramatic moments you never saw coming," Steiner said. "Now it's all these years later and it's a call that has had shelf life, and more importantly, historical significance."

Steiner recalled speaking with Boone in the wee hours of the morning after the home run, talking about the thrill of calling such a historic moment.

"I said, 'Do you have any idea how big a moment you orchestrated here?' He really didn't; it was still just euphoria for him," Steiner said. "I said, 'The good news is you're now an historic figure in Yankees history. The bad news is, you're stuck with me the rest of your life.'"

Kay once told Jeter something similar following one of his many career highlights, which, like almost every other major Yankees milestone of the past 15 years, have been narrated on television by Kay.

"I am connected to so many of Jeter's great moments, it's amazing; The Flip, Mr. November, his 3,000th hit, his last hit at Yankee Stadium. I'm honored," Kay said. "I told him, 'Just to have my voice connected to you for all time, it means something to me.' He said, 'Same back,' which was nice of him to say. It's amazing. In 100 years they're going to listen to Alex Rodriguez's 600th home run or Jeter's 3,000th hit and it's going to be my silly voice doing them. It's kind of neat."

Located on the campus of Monclair State University, the Yogi Berra Museum & Learning Center is a great stop for any baseball fan. (Yogi Berra Museum & Learning Center)

# Visit the Yogi Berra Museum & Learning Center

**WHERE:** 8 Yogi Berra Drive, Little Falls, New Jersey

**WHEN:** Wednesday through Sunday, 12 PM–5 PM

**HOW TO DO IT:** For information, visit yogiberramuseum.org

**COST FACTOR:** Adults $6; Students under 18 $4

**BUCKET RANK:** 🗑️ 🗑️ 🗑️ 🗑️

**T**here are few athletes in America—or anywhere, for that matter—who have been more beloved than Yogi Berra.

His endearing "Yogisms" are a staple of pop culture, while his commercials helped bring his lovable personality to a new generation or two of fans. But let's not forget just how much he contributed to both the Yankees and baseball—not to mention the United States.

His life and legacy are immortalized in the Yogi Berra Museum & Learning Center in Montclair, New Jersey, a project that was near and dear to his heart from the day it opened in December 1998 all the way through his death in 2015.

"He was such a people person, and would often surprise school groups and go hang out with them," said Lindsay Berra, Yogi's granddaughter. "Can you imagine going to the museum thinking you were just going to look at some stuff, then getting the actual tour from Yogi? He loved doing that. He loved being with the kids."

Memorabilia from Berra's life—from his youth in St. Louis to his legendary career to his time serving in the Navy during World War II—is represented in the museum, which is located on the campus of Montclair State University.

"It's not nearly as daunting as Cooperstown," said David Kaplan, the museum's director.

The museum sits next to the university's baseball field, appropriately named Yogi Berra Stadium. The New Jersey Jackals, an independent minor league team in the Can-Am League, call the field home.

"He would stare out the window and watch the guys take BP or shag flies," Lindsay said. "He just loved to be around baseball."

Berra never thought much of his collection, often giving pieces away to friends and family. According to Lindsay, her "Grampa" wore his 1953 World Series ring and his Hall of Fame ring, "but he was more about winning ballgames with his buddies" than worrying about his legacy.

*The Yogi Berra Museum & Learning Center is a great place to learn about the Yankees legend and his incredible life.* (Yogi Berra Museum & Learning Center)

"When Grampa played, he never thought anyone down the line would want to look at his old gloves and bats and baseball cards, so he gave a lot of his things away, or just tucked them away in the basement," Lindsay said. "But once it was all within the four walls of the museum, I think he thought, 'My goodness, this is really neat! This is all my stuff!' As he got older and retired from baseball and wasn't at the ballpark all the time, the museum became a way for him to be around baseball."

A tour through the museum takes roughly one hour, though you may want to budget a little more time if you plan to soak in everything the building has to offer, including the films that run on a loop all day.

Original jerseys from Berra's playing days are on display, as is the bronzed glove he used to catch Don Larsen's perfect game in the 1956 World Series. All 10 of Berra's World Series rings are displayed, along with replicas of every championship ring from Yankees history.

The original plaques that honored Mickey Mantle and Joe DiMaggio on the outfield wall at Yankee Stadium are at the museum, having been replaced in the ballpark by monuments 1996 and 1999, respectively.

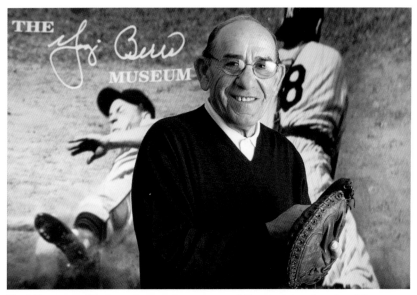
***Yogi Berra used to be a frequent presence at the museum bearing his name.***
(Yogi Berra Museum & Learning Center)

Photos around the museum take you through Berra's life, from his childhood on "The Hill" in St. Louis with his friend Joe Garagiola to his early days with the Yankees. One photo shows Berra with Babe Ruth, a reminder of how long he's been a part of the Yankees family.

"He knew Babe Ruth and he knew Derek Jeter," Kaplan said. "That's just amazing."

There are mementos from the first Yogi Berra Day at Yankee Stadium, which was held in 1959 while he was still an active player. The Yankees would finish third that season—the only season between 1955 and '64 that they did not reach the World Series—so Berra's day was a way to sell some extra tickets. He was presented with a handful of gifts, including a television and patio furniture.

"It was a bad year for them," Kaplan said. "Ted Williams presented him with a fishing rod. It looked like a garage sale."

Another day was held in his honor in 1999, the same day David Cone pitched the third perfect game in Yankees history.

An entire section of the museum is dedicated to Berra's colloquialisms, better known as "Yogisms." Among the more famous are "When you come to a fork in the road, take it," and "It's like déjà vu all over again," though the list runs much deeper than those.

"Barely a day goes by when somebody isn't quoting Yogi," Kaplan said.

At the age of 19, Berra served as a Second Class Seaman in the Navy, playing a significant role in the Normandy Invasion, better known as D-Day. According to the museum, Berra was part of a six-man crew on a Navy rocket boat, firing machine guns and launching rockets at the German defenses at Omaha Beach, later receiving several commendations for his bravery. In 2013, he received the Bob Feller Act of Valor Award in honor of his service.

"I didn't even think about death," Berra told the *Star-Ledger* after receiving the award, which is in the museum. "I figured if you got hit with a bullet, you wouldn't know it. So I just did what I was supposed to do."

That Berra agreed to have part of the museum acknowledge his service was somewhat surprising to his family, which rarely heard him discuss that period of his life.

"Most World War II vets don't talk a lot about their service, so to have that section about that is pretty compelling," Lindsay said.

On the other side of the spectrum, Berra's work as a pitchman is also on display, both in print and television.

Then there's Berra's favorite exhibit: the dozens of love letters he wrote through the years to his wife, Carmen, who he married in 1949 and was with until her passing in March 2014.

"The love letters are one of my favorite parts of the museum," Lindsay said. "Grammy refused to share them, so we never saw them until she agreed to put them in the museum after the renovation. Grampa didn't go to school past the eighth grade, but he had beautiful cursive penmanship and wrote in flowery, complete sentences. College graduates today don't do that on email. He took pride in that."

Suzyn Waldman, the Yankees' broadcaster who orchestrated Berra's reconciliation with George Steinbrenner in 1999, said Berra's love for the museum was evident every time he spoke about it, though nothing brought him more joy than showing people the letters.

"He was so proud of that place," Waldman said. "When they put up the exhibit of the love letters he wrote to Carmen, he wanted me to read every single one of them so I could understand what they had, which was extraordinary. He was so proud of that museum and everything in it. He got such joy being around it."

One of the most recent additions to the museum is the Presidential Medal of Freedom, which was presented posthumously to Berra's family in November 2015, two months after his death. President Barack Obama even referenced one of Berra's own lines in presenting the medal: "One thing we know for sure: if you can't imitate him, don't copy him."

Lindsay was at the forefront of the campaign to honor Berra, launching an online petition to get him nominated. More than 100,000 signatures were collected in 30 days, while Lindsay and other family members spent the summer writing letters to President Obama to support his nomination.

"It was like running a really hard race that I didn't even know I had signed up for," Lindsay said. "Grampa knew about the petition, but didn't understand the online part of it at all. He kept asking me where he could sign. Of course, I wish he could have received the medal while he was still alive, but I know he didn't do anything he did because he wanted a medal. He did it because that was the person he was. Still, it's nice to have the medal in the museum so people can see it for exactly what it is; an exclamation point at the end of my Grampa's exemplary life."

In addition to being a wonderful museum for baseball fans to enjoy, the Learning Center portion of the facility's name is more than just a title. Schools often send classes to the museum for special programs and workshops, often using Berra as the model for character education. Baseball and softball camps are also held each summer.

"It's about character and sportsmanship," said Marty Appel, who authored a children's biography about Berra and has served on the museum's Board of Directors. "Those are qualities you never thought about when he was a player. The museum, his boycott of George Steinbrenner, honors that befell him, it enhanced his image and reputation in the minds of the public in the years after his retirement."

. . . . . . . . . . . . . . . . . . . . . . . . . . . . . .

# Learn the History of Closers: From Short Men to Sandman

**M**ariano Rivera is the gold standard for closers, establishing both the all-time saves record in the regular season with 652 and the most prolific postseason career in history, posting a 0.70 ERA and 42 saves in 96 appearances.

But the Yankees have had a rich history of relief pitchers, one that long predates the save becoming an official major league statistic in 1969.

The Yankees' first relief ace—they were also known as "short men" back in the day—was Wilcy Moore, who burst on to the scene as a

30-year-old rookie in 1927, producing a valuable season for the 110-win team.

Moore was a dirt farmer from Oklahoma who won 30 games in the bush leagues in South Carolina, catching the eyes of scouts. The Yankees signed him, though he started throwing sidearm after hurting his arm the previous season.

"This guy came out of nowhere when no one was paying attention to him," said Brian Richards, curator of the New York Yankees Museum Presented by Bank of America. "The Yankees took a low-risk gamble on him and it had a really high yield."

Moore appeared in 50 games that year, starting 12 and finishing 30. He went 19–7 with a league-best 2.28 ERA, pitching a total of 213 innings despite spending most of the season in the bullpen.

"Miller Huggins put him in the bullpen because he thought he was too weak to throw complete games," Richards said. "Back then, that was an embarrassment if you couldn't go nine innings, but Huggins thought, 'Until we can get him to go nine innings, we'll see if we can get three or four out of him at a time.' That was cutting-edge thinking in those days."

According to Richards, Moore became a cult hero to Yankees fans in 1927, often cheered as loudly as Lou Gehrig or Babe Ruth.

"People fell in love with this guy," Richards said. "The *Times* called him 'the Lifeguard,' because he rescues pitchers from sinking. He was like a Roy Hobbs; he just came out of nowhere."

Moore pitched two innings of relief in Game 1 of the World Series that fall against the Pittsburgh Pirates, then after the Yankees took a 3–0 lead in the series, Huggins decided to let Moore start Game 4.

Moore pitched a complete game, beating the Pirates 4–3 to clinch the Yankees' second World Series title.

"They let him start Game 4 of the World Series, basically as a thank you, because they knew they were going to win the series," Richards said. "He hurt his arm pitching in that game and was never the same after that. He pitched a couple more years, but he was never as effective again. For that one year, he was as good as anyone."

The Yankees would have several strong relievers through the years including Johnny Murphy, Joe Page, Johnny Sain, and Allie Reynolds, who excelled for the Yankees as both a starter and reliever.

"Joe Page in the late 40s, they nicknamed him 'Fireman' and gave him an honorary fire helmet," said Marty Appel, author of *Pinstripe Empire*. "Allie Reynolds, Ryne Duren, Luis Arroyo; they were blessed with a lot of these guys."

As the years went on, relievers began to be used in more specific ways, especially once the save became an official stat. Sparky Lyle compiled 141 saves for the Yankees between 1972 and '78, while Rich "Goose" Gossage had 150 saves with the Bombers between 1978 and '83, picking up one more during a second stint in 1989.

After beginning his career as a starting pitcher, Dave Righetti was moved to the bullpen in 1984 to take over as the closer once Gossage signed with the Padres as a free agent. Righetti would save 224 games over seven seasons for the Yankees, the second-most in team history behind only Rivera.

John Wetteland saved 74 games during his two years with the Yankees, winning World Series MVP honors in 1996. His setup man that season? A skinny 26-year-old named Mariano Rivera.

Rivera took over as the closer in 1997, kicking off a brilliant 17-year run that redefined ninth-inning greatness.

"The difference between Mariano and all the rest was Mariano's longevity," Appel said. "In all of Mariano's years, there were other guys doing it for their teams, but nobody was doing it like that for that long."

Rivera had nine seasons with 40 or more saves, posting a sub-2.00 ERA 11 times. He made 13 All-Star teams, and although he never won a Cy Young Award—he finished in the top five of voting five times—Major League Baseball established an annual award for the American League's best reliever which was named after him in 2014.

"Mariano is by far the greatest reliever that ever was, and I played with Rollie Fingers, who I think is No. 2," Hall of Famer Reggie Jackson said. "Rollie could have done what Mariano did, but he'd pitch five innings. That's been lost. Rollie had the control that Mariano had, he had a bigger breaking ball and he threw 93–95. I've always said with Mariano, he could pitch if home plate was the size of an iPhone. If you want to talk about efficiency for a player, you'd have to go to Ruth's efficiency to match Mariano."

Rivera had some high-profile failures, too. He blew a key save opportunity in the 1997 ALDS against the Cleveland Indians, Game 7 of the 2001 World Series against the Diamondbacks and Games 4 and 5 of the 2004 ALCS against the Red Sox. Despite those rare, costly hiccups, he was about as close to a sure thing as there could be in sports.

"Just an amazing athlete, an amazing competitor, and an amazing person," Joe Girardi said. "I don't think anyone ever wanted to see that era come to an end."

# A Day for Thurman: The Yankees Honor the Captain

Thurman Munson was the heart of the Yankees, a star-studded team that had won two consecutive World Series in 1977–78 to reestablish the Bronx as the home office of baseball.

A seven-time All-Star, Munson had been named Captain of the Yankees by George Steinbrenner in 1976.

"He was a leader immediately," said former Yankees PR man Marty Appel, who worked for the team from 1968 to '77. "He was drafted in '68, he came up in the summer of '69, and he had such a cocky swagger about him that you knew this guy was going to lead us somewhere.

"He had leadership qualities about him. Sometimes you would just get a sense walking through the airport with the team who was in charge here. It was apparent immediately that this guy was going to lead us to greatness."

Munson was the Yankees' first captain in 37 years, filling a position last held by Lou Gehrig in 1939. Only Munson didn't care about the title, Appel said, unaware of the importance of his newfound place in franchise history.

"He didn't appreciate the fact that there hadn't been one since Lou Gehrig," Appel said. "He didn't know from captains, but Mr. Steinbrenner did."

Munson began flying propeller planes during the spring of 1978, eventually flying home to Canton, Ohio, after games to spend a few hours with his family before returning to New York for the next day's game.

During the summer of 1979, he upgraded to a Cessna Citation jet, a machine he wasn't necessarily qualified to fly. Three weeks after purchasing the plane, Munson had a Thursday off-day during which he decided to show off his new toy to his business partner and a flight instructor he knew.

But after making three successful takeoffs and landings, Munson went back up for a fourth. The plane crashed as he tried to land in a field near the runway, breaking Munson's neck. The two passengers escaped, but the Yankee died in the wreckage, unable to get himself out of the plane before it caught fire.

"It was beyond shock," Appel said. "People don't die at that age and ballplayers don't die piloting their own plane. It was just a function of the modern riches that players were starting to accumulate."

The Yankees took the field the following night, August 3, standing at their positions without anybody at home plate while Cardinal Terence Cooke held a memorial service for Munson. They lost a pair of one-run games to the Orioles, then beat Baltimore on Sunday as they prepared to fly to Canton for the Captain's funeral.

"I don't like really remembering it," Reggie Jackson said. "It was such a sad day. A sad time. It left a big void. You always think, 'What would he be like today? Where would he be? What are some of the things you'd be doing with him?' He was a great Yankee and he would have been around."

Bobby Murcer and Lou Piniella delivered eulogies at the funeral, while the team accompanied the casket to the cemetery before boarding a flight back to New York for a night game against the Orioles.

"Everybody was crying," Appel said. "The casket was in the front and you were trying to imagine what he must look like in there having burned to death in an airplane.

"I've had family funerals, but this was more emotional than even those things because of the total shock of it all."

Murcer was Munson's best friend. In *Pinstripe Empire*, Appel wrote that manager Billy Martin told Murcer to go home and skip Monday night's game, but the outfielder insisted on suiting up.

"Skip, I somehow feel I've got to play tonight, if you'll let me," Murcer told Martin, who put the veteran in the lineup.

"Ballplayers have a connection during the season; it's a band of brothers traveling around the country together," Appel said. "Once the season was over, in those days before texts and social media, they didn't call each other in the winter to ask how the kids were doing. They would see each other the following spring. Murcer and Munson did keep in touch. They would call each other. It was an unusual baseball friendship in that sense."

The Yankees trailed the Orioles 4–0 in the seventh inning when Murcer hit a three-run home run to pull his team within a run. Orioles left-hander Tippy Martinez had entered the game with two out in the seventh inning and got the game to the ninth with the one-run lead intact.

Bucky Dent drew a leadoff walk in the ninth to put the tying run on base, then Martinez made an error on Willie Randolph's sacrifice bunt, putting runners at second and third. Murcer was due up, and although Martinez had owned left-handed hitters all season, Martin didn't pinch-hit for Murcer, giving him a chance to be the hero only hours after burying his best friend.

"Tippy was a former teammate of Thurman's; he had come up with the Yankees," Appel said. "He loved Munson and he was angry with himself for not going to the funeral, so it was on his mind that night."

Martinez later told Appel that after throwing two breaking balls for strikes to get ahead 0–2 against Murcer, he decided to throw him a hittable fastball.

"He said, 'Murcer had no hope against me, but then something came over me where I thought I owed Bobby a fastball,'" Appel said. "'It's not going to be 72 mph and over the middle of the plate, but I'm not going to throw him a breaking pitch here and strike him out, which I can do. I owe him one fastball over the black.'"

Murcer lined a single down the left-field line, scoring both runners to give the Yankees an emotional 5–4 walk-off victory.

"If you look at the replay of the game, you see Tippy walking off looking up at the heavens," Appel said.

# Attend the Thurman Munson Awards Dinner

**WHERE:** New York City

**WHEN:** February

**WHAT TO DO:** For ticket information, visit www.ahrcNYCfoundation.org/events

**COST:** $1,000 per ticket

**BUCKET RANK:**

*Diana Munson (center, with JoAnna Garcia Swisher and Nick Swisher)
has helped keep her husband Thurman's memory alive with an annual
fundraising dinner in his name.* (AHRC New York City Foundation)

**T**hurman Munson's memory has been preserved by the Yankees
and their fans, who remember the late captain through his
plaque in Monument Park and his locker, which remains on
display in the Yankees Museum.

Yet on a chilly winter night every February, Munson's memory is
as alive as ever. That's when his wife, Diana, their three children,
and nearly a thousand others gather in midtown Manhattan for the
annual Thurman Munson Awards Dinner.

"His wife is a very special woman and she has kept his memory
alive," Yankees broadcaster Michael Kay said. "He was such a
strong presence after that long drought of championships; he was
there when it started to turn and then was obviously there for the
championships in '77 and '78. He still resonates. Whenever an athlete
dies young, there's a stronger remembrance of them because you

don't remember them in a diminished state; you remember them great."

For more than 35 years, the Thurman Munson Awards have honored athletes—both local and national—for their work on and off the field. The event has raised more than $13 million for the AHRC New York City Foundation, which supports programs such as schools, summer camps, and job training programs to enable children and adults with intellectual and developmental disabilities to lead richer, more productive lives.

"Knowing that we're remembering him while also helping so many people, it's overwhelming and emotional," Diana told the New York *Daily News* in 2015. "I'm very proud of it."

Diana was approached by the AHRC New York City Foundation only months after Thurman died in a tragic plane crash, though she was unsure about lending his name to a fundraising dinner. Knowing Thurman had done work with the charity, she decided to move forward with it, though her expectations were low.

"They said it would probably last two or three years," Diana said. "The first one was very emotional. It was hard for anyone to speak about him. You lose a hero in the prime of his career in the middle of the season; it's almost unheard of. It was uncharted waters. We weren't sure how it was going to go."

Honorees have included more than 30 Yankees, though athletes from local hockey, football, and basketball teams have also received awards, as have Olympians from many different sports.

"I see the respect that these athletes have for Thurman when they speak of him," Diana said. "That's the most touching part for me. Not just baseball, but all fields. He really reached people."

"I think it just tells you how special he was; what he meant to the city, to the community, to the game of baseball," Joe Girardi said.

"This was a special man that perished way too early in life. His legacy lives on and will never be forgotten."

When Bernie Williams received a Munson Award in 2015, he recalled the emotion of seeing Munson's empty locker the first time he walked into the Yankees clubhouse in 1991.

"It is Thurman who is the true legend and Yankee royalty," Williams said. "To be recognized with an award bearing his name is truly special. The family's efforts have helped so many in need. It has kept the legacy of Thurman alive and well."

"I keep thinking to myself that Thurman must be smiling ear-to-ear thinking, 'This guy from Canton, Ohio, came to New York City and all these years later, people are still paying tribute to me,'" Diana said. "It's been amazing."

August 2 is a somber day every year as Munson's family, friends, and fans remember the anniversary of his death. The annual dinner is a different type of celebration, as the Munson family and the New York community come together to honor the man they loved.

"It's a little pause to just reflect on the man that we're honoring and the wonderful times we had through the years," Diana said. "It's not living in the past; it's just paying homage to the past. It's a nice way for us to all give him a hug."

No. 15 shirts are routinely spotted in the stands at Yankee Stadium, though it's not just the fans that watched Munson play that continue to wear his number to games.

"I'm still amazed when you look at the crowd when there's a video of Thurman on the board, you see young kids who weren't even born standing there just enraptured," Kay said. "He certainly has resonated from generation to generation. Dads tell their kids about Thurman Munson and what he meant to the Yankees."

*Derek Jeter and the Yankees were back at City Hall for a celebration after winning the 2009 World Series.* (Mark Feinsand)

# Derek Jeter's Fairy-Tale Ending

**M**uch of Derek Jeter's time with the Yankees had already been a fairy tale. From winning the World Series in his rookie year to collecting his 3,000th hit in front of his home fans, the shortstop had lived a charmed life, but every story of this nature needs a happy ending.

On September 25, 2014, Jeter got exactly that.

More than seven months earlier, the Captain had announced that he would retire at the end of the season, setting up a six-month farewell tour around the majors. The penultimate series was slated to take place at Yankee Stadium against the Baltimore Orioles, while Jeter's final three games would come at Fenway Park.

"I felt really privileged to be able to write his name on the lineup card that day, but I also felt sad knowing that it would be the last time I would do it at home," manager Joe Girardi said. "Derek had a chance to realize his dream. He was able to win a number of championships, to have 3,000 hits, but the focus was never on him. This was a chance to focus on him and what he had meant to the organization. That was really special."

The Yankees and Orioles each scored twice in the opening inning, with Jeter doubling in New York's first run. Some wondered whether they had just witnessed the final RBI—or even the final hit—of Jeter's career.

The game remained tied at 2 until the seventh, when Jeter stepped up with the bases loaded. Jeter's RBI ground out and an error by shortstop J.J. Hardy gave the Yankees a 4–2 lead, while Brian McCann's sacrifice fly made it a three-run game.

Hiroki Kuroda completed eight innings, turning the three-run lead over to David Robertson, the closer who had successfully converted 38 of his 42 save opportunities that season.

But Robertson allowed three runs in the ninth on home runs by Adam Jones and Steve Pearce, stunning the crowd. Jeter's farewell party was suddenly being threatened by the prospect of a Yankees loss.

Jose Pirela led off the home half of the ninth with a single, replaced by pinch runner Antoan Richardson. Brett Gardner bunted Richardson over to second base, putting the winning run in scoring position. And guess who was coming to the plate?

# THE CAPTAIN'S GREATEST MOMENT IN THE BRONX

**D**erek Jeter had a number of great highlights in the Bronx during his 19-year career, from his Mr. November home run in the 2001 World Series to his dive into the stands against the Red Sox in July 2004. He passed Lou Gehrig for the Yankees' all-time hits lead, recorded his 3,000th hit, and even played the role of pitching coach when he and Andy Pettitte were sent to the mound to remove Mariano Rivera from the final game of his incredible career.

But Jeter's finest moment didn't involve a bat, ball, or glove. It was September 21, 2008, the final day the Yankees would play at the old Yankee Stadium.

The Bombers had just beaten the Orioles to finish their final home stand with an 8–2 record, but now it was time to say goodbye. Jeter stood on the mound with his teammates circled around him, took the microphone and spoke from the heart.

"For all of us up here, it's a huge honor to put this uniform on every day and come out here and play," Jeter said. "Every member of this organization, past and present, has been calling this place home for 85 years. There's a lot of tradition, a lot of history and a lot of memories. Now the great thing about memories is you're able to pass them along from generation to generation.

"And although things are going to change next year and we're going to move across the street, there are a few things with the New York Yankees that never change. That's pride, tradition, and most of all, we have the greatest fans in the world. We're relying on you to take the memories from this stadium and add them to the new memories that come at the new Yankee Stadium and continue to pass them on from generation to generation. So on behalf of the entire organization, we just want to take this moment to salute you, the greatest fans in the world."

Jeter hadn't prepared those words, but it's unlikely he could have come up with anything better had he worked on them for weeks.

"To be quite honest, I didn't know what I was going to say," Jeter said later that night. "When I came out of the game with two outs in the ninth, I had to hurry up and think of something. I wanted to acknowledge the fans. All the memories here are because of the fans, so that's the message I wanted to get across."

Jeter led his teammates around the Stadium for a lap to thank the fans while Sinatra's "New York, New York" played them off the field for one final time.

"He represents everything that it is to be a Yankee," Jason Giambi said after hearing Jeter's speech. "From Joe D. to Mickey, he represents the pinstripes."

"You don't want to apply fairy tale aspects to these things, but when Jeter came up, I just didn't have any doubt that he was going to get a hit," Jack Curry of the YES Network said. "He was going to come through there; I didn't know where he was going to hit or how he was going to do it, but there was no doubt that he was going to get a hit there."

Jeter jumped on the first pitch he saw from Evan Meek, shooting it to the opposite field as he had done hundreds upon hundreds of times before. Richardson scored from second base to give the Yankees a 6–5 win—and Jeter the grandest goodbye possible.

"He sealed it by getting the kind of hit we probably saw 40 percent of the time from him: an inside-out swing taking the ball the other way," Curry said. "It was probably about as fitting a finale as a great player could have."

As Jeter was mobbed by his teammates between first and second, several key figures from the dynasty years of 1996–2000 lined up in front of the Yankees dugout. There was Joe Torre, Bernie Williams, Jorge Posada, Mariano Rivera, Andy Pettitte, and Tino Martinez, waiting to congratulate the Captain.

"We've shared a lot of success, a lot of memories together," Jeter said that night. "I guess this is one last one we can share together."

After sharing more hugs with teammates past and present, Jeter strolled one last time to his position, where he squatted down and said a short prayer.

"I wanted to take one last view from short," Jeter said. "I was trying to take a last view in the top of the ninth and then they tied it, and I thought I would have to go back out there. I basically just said thank you, because this is all I've ever wanted to do, and not too many people get an opportunity to do it. It was above and beyond anything I'd ever dreamt of. I don't even know what to say. I've lived a dream, and part of that dream is over now."

Jeter went on to take four at-bats at Fenway Park that weekend as a DH, but he would never play shortstop again. Although his final game took place three days after his memorable night in the Bronx, it was his Stadium farewell that people will always remember.

"You almost expected something magical and special to happen," Yankees broadcaster Michael Kay said. "I said on the air, 'Fantasy becomes reality'—he lives a fantasy life and he handles it very well. You expect those things from him. If he made an out in that final at-bat, I think we would be more shocked than we were that he got the hit. That's what Derek Jeter is supposed to do. That's what he did his whole life, so it was a perfect ending to his Yankee Stadium career."

# Chapter 4

# *A Moment in Time*

*Few franchises have the type of history that the Yankees do, making for more memorable moments than most can recall.*

*"The Yankees once had an advertising campaign with the slogan, 'At any moment, a great moment,'" longtime Yankees broadcaster Michael Kay said. "That really sums up the 25 years I've had in the booth; this team gives you some unbelievable moments."*

*There are far too many to address them all, but get a grasp on the following events and you'll be able to talk Yankees baseball with anybody.*

# Aaron Boone
# Belts the BoSox

The greatest rivalry in baseball has had plenty of highlights through the years, from the sale of Babe Ruth to a number of memorable brawls to Bucky Dent's home run in the 1978 one-game playoff (more on that later).

But no matchup between the two rivals had as much at stake as it did on October 16, 2003.

The Yankees and Red Sox had played 19 times during the regular season, a fierce series that saw the Bombers win 10 times. Once the two teams took care of business in the American League Division Series (the Yankees dispatched the Twins in four games, while the Red Sox needed five games to beat the Athletics), the ultimate showdown was set.

The two teams had met in the American League Championship Series in 1999, but the Yankees proved to be too much for the Red Sox to handle, cruising to a five-game win en route to their second of three straight World Series titles.

This time, things were different.

Boston came into Yankee Stadium and took Game 1, but Andy Pettitte led the Yankees to a Game 2 win. The Yankees took Game 3 at Fenway Park, a tilt remembered most for the bench-clearing brawl that included Pedro Martinez throwing 72-year-old bench coach Don Zimmer to the ground.

A split of the next two games sent the series back to the Bronx, giving the Yankees a chance to wrap it up at home in Game 6. But the Red Sox made a late-inning comeback to force Game 7, marking the first time in major league history that two teams played more than 25 games against each other in a single season.

The Red Sox held a 5–2 lead as the Yankees came to bat in the eighth inning, leaving Boston six outs away from its first World Series appearance since 1986. Martinez—a three-time Cy Young winner considered by many to be the best pitcher in the game—had already thrown 100 pitches, but manager Grady Little sent him back out for the eighth looking to move his team one inning closer to the pennant.

Nick Johnson popped out to start the inning, but Derek Jeter doubled and Bernie Williams singled, pulling the Yankees within two runs. Little went to the mound, seemingly to remove his starter, but he opted to leave Martinez—whose pitch count now stood at 115—in the game.

Hideki Matsui hit a ground-rule double, putting the tying runs at second and third. Up came Jorge Posada, who blooped a two-run double against his Boston nemesis, tying the game as the Stadium rocked with delight.

Aaron Boone had not started that night, and when he entered the game to pinch run later in the inning, it went largely unnoticed.

Boone had come to the Yankees before the trade deadline, hitting .254 with six home runs and 31 RBI in 54 games after replacing Robin Ventura as the starting third baseman. But his postseason had been dreadful; his .161 average and one RBI in the first 10 games prompted manager Joe Torre to sit him in the win-or-go-home Game 7 against the Sox.

With the game tied after eight, Mariano Rivera threw three brilliant innings to bring the Yankees to bat in the bottom of the 11th. There were 56,279 fans in attendance (though I'm sure 200,000 claim to have been there that night), all of them hoping for a chance to celebrate a sixth trip to the World Series in eight years.

Boone stepped to the plate to lead off the 11th against veteran knuckleballer Tim Wakefield, who had retired Matsui, Posada, and Jason Giambi in order the previous inning.

Many fans were likely looking ahead at the top of the lineup getting another chance, with 30–30 leadoff man Alfonso Soriano due up third that inning. Boone never gave Soriano a chance to be the hero, blasting Wakefield's first knuckleball into the left-field stands. The crowd almost didn't know what to do with itself, the shocking home run turning the ground beneath the ballpark into a trampoline.

Boone rounded the bases as the Stadium shook, his teammates rushing to the field to welcome him to the plate. Rivera ran to the mound and collapsed, later calling it the greatest game of his storied career.

"Wow. I can't even talk," Boone told Fox Sports' Curt Menefee on the field only minutes after touching home plate. "So many heroes today; I just happened to run into one. You've got to be kidding me. This is awesome."

Boone's vacant stare told the story. To this day, he struggles to put the words together to describe his feelings rounding the bases that night, calling his memories "foggy" at best.

"Derek told me, 'The ghosts will show up eventually'—and they did," Boone told Menefee. "This is stupid."

The Yankees went on to lose the World Series to the Marlins in six games, but the ALCS win over the Red Sox and Boone's home run will always be remembered as one of the greatest moments in the history of the old Stadium.

As for Boone, he had been penciled in as the starting third baseman for the 2004 Yankees, but he suffered a serious knee injury in January while playing basketball, ending his year before it even began.

The Yankees would trade for Alex Rodriguez to take his place, ending Boone's pinstriped tenure after only 71 regular season and postseason games, but that one swing on a memorable October night guaranteed his place in Yankees lore forever.

# Bucky F'n Dent

Before there was Aaron Boone, there was Bucky F'n Dent.

The Yankees and Red Sox have had a fierce rivalry for nearly 100 years, dating back to the sale of Babe Ruth from Boston to New York and the ensuing "Curse of the Bambino" that haunted Beantown for generations.

Separated by only 200 miles, Yankee Stadium and Fenway Park have witnessed so many memorable moments and spawned so many books and television specials it has become known as the best rivalry in professional sports.

Joe D. versus Teddy Ballgame. Thurman versus Fisk. Manny, Pedro, and Big Papi versus Jeter, Posada, and the Rocket. The names elicit visions of some of the greatest games in the sport's history.

But long before baseball changed its playoff format to allow the Yankees and Red Sox to meet in the postseason, there was never a bigger game between the two rivals than the one-game playoff on October 2, 1978.

The Red Sox led the American League East for most of the summer, while the Yankees lingered in the middle of the division, a sizeable gap separating them from first-place Boston.

On July 19, the Yankees were a whopping 14 games behind the Red Sox, their hopes for a defense of their 1977 World Series title waning by the day.

An 11–4 run helped the Yankees trim the lead to 6.5 games by August 1, but when the calendar turned to September, the deficit remained the same.

Then the Yankees went 9–1 over their next 10 games, culminating with a four-game sweep at Fenway Park that became known as "The Boston Massacre." The Yankees outscored the Red Sox 42–9 in the series, leaving Boston with only a share of first place.

The Yankees actually led the Red Sox from September 13 to September 30, but the Red Sox blanked the Blue Jays on the final day of the regular season and the Yankees were blown out by the Indians, leaving the two rivals tied at 99–63 after 162 games.

"We knew we were a great team," Reggie Jackson said. "We had gone on a run of 21–4, but we got beat by Rick Waits that last day that made us go to Boston. We had both won 99 games. Somebody had to win one more. There had to be a loser, but anyone could have won that game."

The division title would be settled in a one-game playoff at Fenway Park the very next day—the site was determined by a coin toss—with Ron Guidry taking on Mike Torrez, who had pitched for the Yankees the previous season, winning two games in the World Series including the clincher in Game 6.

"Just how big a game it was, the magnitude of a one-game playoff," Dent said of the anticipation leading up to the game. "After 162 games, it came down to one game between us and Boston. It was a crystal-clear day and you could feel the electricity in the crowd.

"Games like that don't happen very often. Two teams that don't like each other, two cities that don't like each other, and we're playing one game for all the marbles."

The Yankees were confident with their ace on the hill. Guidry had gone 24–3 with a 1.72 ERA and nine shutouts that season, leading the league in all three categories. They also had All-Star closer Rich "Goose" Gossage—who won 10 games and led the league with 26 saves—primed to come out of the bullpen.

"With Guidry on the mound and Goose available in the pen, I knew we were going to be tough to handle," Jackson said.

The Red Sox jumped out to a 1–0 lead in the second inning on a leadoff home run by future Hall of Famer Carl Yastrzemski, pushing it to 2–0 on an RBI single by Jim Rice, another player destined for Cooperstown.

The Yankees had managed only two hits through six innings against Torrez, leaving them nine outs away from the end of their season.

"As the game went on, you could feel it starting to build," Dent said. "Torrez was throwing a good game and Guidry was pitching well."

Torrez retired Graig Nettles to open the seventh, but Chris Chambliss and Roy White followed with singles, putting the tying runs at first and second. Jim Spencer pinch hit for Brian Doyle, flying out to left field for the second out of the inning.

Dent stepped to the plate, hitless in his first two at-bats that day against Torrez.

"I wanted to pinch hit but didn't have anybody to play," Yankees manager Bob Lemon said years later in an interview with MLB Productions.

Dent fouled a ball off his left ankle, taking a few minutes to shake it off. As he stepped to the plate, Mickey Rivers noticed that Dent's bat was cracked, so he handed him his lumber to finish his at-bat.

Torrez hung a slider on the next pitch that Dent drilled high to left field toward the Green Monster, Fenway's signature 37-foot-high wall. Most people—Dent included—thought it would hit the wall, but as Bill White told television viewers that day, it most certainly did not.

"Deep to left!" White said on the broadcast. "Yastrzemski will not get it—it's a home run!"

The ball squeaked over the Monster and landed in the netting high above Lansdowne Street, giving the Yankees a 3–2 lead.

"I didn't realize the impact of the home run until it was all over with," Dent said. "At 3–2, the Red Sox had a great lineup and anything can happen in Boston. Rounding the bases, I just thought, 'We're ahead.'"

Jackson, who along with Nettles had led the Yankees with 27 home runs that season, was not surprised to see Dent come up with the big home run despite hitting only four all season.

"He was a good player, so for him to do something like that was not out of the ordinary to me," Jackson said. "He was a very sound player. For him to hit a fly ball over the Green Monster was not that difficult for him to do. I never thought, 'We should be hitting for Bucky' or 'We need to get past Bucky here.' He got hits, and when he hit a home run, it was like Willie Randolph—it meant something. When they hit one, it was usually going to matter for us."

The Yankees added another run in the seventh on Thurman Munson's RBI double. Gossage replaced Guidry with one out in the seventh, the Yankees holding a 4–2 lead, then Jackson took Bob Stanley deep for a solo home run, pushing the lead to three runs.

The Red Sox scored twice against Gossage in the eighth, trimming the lead to 5–4. But the intimidating closer retired Yastrzemski to end the game with the tying run at third base, clinching the division title for the Yankees, who went on to win their second straight World Series title thanks to the heroics of an unlikely power source.

After the season, Dent's friend Joe Illigasch, who worked for CBS' *60 Minutes,* told the shortstop his life would never be the same thanks to his timely home run.

"He said, 'That home run is going to change your life.' I said, 'Get out of here!'" Dent said. "He was right. It did. Sports is about moments and that was a big moment. It seemed like the whole world was watching. Everybody I talk to remembers exactly where they were at that moment. It doesn't happen very often, so I feel grateful to be a part of history like that—especially with the Yankees."

# Jeffrey Maier Lends a Hand

The atmosphere at the old Yankee Stadium was unlike any other in baseball. Thanks to the architecture of the ballpark, players would often speak of the feeling that the fans were right on top of them.

In Game 1 of the 1996 American League Championship Series, one fan took that literally.

Jeffrey Maier, a 12-year-old from Old Tappan, New Jersey—a 30-minute ride to Yankee Stadium—got an opportunity to attend his first postseason game in the Bronx when family friends had an extra ticket. The friends, according to a guest column Maier wrote for Bleacher Report in 2014, were Orioles fans, so their invitation would come back to haunt them and the entire Baltimore fan base.

It also may have helped launch the latest Yankees dynasty.

The Orioles and Yankees had battled in the American League East all season, a four-game New York sweep at Camden Yards in July giving Joe Torre's club a healthy lead they would ultimately protect for the Yankees' first division crown since 1981.

The Yankees got past the Rangers in the first round, while the Orioles beat the Indians to set up an all–AL East matchup in the ALCS. The Red Sox may have been the Yankees' traditional rival, but the Orioles had become the team Yankees fans loved to hate that season.

Baltimore had a penchant for hitting the long ball, setting a major league record with 257 home runs that season, led by an unlikely 50-homer season from speedy center fielder Brady Anderson. The roster included future Hall of Famers Cal Ripken Jr., Roberto Alomar, and Eddie Murray, lending plenty of star power to the lineup.

Rafael Palmeiro, who would hit 3,000 home runs and collect 3,000 hits in his career before his performance-enhancing-drug suspension ultimately kept him out of Cooperstown, had a monster season in 1996 with 39 home runs and 142 RBI.

The two teams opened the ALCS at Yankee Stadium on October 9, exchanging runs in the early innings, while Palmeiro put the Orioles ahead with a fourth-inning home run against Andy Pettitte.

Baltimore led 4–3 heading into the eighth inning, leaving the Yankees with six outs to tie the game. Setup man Armando Benitez was trying to get the ball to closer Randy Myers as the Orioles looked to steal home-field advantage with a Game 1 victory.

Jim Leyritz—who had hit a memorable home run in the previous year's ALDS and would go on to hit the biggest homer of the 1996 World Series against the Braves—took a called third strike to open the eighth. That brought star rookie Derek Jeter to the plate.

Jeter hit 10 home runs in his rookie campaign, so the last thing on his mind was taking Benitez deep. Jeter jumped on Benitez's first pitch and drove it the opposite way, sending right fielder Tony Tarasco—who had taken over for Bobby Bonilla as a defensive replacement that inning—toward the wall.

Tarasco tracked the ball and appeared to have a read on it, putting his glove up in anticipation of making the catch. As he looked up to make the play, Tarasco's back hit the wall and the ball disappeared, clearing the fence for a game-tying home run.

Confusion ensued. Even Bob Costas, calling the game for NBC, was unsure of what had just happened.

"And what happens here?" Costas shouted. "He contends that a fan reaches up and touches it! But Richie Garcia says no, it's a home run!"

Tarasco immediately pointed up at the fans, rushing over to argue with Garcia, the right-field umpire, that a fan reached over and swiped the ball away from the field of play. Garcia pointed up at the stands, making his official ruling that Jeter's ball was a home run, knotting the game at 4.

Jeter himself seemed uncertain about what had happened, running hard to second base before slowing into a home run trot a few strides later.

Orioles manager Davey Johnson came out of the dugout to argue, while an animated Tarasco pleaded his case. Anderson came over from center field to lend his two cents, then Benitez made his way out to right field from the mound to argue that it should not be a home run.

Johnson ushered his players away from Garcia, then resumed his angry appeal that the play should have been ruled interference.

Upon seeing the review, Costas and his two broadcast partners—Bob Uecker and Joe Morgan—acknowledged that a fan had grabbed the ball before it descended into Tarasco's glove, or at worst hit the top of the wall for a double.

Maier didn't actually catch the ball, which glanced off his glove and into the stands, retrieved by another fan. While Johnson argued the call, Maier was hoisted onto the shoulders of an adult Yankees fan, the kid pumping his fist and high-fiving other fans as they celebrated his team's new life in the game.

Once replays made it clear that Maier had altered the course of the game, stadium security took him to an area where media members promptly interviewed the Yankees' 26th man.

With no instant replay to lean on, the call stood and the game resumed. It remained tied into extra innings, ending when Bernie Williams led off the bottom of the 11th with a walk-off home run against Myers.

Baltimore filed an official protest with Major League Baseball, noting Garcia's confession after the game that he had blown the call. The Orioles called it "an extraordinary protest based on extraordinary events," asking the league to reverse the decision and replay the game from that point.

"The best interests of the game demand no less," the protest said.

MLB didn't agree, allowing the call—and the Yankees' victory—to stand.

The Yankees went on to beat the Orioles in five games, then beat the Braves in the World Series for their first championship since 1978.

Maier went on to play baseball at Wesleyan University in Connecticut, though he went undrafted and his dream of playing professionally was never realized. He now lives in New Hampshire with his wife and their two children. He has attended only a handful of games after that infamous night, though he remains a Yankees fan.

"It's a play that whether or not it matters to me, it's a play that's important to the Yankees and it has a place in the history of the game," Maier told the *Daily News* before the Yankees and Orioles faced off in the 2012 ALDS. "I've embraced that."

Who knows whether the Yankees would have gotten past the Orioles without Maier's help, but one thing is for certain: none of us would know Maier's name if not for his involvement in one of the most controversial plays in recent memory.

# Doc Gooden Makes a House Call

There was no bigger star in New York in the mid-1980s than Dwight Gooden, the unhittable Mets pitcher known to most as "Dr. K" or "Doc."

The National League's 1984 Rookie of the Year and 1985 Cy Young Award winner, Gooden went 58–19 with a 2.28 ERA during his first three seasons in the majors, capping it by helping the Mets to the 1986 World Series title.

But substance abuse and injuries sidetracked Gooden's career, culminating in a 60-day suspension in June 1994 for a positive cocaine test. He tested positive again during his suspension, prompting Major League Baseball to suspend him for the entire 1995 season.

Gooden signed with the Yankees as a free agent in February 1996, but the start of his season went so badly, he was demoted from the rotation to the bullpen after going 0–3 with an 11.47 ERA in his first three starts.

When David Cone's season was interrupted due to an aneurysm, Gooden was thrust back into the rotation.

"I was sad for David, especially because he was a close friend," Gooden told *Yankees Magazine* in 2016. "But I also looked at it as my last shot to stay in the big leagues."

On May 8, Gooden gave up three runs in the first inning against the Tigers, then proceeded to retire 22 consecutive batters as he pitched through the eighth.

Six days later, Gooden was slated to take the mound at Yankee Stadium, though 24 hours before the game, it was no sure thing he would pitch at all. Gooden's father, Dan, was scheduled to undergo open heart surgery on May 15, so Gooden had bought a plane ticket and planned to fly to Tampa to be with his parents, skipping his start against the Mariners.

"When I woke up that morning, I started to think that my dad would probably want me to pitch," Gooden said. "I began to think about all the days we spent together at the park when I was a kid. He always talked to me about being a man and putting the job first. So I said, 'You know what, I'm going to pitch, and then I'll go home.'

"I called my mom to tell her that I was going to stay in New York, and she didn't take it that well. She was making me feel guilty, and when she started to say, 'You know what could happen...' I hung up the phone on her. After that, it felt like a dark cloud was over me all day, and I really couldn't focus. All I could think about was my childhood."

Gooden walked Darren Bragg to open the game. Alex Rodriguez—playing in his first full season in the majors—launched a ball to deep center field, where backup Gerald Williams chased it down and made a spectacular play, then threw the ball to the infield to double up Bragg at first base.

"I was hurt, nursing an injury," said Bernie Williams, the regular center fielder, who was on the bench that night. "Gerald was in center field instead of me and he made an unbelievable catch in the first inning that was probably one of the better plays that saved the no-hitter from the get-go. If he didn't make that play, we're not talking about that no-hitter today."

"If he doesn't make that catch, I'm down 1–0 and A-Rod is on third base with no outs and Ken Griffey Jr. is coming up," Gooden said. "That catch changed the whole dynamic of that game."

A-Rod had taken a great swing against Gooden, but he could tell there was something different about the 31-year-old that night.

"I remember early on how electric Doc's stuff was that night," Rodriguez said. "I hit second, and I remember him having an extra foot on his fastball. He was throwing well, elevating his fastball, and he had a really sharp breaking ball that he was throwing for strikes. I thought, 'This is a different Dwight Gooden,' and going back to the dugout and telling guys, 'He's got good stuff. Make sure you're ready to hit.'"

Gooden issued a walk in each of the first three innings, but he finally retired the side in order in the fourth and fifth. Bragg reached on an error by Tino Martinez to open the sixth, but Gooden got A-Rod to ground out, struck out Ken Griffey Jr., then watched Edgar Martinez line out to center to end the inning.

"The more zeros I put up, the more confidence I was gaining," Gooden said. "I was walking out to the mound with more of a swagger. Even though I wasn't the Doc Gooden of '85, I felt like I was back that night."

Gooden thought about his father a lot during the early innings, but when he walked out for the sixth, it occurred to him what was developing on the mound that night.

"When I took the mound in the sixth inning and realized that I hadn't given up a hit I just said, 'Wow, is this really happening?'" Gooden said. "From that point on, I forgot about my dad's situation. That's when it began to feel like 1985 again."

As the innings went by, Gooden's teammates were anxiously watching every pitch.

"I was shaking on the bench," Andy Pettitte said. "I've seen several no-hitters and whenever I get to those moments and I know it's close, I'm so nervous. It's like when I'm deer hunting and a big deer comes along, I get buck fever. That's what I felt like sitting on the bench. The nerves, the anticipation; I felt like a fan. You're so helpless."

By the ninth, Gooden was physically and mentally exhausted, but he was determined to finish off his bid for history.

"That ninth inning was all about adrenaline and guts," Gooden said.

Holding a 2–0 lead, Gooden wasn't just trying to complete the no-hitter; he was trying to lock down a win. He walked A-Rod to open the ninth, then Griffey hit a grounder that Tino Martinez snagged about 30 feet to his right, diving back to first base to record the first out of the inning.

"I was like a boxer in the last round just trying to hang on," Gooden said. "Tino Martinez made an incredible play at first base on a ground ball that Griffey hit. That saved the no-hitter."

A walk of Edgar Martinez put the tying run on base, while a wild pitch put the two runners into scoring position. Pitching coach Mel Stottlemyre came to the mound to check on Gooden, but there was no way the veteran was handing the ball over.

Gooden dug down deep and struck out Jay Buhner for the second out, leaving Paul Sorrento as the only hitter standing between himself and history.

"The last pitch of the game was actually the worst pitch I threw that night," Gooden said. "I threw Paul Sorrento a hanging curveball that was right over the plate, and he popped it up. You've got to have some luck to pitch a no-hitter."

Derek Jeter squeezed the ball for the final out, setting off a loud celebration at the Stadium.

"It was amazing; there was a lot of drama to it," Yankees broadcaster Michael Kay said. "It didn't look like Doc had much left, so the sheer joy on his face for a guy who had been through so much—a lot of it self-inflicted—when he got the final out, it was neat."

Gooden hugged catcher Joe Girardi as teammates began to mob them. Bernie Williams and Jim Leyritz hoisted Gooden on their shoulders, carrying him off the field before he came back out for a curtain call.

"I was thinking about how not that long before, I couldn't stay clean for more than a day," Gooden said. "I thought about how I would be in a hotel room crying because I thought my life was over. I couldn't believe that after being out of baseball and then nearly released by the Yankees, I was getting carried off the field at Yankee Stadium."

Those same teammates that were living and dying with each pitch over the final few innings were elated as they celebrated with Gooden.

"He was instrumental for me as a young pitcher on that staff," Pettitte said. "The way he treated me, it just made it even more special. Knowing what he went through in his life, the ups and downs, to be able to come full circle and to do that on that stage at Yankee Stadium, it was awesome."

"He never threw a no-hitter anywhere else when he was more dominant than anything," Leyritz said. "To do it in a Yankees uniform, it was really cool. Those type of stories were what that whole year was about."

Even Gooden's opponents that day understood the significance of his incredible accomplishment.

"He had been through so much," Rodriguez said. "I came up watching that Mets team very closely with Keith Hernandez, Darryl Strawberry, and Doc, so while you certainly don't stand in the box cheering for him because you want to get hits and do well, when he has a night like he did that night, it was his career coming full circle. It was true redemption. I was happy for him."

Gooden flew home to Tampa the following day to be with his family. When his father came out of surgery, he gave him the ball from the final out of his historic performance.

# Yankees Slam the Athletics Again and Again and Again

O ver 130-plus years and nearly 200,000 games, no team in history had ever hit three grand slams in the same game.

So when Curtis Granderson stepped to the plate with the bases loaded in the eighth inning on August 25, 2011, he had no idea he was about to make history.

Granderson clubbed a grand slam against Oakland right-hander Bruce Billings, becoming the third Yankee to go deep with the bases loaded that afternoon. It wasn't until the news flashed on the scoreboard that the Yankees learned they were the first team ever to accomplish the powerful feat.

"I'm surprised it hadn't been done before with all the great teams and great individual hitters that have come throughout the course of the game," Granderson told reporters after the game. "The fact that we as a team have done something that all the teams that have ever played this game have never done before, especially all the offenses...it kind of speaks to what this offense is."

The Yankees had hit a pair of grand slams in a game only three times during their illustrious history: Tony Lazzeri hit two on May 24, 1936; Dave Winfield and Don Mattingly each hit one on June 29, 1987; and Bernie Williams and Paul O'Neill had a slam apiece on September 14, 1999.

The day actually started out quite poorly for the Yankees, who found themselves trailing Oakland 7–1 in the fourth inning thanks to a terrible outing by starter Phil Hughes.

"They were really far behind early, and [YES Network president of production and programming John Filippelli] called me in the booth and said, 'Don't give up on the game and kill the audience. It doesn't mean they're out of it, but it sounds like you guys have given up on the game,'" Yankees TV voice Michael Kay recalled. "It ended up being very prescient."

After Russell Martin hit a solo shot in the fourth, Robinson Cano got the comeback rolling with a grand slam to right field against Athletics starter Rich Harden in the fifth, bringing the Yankees within a run.

At that point, they had no thoughts of making history. They were just hoping to win the game.

"It's definitely a roller coaster of emotions during the course of the day," Granderson said.

Martin put the Yankees ahead in the sixth with his second homer of the day, this one coming with the bases juiced against righty Fautino De Los Santos. The Yankees had loaded the bases with a hit batter, a walk, a wild pitch, and an intentional walk, but Martin cleared them with one big hit to right field.

"They got a little erratic and we have professional hitters on our team who are willing to take balls and take good at-bats," Martin said after the game. "We were patient enough to wait for our pitch and drive it."

Martin's second homer was part of a 5-for-5 day, making him the first Yankees catcher since Elston Howard in 1959 to have five hits in a game. He drove in a career-best six RBI that day.

The Yankees went on to score six more runs in the seventh, though they only had two hits in the inning as Oakland's bullpen issued an astonishing seven walks in the span of 11 batters.

During that inning, which saw the Yankees have seven opportunities with the bases loaded, Granderson thought to himself, *Are we going to get another one?*

It didn't happen in the seventh, but when Granderson came to bat with the bases full in the eighth, he unloaded on Billings' sixth pitch of the at-bat, belting it deep to right center to make history.

"I've never been involved in such a game," Alex Rodriguez said. "Three grand slams, three different guys. That's why it's fun to come to the park every day; you never know what you're going to see. We may never see that again for a long time."

"It happened so fast, you didn't realize the historical perspective of it until later on," Kay said.

The three grand slams traveled a combined estimated distance of 1,155 feet.

"You have to be pretty fortunate," manager Joe Girardi said, "because you have to get the bases loaded a lot. It's a pretty crazy accomplishment."

By the end of the day, the Yankees had come to bat with the bases loaded an incredible 16 times. They were 6-for-13 with two walks and a sacrifice fly.

"You're not going to see it again, probably," said Derek Jeter. "You can't explain it."

The crowd of 46,369—at least those that waited out the initial 89-minute rain delay that postponed the start of the game—went on to see a 22–9 Yankees win as the Bombers tied an 80-year-old team record for most runs in a home game.

"You feel pretty good about your chances of winning when you get 12 runs on three swings," Girardi said. "There have been so many gifted players that have come through here, so just to get a chance to play with them, manage them and watch them has really been amazing."

The game also included Jorge Posada's first and only career appearance at second base, as he fielded a grounder for the final out of the game.

"This game has been played for a long time; pretty much everything has already happened," Martin said. "I'm waiting to see who hits four. I don't know if it will ever happen. We'll see. But three is pretty cool."

. . . . . . . . . . . . . . . . . . . . . . . . . . . . . . . . .

# A-Rod's Epic Night

Alex Rodriguez has had plenty of big days in his career. When you've hit nearly 700 home runs, that's pretty much a given.

He hit multiple home runs an incredible 62 times during his 22 seasons, including five three-homer performances. Only six other players have had that many, putting A-Rod in an exclusive club.

None of them drove in 10 runs in their three-homer games, making Rodriguez's one of the most productive days a player has ever had.

Tony Lazzeri of the Yankees was the first player in history to hit three home runs while driving in at least 10 runs in the same game, collecting 11 RBI in a 25–2 win over the Philadelphia Athletics on May 24, 1936.

It would be 13 years until another player accomplished the feat, as Walker Cooper of the Reds had a three-homer, 10-RBI game against the Cubs in 1949. As of 1992, only four players had ever posted those numbers in a single game, with Boson's Norm Zauchin (1955) and Fred Lynn (1975) joining the club.

St. Louis' Mark Whiten (four homers, 12 RBI on September 7, 1993) and Boston's Nomar Garciaparra (three homers, 10 RBI on May 10, 1999) were the fifth and sixth players to accomplish the feat.

A-Rod made it seven on April 26, 2005.

"I remember it being a warm night at the Stadium; good crowd," Rodriguez said. "I always enjoyed facing Bartolo Colon."

Rodriguez had experienced plenty of success against Colon since the right-hander debuted in 1997, batting .350 (14-for-40) with three home runs, five doubles, and six RBI over 15 games.

"Bartolo Colon would always challenge you," Rodriguez said. "As a pitcher, he would never hold back. That's one of the reasons he was so successful and has had such a long career; he pitched to guys, had a lot of conviction and wouldn't walk you. If you were going to beat him, it was going to be early, because he wasn't going to pitch around you."

Although the Yankees were 8–11 through their first 19 games in 2005, A-Rod was off to a decent start, hitting .280 with four home runs and 15 RBI.

A-Rod stepped to the plate with two runners on and two out in the first inning, launching Colon's 2–2 pitch over the 399-foot sign in left-center field.

His second at-bat came in the bottom of the third with one man on and two out. This time, A-Rod belted a 1–0 pitch from Colon, sending it over the retired numbers and into the visitors bullpen.

"After the two home runs, that's all anybody was thinking, even the players," manager Joe Torre said that night. "Players don't normally get caught up in that stuff, but everybody in the dugout became a fan. It was quite an incredible thing."

When A-Rod came up in the fourth inning for his third at-bat, the bases were loaded with two out. Colon wouldn't possibly give him another pitch to hit, would he? Even a bases-loaded walk would be better than the alternative.

"In a weird way, because it's Bartolo, I felt like he was going to keep coming at me," Rodriguez said. "I felt like he felt that he was due to get me out."

# A CLOSE SECOND

**I**f A-Rod's night against the Angels was a game for the ages, then his performance in his final regular season inning of 2009 was an inning for all time.

Having missed the first 28 games of the season following March hip surgery, Rodriguez returned to the lineup on May 8 in Baltimore. He launched the first pitch he saw for a three-run home run, giving CC Sabathia all the support he needed in a 4–0 win.

The late start all but ensured that A-Rod's 11-year streak of 30-homer, 100-RBI seasons would come to an end. He went into the final game of the season at Tropicana Field with 28 home runs and 93 RBI, needing two home runs and seven RBI to keep the streaks alive.

"You think about it once, but you realize it's not realistic to do," Rodriguez said. "First, how many times do you get to hit a couple of home runs and drive in seven runs? More than that, you usually don't get enough opportunities to drive in seven runs. You talk about it and laugh about it tongue-in-cheek, but it's nothing you even think about for real until the opportunity comes up."

The Yankees entered the sixth inning without any runs, trailing the Rays 2–0. Manager Joe Girardi planned to lift his starters after the sixth to get them some extra rest before the postseason, making it a near certainty that A-Rod would fall short of both milestones.

He came to bat against Wade Davis with two runners on base, launching a three-run home run that brought him to 29 and 96. Still, the third baseman was unlikely to hit again in the inning, let alone get an at-bat with the bases loaded.

Andy Sonnanstine replaced Davis after two more runners reached base, then the Yankees scored three more runs against the reliever.

With runners at second and third and two out, the Rays opted to intentionally walk Mark Teixeira, giving A-Rod his shot with the bases loaded.

A-Rod crushed an 0–1 pitch to deep right-center field, capping his unthinkable inning with a grand slam that left him with exactly 30 home runs and 100 RBI, extending his streak to 12 years with both.

A season that had started with a performance-enhancing-drug admission and major hip surgery ended with an extraordinary, improbable inning. The real fairy tale was yet to come, as A-Rod had a huge October, helping the Yankees to their 27th World Series title.

"You could have forecasted that it would be an awesome year," Rodriguez said. "My first swing of the season was a three-run home run on the first pitch I saw against Jeremy Guthrie in Baltimore while Sabathia threw a complete game. Then the last pitch I saw was a grand slam to take me to 30 and 100 and help us win. That year had magic written all over it from the start."

He worked the count full before unloading on Colon's seventh pitch of the at-bat, sending it soaring to center field. The ball glanced off the front of the batter's eye "black" section, giving A-Rod three home runs and nine RBI in his first three trips to the plate as the Yankees jumped out to a 10–2 lead.

"You can do that in Nintendo, stuff like that," said Jason Giambi, who saw all three blasts from the on-deck circle. "It was pretty incredible to watch. That was a lot of fun."

"I was thinking, 'How is he getting so many chances against Bartolo?'" said Joe Girardi, who was Torre's bench coach at the time. "Nine RBI against one guy? That's amazing."

Rodriguez, whose previous best had been seven RBI in one game, singled in the sixth inning against righty Kevin Gregg, driving in his

10<sup>th</sup> run of the night. He came up short in his bid for a fourth homer, making his only out of the night in the eighth, a hard fly ball to center against 23-year-old left-hander Jake Woods.

The last player prior to A-Rod to drive in nine runs in a game for the Yankees was Danny Tartabull in 1992. Lazzeri remains the only player ever to top A-Rod's feat, his 11 RBI remaining the single-game standard for the club.

"Your mouth has to drop open when you see something like that," Torre said. "That was certainly worth the price of admission."

"That was a vintage example of what Alex could be on the right day at the right moment," said Yankees broadcaster Michael Kay. "The thing that stood out to me was that he made it look so easy; it didn't look like he was laboring to do it. Like I said at the time, Alex Rodriguez had an unbelievable month on a Tuesday night. Players would kill to do that over two weeks and he did it on one day."

Six years later, Colon would sign with the Yankees, playing with A-Rod as teammates for the first time.

"I told him he is going to have two less home runs now because we are on the same team," Colon said through a translator.

A-Rod wound up with two more three-homer games during his tenure with the Yankees, repeating the feat in 2010 in Kansas City and again in 2015 in Minnesota. But his epic night in the Bronx against Colon and the Angels remains his greatest single game, as much for the surroundings as the results.

"To do it at home, to do in the Bronx, and for the last one to be a grand slam, that put an exclamation point on the night and made it historic," Rodriguez said. "Without a question, when I think about *the* three-run homer game, that's the one I think of. The 10 RBI, us winning the game and the fans going crazy, all of that makes that one something I'll remember forever."

# Gator Gets the Crowd on Its Feet— Over and Over Again

Ron Guidry announced his arrival in the major leagues in 1977, winning 16 games with a 2.82 ERA as he helped the Yankees to their first World Series title in 15 years.

In 1978, however, Guidry took his game to the next level.

The left-hander posted one of the most remarkable seasons of all time, going 25–3 with a 1.74 ERA. He threw 16 complete games and a league-high nine shutouts, holding hitters to a .193 batting average and .528 OPS for the season.

"Guidry was something special," said Marty Appel, the Yankees' longtime PR executive. "There was no way that a guy like him without big baseball-player arms could throw that hard and be so effective, but he was. In the 1976 World Series, he only appeared as a pinch runner, so nobody saw him coming as the great player that he was."

On May 23, Guidry began a five-start stretch that saw him go 5–0 with four complete games and a 1.22 ERA. With four double-digit strikeout games, Guidry fanned 49 batters over 44⅓ innings as he improved to 10–0 in his first 13 starts.

"He mowed through lineups like a man playing with boys," Willie Randolph later said of his teammate.

As it turned out, all of that was little more than an appetizer for the main course.

Fresh off a three-hit shutout of Oakland only five days earlier, Guidry took the mound on June 17 for a Saturday-night start against the Angels.

The left-hander left the bullpen following his pregame warmups and believed his seven-start streak of pitching at least eight innings would end that night.

"What's the earliest you've ever come into a game?" Guidry asked closer Sparky Lyle, according to a 1998 *Daily News* story celebrating the 20th anniversary of the game. "I feel like I don't have anything."

Bobby Grich hit a leadoff double to start the game, reaffirming Guidry's fears. But a strikeout of Rick Miller, a comebacker by Dave Chalk, and a strikeout of cleanup hitter Joe Rudi left Grich stranded at third.

Two innings later, Guidry allowed back-to-back, two-out singles by Miller and Chalk, putting the tying run at third base. Guidry struck out Rudi for the second time, ending the threat with his sixth K of the night.

Guidry struck out the side in the fourth, fanned two more in the fifth, and struck out all three batters in the sixth, giving him 14 Ks through six frames.

"The entire bench was laughing, because we felt we were overmatched," said Nolan Ryan, baseball's all-time strikeout leader.

Sensing something special, the crowd of 33,162 began to stand and cheer every time Guidry got to two strikes against a hitter. That's standard operating procedure in the Bronx these days, but as of that day, it had never been done before.

"That was the absolute first time," Appel said. "History happened right there and you could actually say, 'This is where it began.' That was the day that everybody stood up."

"I know they're behind me on every pitch, and when I don't strike out a batter it's like I let them down," Guidry told the Associated Press.

A strikeout of Brian Downing to end the seventh gave Guidry 15, tying the Yankees' club record set by Bob Shawkey in 1919. He broke the record with a strikeout of Ike Hampton to start the eighth, finishing that inning with 16.

Chalk and Rudi both struck out to start the ninth, giving Guidry 18 strikeouts through 8⅔ innings. He had already eclipsed Frank Tanana's American League record of 17 strikeouts by a lefty, but one more K to end the game would put Guidry alongside Ryan, Tom Seaver, and Steve Carlton as the only men ever to strike out 19 batters in a nine-inning game.

"The fans help him tremendously," Tanana told the AP. "They get up and cheer when he gets two strikes on a batter. Everyone gets excited, even the umpires, and he gets an extra yard on his fastball.

"I was excited from knowing what he's going through. From knowing how invincible and unbeatable he felt. It's a special feeling knowing you're in command and they've got no chance. You don't get that feeling every time you walk on the mound."

Don Baylor singled to center field with two out, but with the Yankees holding a 4–0 lead, that was just fine with the fans. The game was well in hand, and now Guidry would have another crack at the record-tying strikeout.

But Ron Jackson, who had already struck out once in the game, hit a ground ball to third base, closing the book on Guidry's incredible day.

The final line: nine innings, four hits, no runs, two walks, 18 strikeouts. He struck out every Angels hitter at least once, including Rudi four times.

"If you saw that pitching too often, there would be a lot of guys doing different jobs," Rudi said after the game.

Guidry went on to win the only AL Cy Young Award of his career that season, also finishing second behind Boston's Jim Rice in the MVP voting. Guidry got the last laugh on Rice, of course, picking up the victory against the Red Sox at Fenway Park in the one-game playoff between the two rivals.

The lefty—now known as "Louisiana Lightning"—beat the Royals in Game 4 of the ALCS to send the Yankees back to the World Series, then pitched a complete game in Game 3 against the Dodgers to help the Yankees win back-to-back titles.

His 18-strikeout game is considered one of the most dominant performances of all time, easily the best game of a career that led to his No. 49 being retired by the Yankees. Yet when he looks back on his historic season, Guidry's memorable game isn't what comes to his mind.

"When I think of 1978," Guidry said, "All I really think about is that we won the World Series."

# Jim Abbott Makes Unexpected History

Jim Abbott had been defying the odds for years.

Born without a right hand, Abbott became an All-American pitcher at the University of Michigan, pitched for the gold medal–winning United States Olympic team in 1988, and was drafted in the first round by the California Angels that same year.

But on September 4, 1993, Abbott pitched the game of his life, throwing a no-hitter against the Cleveland Indians at Yankee Stadium.

*Jim Abbott was born with only one hand, but he used it to make history with his no-hitter in 1993.* (AHRC New York City Foundation)

"I didn't talk about it much back then, but playing with one hand, I always wanted to be good," Abbott said. "I didn't want to just make it. If there was something for little kids to look to who had similar challenges as I did, I thought it could be more impactful if there was something credible, an achievement behind it.

"Not just making it, not just participating, but getting to the major leagues and being good. I don't know to what degree I was able to do that, but the no-hitter in some ways is symbolic of something good. I'm proud of it for those reasons. Some amazing things can happen in this world if you can stay determined, creative and find your own way of doing things."

Abbott had been rocked for seven runs on 10 hits and four walks in just 3⅔ innings only six days earlier at Cleveland Municipal Stadium, one of his worst starts in what had become a disappointing season. He wasn't thinking of making history on that sunny Saturday in the Bronx; he was simply hoping to give the Yankees a chance to win.

"I remember getting knocked out of the game in Cleveland, changing from my uniform into shorts and I went running, trying to kill some of the frustration," Abbott said. "It had been a frustrating season. That game in Cleveland was terrible, so a no-hitter in my next start against the same team couldn't have been further from my mind."

Abbott, catcher Matt Nokes and pitching coach Tony Cloninger got together to go over the scouting reports before the game, forming a plan to counter the beating Abbott had taken in his previous start.

That included throwing more breaking balls earlier in the count, something he had not done in Cleveland.

"The emphasis was just on trust and belief," Abbott said. "Matt was very enthusiastic about that; coming off the start before, he was eager to change the mindset. I think the previous start may have helped me kick in the concentration early, because you knew things could get away from you early."

The Indians were a young team anchored by All-Stars Albert Belle and Carlos Baerga, stellar leadoff man Kenny Lofton, and a pair of youngsters named Jim Thome and Manny Ramirez, who were only 22 and 21, respectively. Ramirez had made his major league debut only two days earlier, hitting two home runs against the Yankees in his second career game.

"They were young, but man, they could hit," Abbott said. "They were a strong hitting team. Ramirez had just been called up, Baerga had a high average; it was a good lineup with no breaks in there. A lot of it was forgetting about the lineup and trying to focus on throwing each pitch the best I possibly could."

The Yankees staked Abbott to a 3–0 lead with a three-run third inning, and although the left-hander had walked a batter in each of the first two innings, he had yet to allow a hit to that point.

Abbott induced three ground-ball outs in the fourth, then after a leadoff walk of Randy Milligan in the fifth, he got Ramirez to ground into a 6-4-3 double play before retiring Candy Maldonado to keep his no-hitter alive through five innings.

Randy Velarde hit a solo home run in the bottom of the fifth, right around the time Abbott realized he was more than halfway to history.

"By the fifth inning, we were leading 4–0 and I looked up at the scoreboard," Abbott said. "It wasn't a perfect game by any means; I had walked some guys and was a little erratic trying to find that aggressiveness within the zone. But I looked up and noticed they didn't have any hits yet.

"It had been the furthest thing from my mind, but from that point on, once it enters your mind, it's hard to move your concentration away from that thought. Then the crowd starts catching up with it, your teammates aren't talking to you in the dugout. It gets more and more special as the game progresses."

Abbott worked around his fourth walk of the day in the sixth, then needed only six pitches to get through the seventh, leaving him six outs from one of the most improbable games the stadium had ever seen.

Some pitchers might have let the enormity of the situation overwhelm them. Not Abbott.

"When he joined the Yankees, I asked him about the pressure of playing in the major leagues," said Yankees radio analyst Suzyn Waldman, who was covering the team for WFAN at the time. "He said, 'That isn't pressure; playing in the Olympics is pressure.'"

Abbott called his team's defense that day "amazing," recalling several plays that kept his historic bid alive, including Mike Gallego's play on a Lofton chopper in the third inning. With one out in the seventh, Wade Boggs made a diving stop at third base on a ball hit by Belle, throwing him out at first by a half-step.

"The stadium just went crazy," Abbott said. "What had been a quiet tension, there was this release. The secret was out that everyone was thinking about a no-hitter."

After striking out Ramirez and retiring Maldonado on a ground ball to start the eighth, Abbott walked Thome, who was hitting eighth that day. Sandy Alomar Jr.—who had driven in four runs against Abbott the week before—pinch hit for Junior Ortiz, presenting a challenge for the Yankees pitcher.

Alomar grounded out to third base to end the inning, sending the stadium into a frenzy as Abbott walked back to the dugout needing only three more outs. He had overcome so much during his 25 years, but this was setting up to be the biggest day of his baseball life.

"It added a lot more emotion to it," said Yankees broadcaster Michael Kay, who called the game on radio. "He was a good guy, so you liked him. You just felt good for him. He was a guy that had defied the odds his entire life, so for him to throw a no-hitter was going to be pretty cool."

Abbott had thrown 107 pitches when he took the mound in the ninth. Lofton grounded out to start the inning, then Felix Fermin hit a deep fly ball to left center that Abbott thought might end his bid, but Bernie Williams chased it down, saving the no-hitter with a stellar play.

Baerga, Cleveland's best overall hitter, grounded out to shortstop for the final out. As Abbott watched Velarde's throw settle in Don Mattingly's glove, he transferred his glove to his right arm and pumped his left hand as his teammates began to mob him on the mound. Nokes ran to the mound and gave his pitcher a bear hug, not wanting to let go.

"I thought he was the most extraordinary person I had ever met," Waldman said. "When he had his no-hitter and Velarde made the last play, it was the most extraordinary moment. I wasn't crying, but I was almost hyperventilating because it was so remarkable. Who would have ever thought that could happen? Those things stay with you."

Abbott had enjoyed success with the Angels, finishing third in the American League Cy Young vote in 1991 after going 18–11 with a 2.89 ERA. But this day in the Bronx was different. He had thrown the first no-hitter by a Yankee since Dave Righetti a decade earlier, becoming only the fourth Yankee to accomplish the feat on their home field.

"It adds to it exponentially," Abbott said. "The fans treated me incredibly well and were very supportive. The pinstripes, there was something special about walking on the field as a Yankee—and I didn't grow up as a Yankees fan by any stretch of the imagination.

"The feel in the ballpark that day, the connection with the fans, that stadium, that uniform, it made it all so special. There's such a great history with the Yankees organization. I was there for only two years, but I'm very proud to have a small sliver, a moment at Yankee Stadium like that."

Abbott pitched only two seasons with the Yankees, going 20–22 with a 4.45 ERA in 1993–94. Yet every time he travels to New York, he's welcomed by the locals as if he had been a lifelong Yankee, something that has meant a lot to him over the past two-plus decades. He credits the replays of the game on the YES Network for keeping the game fresh in people's minds, allowing him to remain in the fans' consciousness more than 20 years after his big day.

"I enjoy it greatly," Abbott said. "My Yankees career was up and down to say the least; maybe a disappointment in the Yankees' eyes. But to have that connection to the Yankees organization and the city, it's something that I really cherish.

"There was success in my career, but the no-hitter stands as a symbol. It's something people can connect to. Amazing things can happen coming from Flint, Michigan, playing with one hand, ending up in Yankee Stadium and pitching a no-hitter. It's a cool story."

· · · · · · · · · · · · · · · · · · · · · · · · · · · · · · · · · · ·

# Reggie Jackson Becomes Mr. October

There was a time when Reggie Jackson was simply Reggie Jackson.

A six-time All-Star, Jackson had established himself as one of the game's biggest stars during the first decade of his career. His first eight seasons, all with the Oakland Athletics, saw him hit 253 home runs and collect two World Series rings, winning MVP honors in the Fall Classic in 1973.

But he didn't have a nickname. He was just Reggie.

That all changed on the night of October 18, 1977, when Jackson turned Yankee Stadium into his own Home Run Derby, launching three homers against the Los Angeles Dodgers in Game 6 of the World Series to help the Yankees wrap up their 21$^{st}$ championship.

"The Stadium held 58,000 at the brim," Jackson said. "I've probably met 158,000 that tell me they were there. I always say, 'You're lying. I've already met 60,000 people that were there!'"

Jackson had joined the Yankees before the 1977 season, signing a five-year contract worth $3 million. Jackson, the self-proclaimed "straw that stirs the drink," had a successful debut season in pinstripes, hitting .286 with 32 home runs and 110 RBI, reaching his seventh All-Star team—and the first of what would be eight straight for him. There was also plenty of controversy, as Jackson feuded with manager Billy Martin and was vilified by some, always in the spotlight of what became known as the Bronx Zoo.

The Yankees won 100 games and the American League East title, but Jackson wasn't signed to win the division. He was brought to the Bronx to help win a World Series, something the Yankees hadn't done since 1962, a lifetime in the eyes of Yankees fans and certainly of the team's owner, George Steinbrenner, who bought the team in 1973.

The Yankees had lost the World Series in 1976 to Cincinnati's Big Red Machine, which swept the Bombers in four games and celebrated at Yankee Stadium.

Jackson had a very quiet AL Championship Series against the Royals, hitting .125 with no home runs and one RBI. Still, the Yankees won the best-of-five series 3–2, advancing to the World Series against Tommy Lasorda's Dodgers.

The teams split the first two games in the Bronx, but the Yankees won Games 3 and 4 at Dodger Stadium before losing Game 5, returning home with a chance to clinch on their home turf.

Jackson was hitting .353 (6-for-17) with two home runs and three RBI in the first five games, but as he took the field for batting practice before Game 6, he had a feeling he was saving his best for last.

"When we played back in those days in the World Series, the stadium was full when we were taking batting practice," Jackson said. "When I hit, the stadium was packed."

Jackson recalled seeing several sportswriters hanging around the batting cage as he walked out from the dugout. Dick Young, Jim Murray, Dave Anderson, Ira Berkow, and Bob Ryan were among those watching, as were several Dodgers including Lasorda, starter

Burt Hooton, and reliever Elias Sosa, who would become central figures later that evening.

"The Dodgers and Burt Hooton were watching my BP, and it was probably the best one I ever had," Jackson said. "It was a fun day.

"I hit last in the group, probably took 50 swings and hit about 35 balls over the wall. When I walked out of the batting cage, I got a standing ovation from the stadium. I said to Dick Young and Dave Anderson, 'I sure hope I didn't leave it here.'"

Jackson drew a four-pitch walk in the second inning, scoring on Chris Chambliss' home run as the Yankees tied the game 2–2.

He came to bat in the fourth inning with Thurman Munson at first base and the Dodgers leading 3–2. That lead evaporated when Jackson saw his first strike of the night, drilling Hooton's offering into the right-field seats to give the Yankees another lead.

Sosa was on the mound when Jackson stepped to the plate in the bottom of the fifth, the Yankees now holding a 5–3 lead. Willie Randolph stood at first base with two out in the inning, but he didn't stay there long.

Jackson launched Sosa's first pitch into those same right-field seats, his second home run of the night and fourth of the series giving the Yankees a 7–3 lead. Yankee Stadium shook with delight as the legendary Howard Cosell gushed in the ABC broadcast booth.

"What a World Series for Reggie Jackson!" Cosell said. "First pitch right in his wheelhouse. Reggie Jackson, now well on his way to becoming the Most Valuable Player in the 1977 World Series."

Little did Cosell know.

Jackson led off the home half of the eighth inning with the Yankees still leading 7–3, only three outs away from bringing the Commissioner's Trophy back home to the Bronx.

As Jackson stood in the on-deck circle, he saw knuckleballer Charlie Hough warming up for his second inning of work. It was almost too good to be true, Jackson thought.

Jackson had hit eight home runs against Wilbur Wood and his knuckler, more than any other pitcher. He had also gone deep twice against Eddie Fisher, another knuckleballer, and once against Hoyt Wilhelm.

"I hit the knuckleball well, so I thought, 'They must not know I hit knuckleballs good,'" Jackson said. "He was running to the mound and I thought, 'Man, I hope he gets in here fast.'"

No player other than Babe Ruth had ever hit three home runs in a World Series game, the Babe doing so in both 1926 and 1928. That was about to change.

Just as he had in each of his previous two at-bats, Jackson crushed Hough's first pitch—a knuckleball, what else?—and deposited it into the "batter's eye" black section in center field, a shot estimated at about 450 feet that Cosell termed "a colossal blow."

"What a way to top it off!" Cosell exclaimed. "Forget about who the Most Valuable Player is in the World Series! How this man has responded to pressure. What a beam on his face; how can you blame him? He's answered the whole world!"

Jackson was mobbed by his teammates as he returned to the dugout, then stepped out for a curtain call as the fans continued to chant and cheer.

"I was probably running a foot off the ground," Jackson said of his third and final home run trot. "There was a picture in the *Daily News* of me between second and third, literally in my steps with both feet off the ground. It was a perfect picture for me on that night, because I felt like I was six to eight inches off the ground. It was really cool."

Jackson, who was the clear-cut choice for series MVP, earned the nickname "Mr. October" for his incredible accomplishment, a name that sticks with him to this very day.

# One Is Not Enough for Allie Reynolds

Throwing a no-hitter is a special accomplishment, one achieved by only nine players in Yankees history.

Of those nine, only one of them ever did it twice. And he did it in the same season.

Allie Reynolds was one of the greatest—and most underappreciated—pitchers in the Yankees' rich history, playing an integral role on six World Series championship teams.

Five of those came during an incredible five-year stretch from 1949 to '53, when the Yankees captured five consecutive titles—the first time that had ever been done—beating the crosstown Brooklyn Dodgers in three of those World Series.

"I feel like that whole era gets overshadowed; the early 1950s," Yankees Museum curator Brian Richards said. "People always seem surprised to find out the team won five championships in a row. I think our collective memory skips from Joe D. right up to Mickey, fast forwarding to Mickey's Triple Crown season and then to Mantle and Maris in 1961. The heart of those teams was the starting pitching with Allie Reynolds, Vic Raschi, and Eddie Lopat."

"There were better teams; Brooklyn, on paper, was supposed to be better than the Yankees," said Yankees historian Tony Morante. "But these guys knew how to win."

Nobody more so than Reynolds, who went 131–60 with a 3.30 ERA during his eight-year career in pinstripes. The man known as "Superchief" also excelled in the postseason, going 7–2 with five complete games—and four saves!—in 15 World Series appearances.

"He wasn't really flashy, wasn't showy," Richards said. "He was a quiet, stick to yourself, gruff kind of guy. But he was a hell of a pitcher; a big-game, big money pitcher. If there was one game you needed to win, he was probably the guy you wanted on the mound."

Reynolds, Lopat and Raschi formed a terrific trio atop the Yankees rotation, though Reynolds offered manager Casey Stengel an additional weapon, often pitching out of the bullpen between starts.

"One of the greatest pitchers in Yankees history for the big game," Morante said. "This guy wasn't afraid to come inside. He wasn't a pitcher you wanted to face, especially in a clutch situation. "

On July 12, 1951, Reynolds threw a no-hitter against the Cleveland Indians, beating Bob Feller by a 1–0 final at Cleveland Municipal Stadium. It had been the Indians who traded Reynolds to the Yankees in October 1946 for second baseman Joe Gordon, a deal Joe DiMaggio supposedly helped cinch when Yankees executive Larry MacPhail consulted him regarding which Indians pitcher other than Feller (he was not on the trade block) they should acquire.

"Take Reynolds," DiMaggio was quoted as saying in Reynolds' 1994 *New York Times* obituary. "I'm a fastball hitter, but he can buzz his hard one by me any time he has a mind to."

Reynolds took the mound for his final start of the regular season on September 28, the Yankees having held off both the Indians and Red Sox to win their third straight American League pennant. He was on his way to an easy 8–0 decision against Boston, which had no hits through the first eight innings.

With two out in the ninth, Ted Williams hit a pop-up that Yogi Berra misplayed, giving the Splendid Splinter one more crack at ruining Reynolds' bid for history.

"People were worried Reynolds would lose the no-hitter because of that," Morante said. "But he induced another pop-up against Ted Williams. He stepped up it and brought his best that day."

Reynolds became the first American League pitcher to record two no-hitters in the same season and only the second pitcher to accomplish the feat at all, joining Johnny Vander Meer, who threw back-to-back no-hitters for the Reds in 1938.

In his *New York Times* obit, Reynolds was quoted as downplaying the significance of throwing two no-hitters in the same season.

"A no-hitter is not the best standard by which to judge a pitcher," Reynolds said. "That's just luck. I've pitched four games better than the no-hitters and lost three of them."

Lucky or not, Reynolds remains one of only five men in baseball history to throw two no-hitters in the same season. The others are Vander Meer, Virgil Trucks (1952), Nolan Ryan (1973), and Max Scherzer (2015).

Richards ranks Reynolds in the top 10 of the Yankees' all-time pitchers, saying he very well might be in the top five.

"People talk about the top five or 10 Yankees and they only mention the hitters," Richards said. "We are the Bronx Bombers, so the pitching gets overshadowed. Even in 1961, everyone knows the M&M boys, but Whitey Ford won 25 games and the Cy Young Award and Luis Arroyo was the best reliever in baseball for one year. They get overshadowed, but their contributions were no less significant."

Reynolds, who was such a great athlete that he was once drafted by the New York Football Giants as a halfback, had a Monument Park plaque dedicated to him in 1989, five years before his death.

"He was the best of the three starters; you think of Raschi-Reynolds-Lopat as if it's one word," said Marty Appel, author of *Pinstripe Empire*. "Reynolds is the one that has a plaque out in Monument Park—the other two don't. He was a very smart guy, an American League player representative. He should be in the Hall of Fame."

# Derek Jeter Becomes Mr. November

As the clock struck midnight, history was about to be made. Nobody knew who would create it, but with Game 4 of the World Series tied in the 10th inning, the Yankees and Diamondbacks became the first teams ever to play meaningful baseball in the month of November.

There had already been a magical moment at Yankee Stadium an inning earlier when Tino Martinez delivered a game-tying, two-run home run against Arizona closer Byung-Hyun Kim with two out in the bottom of the ninth.

The stadium—filled with fans looking for a distraction less than eight weeks removed from the horrific terrorist attacks of 9/11—was buzzing after Martinez's clutch blast, but if the Yankees didn't finish the job, they would find themselves down three games to one, leaving them no margin for error against Randy Johnson, Curt Schilling, and the Diamondbacks.

Jeter stepped to the plate with two out in the 10th, Kim still on the mound for his third inning. As he fouled off the first pitch of the at-bat, the Stadium scoreboard clock read 12:00, officially flipping the calendar to November.

"People always ask me if I plan calls," said Michael Kay, who was calling the game with John Sterling on Yankees radio. "I remember looking at the clock when it passed 12:00 and I thought, 'Wow, this is the first game ever played in November. If someone hits a home run, he'll be Mr. November.'"

Jeter worked a full count against Kim, who tried to put the shortstop away with a slider on the ninth pitch of the at-bat. But Jeter—who was 1-for-15 in the series to that point—launched the ball to right field, clearing the wall for a walk-off home run and a 4–3 Yankees victory that evened the series at two games apiece.

"Swung on and drilled to right field, going back Sanders, on the track, at the wall—See Ya! See Ya! See Ya! A home run by Derek Jeter!" Kay called on the broadcast. "A game-winning, walk-off home run by Derek Jeter! He is Mr. November!"

Jeter—who had never hit a walk-off homer in his career—admitted after the game that he didn't know if he had hit it well enough to clear the wall.

"When I first hit it, I had no idea whether it was going to go out, but once it goes out, it's a pretty special feeling," Jeter said. "I've never hit a walk-off home run before so it was a special experience.

"That's the beauty of the postseason. Regardless of how you've done, every time you come up you have a chance to do something special."

The Fox broadcast had shown a fan in the stands holding a sign reading Mr. November during the at-bat, flashing back to him after Jeter crossed the plate.

"Did that guy bring that with him? Did he just have it ready?" Jack Curry of the YES Network wondered. "Whoever that guy was, you have to believe he had Jeter in mind when he made that sign, whether he just made it an inning earlier or carried it into the stadium. It's not as if Jeter needed to cement his status or legacy any more, but that shot absolutely did it. What an amazing moment. It just added to who Jeter already was and what he would become."

Kay, who would also call Jeter's 3,000th hit and his game-winning hit in his final Yankee Stadium appearance, wasn't shocked that it was Jeter who came through with the big moment in that game.

"I was prepared for him to do something special, but when he hits the home run, it surprised you," Kay said. "When he does something special, it doesn't, but a home run? I guess it just fits the narrative with Derek Jeter."

Amazingly, the Yankees provided equal drama the next night. Scott Brosius repeated Martinez's feat, drilling a game-tying two-run shot against Kim with the Yankees down to their final out. Alfonso Soriano finished it off three innings later, his RBI single completing the three-game Bronx sweep and sending the Yankees back to Arizona needing only one win for their fourth consecutive championship.

Throw in the emotional ceremonial first pitch that President George W. Bush threw before Game 3, and it was three days for the ages at Yankee Stadium.

"Those three games were probably the three most memorable games that I've ever been a part of," said Paul O'Neill.

With virtually everybody in the country outside of Arizona pulling for New York in the wake of 9/11, the Yankees returned to Phoenix looking to finish off the Diamondbacks.

Arizona crushed the Yankees in Game 6, setting up an epic Game 7 matchup of Roger Clemens and Curt Schilling. The Diamondbacks scored the game's first run in the bottom of the sixth, but the Yankees tied it in the seventh on Martinez's RBI single against Schilling.

Soriano led off the eighth with a solo home run, giving the Yankees a 2–1 lead. All that was left for the Yankees were six outs by Mariano Rivera, who struck out three in a scoreless eighth.

"Sitting in that press box and Mariano Rivera coming into the game, you thought that story was going to have a perfect ending for the Yankees and for New York," Curry said. "We all know what 9/11 meant and how many people latched on to baseball as something that could help get them through such an awful, dreary period in

# "PAUL O-NEILL! PAUL O-NEILL!"

**T**he Yankees won four World Series titles between 1996 and 2000, putting together one of the most recent great dynasties in professional sports.

The foundation of that run was the core of homegrown players including Derek Jeter, Mariano Rivera, Bernie Williams, Jorge Posada, and Andy Pettitte, a group of All-Stars developed in the Yankees' minor league system before finding a longtime home in the Bronx.

But another crucial cog in the machine was a veteran acquired in a trade with the Cincinnati Reds after the 1992 season: Paul O'Neill.

Nicknamed "The Warrior" by owner George Steinbrenner, O'Neill became a fan favorite through his intense style of play, his need for perfection at the plate—and of course, his infamous temper that left a number of dugout water coolers wishing they had been placed elsewhere.

O'Neill was selected to four American League All-Star teams during his nine-year tenure with the Yankees, winning the AL batting title during the strike-shortened 1994 season.

With four Yankees World Series rings already secured, O'Neill's place in Yankees history was set. He hadn't officially announced that he planned to retire at the end of the World Series, but word began to spread that this was it for O'Neill, prompting the sellout crowd at Yankee Stadium to offer one last gift to their right fielder.

As he took the field in the top of the ninth inning of Game 5 of the 2001 World Series, O'Neill was shocked to hear the entire Stadium chanting his name. The Yankees trailed the Diamondbacks 2–0, but that didn't stop the fans from showering O'Neill with love in what was likely his final inning in the Bronx.

"You don't know how to react," O'Neill said. "Everything you do on a field, you've practiced it. You've dreamed about those things when you're five years old in the backyard. It was the most unbelievable night."

An emotional O'Neill kept his composure in right field as the fans chanted his name throughout the inning. He received a standing ovation from the crowd as he walked in at the end of the frame, tipping his cap to the fans before heading into the dugout.

Scott Brosius extended O'Neill's time at the Stadium with a two-out, game-tying home run in the bottom of the ninth, while Alfonso Soriano made it a night to remember, lifting the Yankees to a win with a walk-off single in the 12th.

"A strange time because we were losing when it started happening," O'Neill said. "But to win that game, go home and celebrate a win, think about what the New York fans just did, how do you explain it?"

their lives. I thought Mariano was going to put a perfect bow on that present."

Rivera came out for the ninth looking to clinch another World Series for the Yankees. But Mark Grace singled, then Rivera made a throwing error on Damian Miller's sacrifice bunt, putting the tying and winning runs on base.

Jay Bell tried to bunt the runners over, but Rivera pounced on the ball and threw out the lead runner at third base. It didn't matter, as Tony Womack followed with a double, scoring pinch runner Midre Cummings to tie the game.

"For a guy that had been so great for so long and had just closed out three straight World Series, there was just a feeling of shock when he doesn't end up doing that," Curry said.

Rivera hit Craig Counsell to load the bases, bringing Luis Gonzalez to the plate with one out. The Yankees brought the infield in, but Gonzalez blooped a single over Jeter's head into center field, setting off a celebration at Bank One Ballpark while stunning the three-time defending champs.

"I always say if you get a World Series with one 'Forever' game, you're doing okay; if you get two, it's unbelievable," Kay said. "They had three of those games out of seven. The Brosius home run, the Tino home run, Jeter's Mr. November homer, Mariano blowing a save in Game 7. I think it might be the best World Series of all time."

# Dave Righetti's Memorable Independence Day

July 4 has always been an important day in Yankees history. Lou Gehrig's legendary speech took place at Yankee Stadium on Independence Day in 1939, while owner George Steinbrenner was born on the same day nine years earlier. Add in the fact that it's a national holiday made for afternoon baseball and the date has significance every year.

The holiday matinee in 1983 featured the Yankees and Red Sox in the final game of a four-game series. Boston had won two in a row and was looking for the series win, and with the All-Star break beginning the next day, the Yankees were trying to earn a split before parting ways for the next three days.

Steinbrenner wasn't at the stadium that day, but there was a special guest sitting in the owner's box: Richard Nixon.

Dave Righetti, a 24-year-old pitching his third full season with the Yankees, had pitched well during the first half, going 9–3 with a 3.53 ERA in his first 16 starts. Because he was pitching Monday, he was not eligible to pitch in Wednesday's All-Star Game at Chicago's Comiskey Park, so he was left off the team, much to his dismay.

"I thought I had pitched well enough to make it," Righetti told *Yankees Magazine* in 2012. "They told me before the weekend that because I was pitching Monday they couldn't use me in the All-Star Game, which was Wednesday. That didn't make it any easier to take."

Instead of representing the American League, Righetti planned to spend his break in Atlantic City and catch a Beach Boys concert with teammate Graig Nettles. But he had one more game to pitch before they headed down the New Jersey Turnpike, so he was determined to make the most of it and end his first half on a high note.

"I was a young kid still trying to prove my way," Righetti said. "That's what I remember: being hot and wondering what I was going to do for the All-Star break, honestly.

"I just wanted to go out on a good note, you know? Playing them, they were hot. Of course it was hot out, but at that age I didn't care about the heat or any of that."

Righetti recalled the atmosphere at the stadium, which he called "different" than usual. A man on a parachute flew the United States flag into the ballpark before the game, while several raffles were held for fans.

"That's almost minor league, and I don't remember seeing it ever again," Righetti said. "But that was part of the festivities that day for July 4, I guess."

With 41,077 in the stands, Righetti took the mound on a steamy, 94-degree day. Nettles was out of the lineup with conjunctivitis, replaced by 41-year-old Bert Campaneris. Several other regulars were out of the lineup against Boston lefty John Tudor: first baseman Ken Griffey, second baseman Willie Randolph, and center fielder Jerry Mumphrey all sat out. Rookies Don Mattingly and Andre Robertson took the two infield spots, while 39-year-old Lou Piniella played left field, shifting Dave Winfield to center field.

"Fourth of July, against the Red Sox," Mattingly said. "It was pretty intense."

The way Righetti started the game, it wouldn't have mattered who was behind him in the field. The southpaw struck out seven of the first nine Red Sox he faced, using his fastball to overwhelm Boston's hitters the first time through the lineup.

Detailed pitch counts weren't recorded at the time, but Righetti knew he had thrown a lot of pitches when he struck out Dwight Evans for his eighth K of the day. He needed some quick outs or he wouldn't be around to finish what he started.

As well as Righetti was pitching, Tudor was matching him zero for zero. The game remained scoreless into the fifth when Robertson singled in Steve Kemp for the first run of the afternoon. Don Baylor hit a solo home run in the sixth, giving Righetti a two-run cushion.

Righetti walked future Hall of Famer Jim Rice with one out in the seventh—"Not the worst thing to do," he later told *Yankees Magazine*—before getting Tony Armas to ground into a 6-4-3 double play to end the inning with the no-hitter intact.

"I still wasn't thinking about a no-hitter at that point because I had pitched a lot of one-hitters in the minors and knew anything could go wrong," Righetti told *Yankees Magazine*. "The score was still close [enough] that my only concern was winning the game."

He may not have been thinking about history, but he was the only one. When he retreated to the clubhouse between innings, Righetti heard the Yankees' radio broadcasters mention his no-hitter.

Evans hit a long fly ball down the right-field line to open the eighth, but Kemp made a superb catch to keep the no-hit bid alive. That, Righetti said, was the first time he believed he could actually get the no-no.

"Dewey was a big out in that spot," Righetti told *Yankees Magazine*. "You knew then, this could be it. I was pretty tired at that point, but Kemper's catch was a shot of adrenaline for me."

Righetti got two more fly balls to end the eighth, though neither put a scare into him the way Evans' ball had.

Now up 4–0 thanks to Kemp's two-run single in the eighth, Righetti had the game well in hand. Now it was about making history.

No Yankee had thrown a no-hitter since Don Larsen's perfect game in the 1956 World Series, while the last regular season no-hitter by a Yankee came in 1951 when Allie Reynolds threw his second of that season. Only one other left-hander—George Mogridge in 1917—had accomplished the feat for the Yankees.

Righetti walked Jeff Newman to start the ninth, which he feared he might regret since it meant Wade Boggs—who was hitting .361— would get another at-bat unless the lefty induced a double play.

Righetti did get two ground balls against the next two batters, though the Yankees were unable to turn a double play.

"It could be the biggest day of Righetti's career," Yankees play-by-play announcer Frank Messer said with one out to go. "Don't tell me he doesn't know it. There's never been a pitcher that did it that did not know it was coming."

Boggs stepped to the plate, bringing one thought to Righetti's mind: *Don't let this end with an infield hit.*

Given the way Righetti fell off the mound toward third base, he was concerned about Boggs beating out a tapper between the mound and Mattingly. He pounded Boggs with fastballs before striking him out with a slider to secure his place in history.

"He struck him out!" Messer said. "Righetti has pitched a no-hitter!"

Righetti celebrated with catcher Butch Wynegar and the rest of his teammates, collapsing into his catcher's arms out of joy and exhaustion.

"After you're busy pitching and trying to get through it, it was obviously hot, then afterward the atmosphere of doing it and thinking, 'Oh shit, now what?'" Righetti said. "Because you can't hide now, right? You do something like that people expect you to do good things here and there.

"With Mr. Nixon there and George's birthday, July 4, and the anniversary of Lou Gehrig's day and all that, all those things kept coming in and I'm going, 'Wow, what timing.'"

Righetti has few mementos from his game; his locker was nearly empty by the next day, as some items were sent to the Hall of Fame and others simply disappeared. One souvenir Righetti cherishes is a letter sent to him by Nixon congratulating him on the no-hitter.

Back in those days, Righetti said, Steinbrenner didn't allow players to make public appearances during the season, but Righetti had people pulling at him from all sides.

"You can imagine all the people who wanted me to do a radio or TV show or anything; I was scared to death to do all that," Righetti said. "Letterman started the year before and he wanted me on, so I missed out on that."

Righetti and Nettles headed to Atlantic City after the game, where the 24-year-old learned quickly the rewards that come with pitching the type of game he did.

"They took care of us a lot, gave us a nice room," Righetti said. "That was pretty cool."

# The Biggest Swing of Chris Chambliss' Career

The year was 1976.

It had been 12 years since the Yankees had won an American League pennant, a virtual eternity for a team that had captured 29 of them between 1921 and 1964.

Manager Billy Martin had guided the 1976 club to 97 wins during the regular season, setting up a best-of-five American League Championship Series showdown with the Kansas City Royals, who won the AL West with a 90–72 record.

The Yankees had gone 5–7 against the Royals during the regular season, so they knew this was not going to be an easy series despite their superior overall record.

Still, this was the first postseason appearance for the Yankees under owner George Steinbrenner, who predicted when he bought the team in 1973 that he would get back to the top of baseball within three years. Anything short of a trip to the World Series would have to be considered a failure.

The two teams split the first two games in Kansas City, then the Yankees won Game 3, their 5–3 victory powered in part by Chambliss, who homered and drove in three runs.

But two Graig Nettles home runs in Game 4 were not enough to wrap up the series for the Yankees, who would host the decisive Game 5 on their home turf in the Bronx.

The two teams each scored twice in the first inning, then after the Royals took a 3–2 lead in the second, the Yankees answered with two in the third and two more in the sixth, taking what appeared to be a commanding 6–3 lead.

But George Brett—the AL batting champion not known much for his power—swatted a three-run homer in the eighth against Grant Jackson, moving the tie game to the ninth inning with a trip to the World Series on the line.

Chambliss was set to lead off the bottom of the ninth, but a home run was the last thing on his mind when he stepped in against right-hander Mark Littel.

"I had learned to that point that thinking home run was not too good because I didn't have good swings when I tried to hit a home run," Chambliss told ESPN.com in 2010.

Littel's first pitch made its way to the plate and Chambliss took a big swing, driving it to right-center field.

"He hits one deep to right center! That ball is out of here!" Yankees broadcaster Phil Rizzuto declared. "The Yankees win the pennant! Holy cow! Chris Chambliss on one swing, and the Yankees win the American League pennant! Unbelievable! What a finish. As dramatic a finish as you'd ever want to see!"

As dramatic as Chambliss' blast was, it was nothing compared with the drama the 27-year-old experienced rounding the bases.

"What made me go after the first pitch? Because it looked good," Chambliss said. "It was high. It was over the plate. I'm an aggressive guy so I swung at a pitch in a zone that I thought that I could get a good swing at."

After watching the ball go out, Chambliss threw his arms up in victory, greeted at first base by first-base coach Elston Howard, a legendary Yankee who was a part of 10 pennant winners and four World Series champions during his own playing career.

"I knew it was gone right away," Howard told Frank Messer during the celebration in the champagne-soaked clubhouse. "I went halfway up the line to meet him. It was really a thrill to see that ball go."

"I have never seen Chambliss show this much emotion since he's been with the Yankees," Rizzuto told viewers.

Thousands of fans mobbed the field, celebrating the best night the Bronx had seen in more than a decade as if they were in a college field house reveling in a big basketball upset. Chambliss could barely complete his home run trot, fighting his way through fans from second base all the way to home plate.

"The safest place to be is up here in the booth," Rizzuto said as he observed the pandemonium on the field. "These are the happiest Yankees fans you have seen."

Chambliss was even knocked down by some fans between second and third base, falling momentarily before continuing his lap.

"I remember tripping," Chambliss said. "I went down to one knee. Somebody tried to steal my helmet from behind. From then on it was like, 'How do I get myself to the dugout?'"

After rounding the bases, Chambliss made a beeline for the dugout, disappearing to the clubhouse with his ecstatic teammates. Several teammates asked him if he actually touched home plate, fearing the home run would not count, so Chambliss grabbed a pair of security guards and made his way back to the field.

When he got there, there was one problem. Home plate was missing, taken by fans, along with the three other bases, the pitching rubber, the on-deck circles, and anything else that wasn't nailed down. Chambliss stepped on the area where the plate had been before returning to celebrate with his teammates.

"I saw about 50,000 people touch home plate," Thurman Munson told the *Daily News* that night. "He could have been one of them. I want to see them take it back."

Chambliss' home run was a high, towering shot, leaving fans and the two teams in suspense until it settled over the outfield wall.

"The home run he hit, to me, it defied science; it felt like it was up in the air forever," said Marty Appel, the Yankees' public relations director at the time. "It didn't clear the fence by that much, so you weren't sure if it was going to be it. It was the most exciting moment of real time during my stint with the Yankees. Why isn't it as important or famous as Bobby Thompson? I don't know. It should be."

Just as it would happen 27 years later when Boone hit his own pennant-winning walk-off home run, the Yankees went on to lose the World Series. But even that doesn't lessen the impact of Chambliss' legendary moment.

"When I see it I'm proud," Chambliss said. "I'm happy that I was part of a special moment in Yankee history."

. . . . . . . . . . . . . . . . . . . . . . . . . . . . . . . . . . .

# A Perfectly Surprising Day for David Wells

When David Wells woke up on Sunday, May 17, 1998, he felt far from perfect. Scheduled to start against the Minnesota Twins, he was just hoping he would make it through five innings.

The left-hander known for his hard-partying ways had spent the wee hours of Saturday night (and Sunday morning) having fun with members of the *Saturday Night Live* cast and crew, attending one of the show's legendary after-parties.

Although the small-market Twins were in town, the ballpark was packed for "Beanie Baby Day," as fans in attendance received a limited edition stuffed bear. It doesn't sound like a big deal, but the country was in the midst of a Beanie Baby craze that had people in a frenzy trying to get their hands on one of these collectibles.

Wells arrived at Yankee Stadium that morning and went through his normal pregame routine.

"I was just trying to avoid everybody," Wells said. "I just thought, 'I better get through this and make sure I do my job.' I didn't look the hottest, but I just wanted to keep the team in the ballgame and give the team a chance to win. I went through my routine like I always did, but it didn't work out too well."

Wells felt like hell as he warmed up in the bullpen, so when he heard pitching coach Mel Stottlemyre tell someone that Wells looked good before the game, the southpaw was incensed.

"I told Mel, 'Stop patronizing me!'" Wells said. "My curveballs were like 49 feet and I had a really bad bullpen. I threw two balls out of the stadium that day; I just couldn't get into any rhythm. I walked out of there and said, 'Let's just go. We'll see what happens.' Something clicked from the walk from the bullpen to going out to the mound. It just clicked."

Wells retired the Twins on just nine pitches in the first, getting off to the quick start he needed. He needed 13 pitches to get through the second and 19 more in the third, leaving him with 41 after three innings.

After he retired the side in order in the fourth, Wells went back to the clubhouse to get a bottle of water. The radio broadcast was coming through the clubhouse speakers, which spooked the pitcher when he heard the words for the first time.

"I could hear Michael Kay saying, 'David Wells has a perfect game' and I started shouting 'La la la la!'" Wells said. "I ran out of the lounge and went into the dugout, went through my routine, and just tried to avoid what was going on. I went out to the mound and forgot about it a little bit."

Two strikeouts during a perfect fifth had fans believing they might be witnessing something special. The crowd grew louder with each out, but it was the other 24 guys in the dugout that told Wells this was a different kind of game.

"By the sixth inning, I realized something was going on," Wells said. "I sat next to [Scott] Brosius and Tino [Martinez], and they got up and walked away from me. Talk about being lonely. I just went with it."

The one teammate that wasn't observing baseball's unwritten rules was David Cone, Wells' best friend on the team. While the rest of the dugout avoided Wells at all costs, Cone knew his buddy needed to be distracted.

"Coney started jumping on me, saying, 'Break out your knuckleball.' I was like, 'I don't throw a knuckleball, dude!'" Wells said. "He was just trying to get my mind off of what was going on. I was just trying to go out there and play catch with Jorge [Posada]."

"He kept walking by me. I could tell he needed somebody to say something to him," Cone said. "Rather than the normal 'Keep it going,' I just chose to kind of fuck with him and said, 'Show me something; break out that knuckleball.' I tried to make him laugh— and he did. If he would have given up a hit, he probably would have blamed me to this day, so there was some risk involved. But it worked."

Wells went out and struck out two more batters in the sixth, leaving him nine outs from history. As he returned to the dugout, Cone continued to rib his teammate, deriding him for not giving the knuckleball a try.

"The next inning, he came back in and I said, 'You're a fucking pussy. You didn't throw it.'" Cone said. "He looked at me and laughed again, but I thought, 'That's enough. I better walk away.'"

# "WHO'S THE FAT GUY?"

**Y**ou would think that throwing a perfect game in Yankee Stadium would make you one of the most famous people in the world—or at least in New York.

But a couple days after David Wells captivated the baseball world by accomplishing that feat with his perfect game against the Twins, there was at least one person who wasn't all that impressed.

After the game Sunday afternoon, Wells received a visit from Billy Crystal, who was shooting the movie *Analyze This* in Brooklyn with Robert De Niro.

"David said, 'I love De Niro, he's my favorite,' so I invited him to the set," Crystal said. "We were doing this big shootout scene at the end with Chazz Palminteri and all these stunt guys, and I'm with Bob talking about the scene with the director, Harold Ramis, when Wells gets out of an SUV with a big canvas bag. He was giving autographed baseballs to the crew, who all knew he had thrown a perfect game."

The crew might have understood the magnitude of Wells' feat, but De Niro—who Crystal said "is not a baseball guy"—did not. According to Crystal, here's how the conversation went from there:

> De Niro: "Who's the fat guy?"
> Crystal: "That's David Wells."
> De Niro: "Who's that?"
> Crystal: "Bob, he just threw a perfect game for the Yankees!"
> De Niro: "What do you mean a perfect game?"
> Crystal: "27 up, 27 down, no hits, no runs, no errors; nobody got on base."
> De Niro: "Sounds boring."

Joe Girardi wasn't catching that day, but he would be behind the plate 14 months later when Cone threw a perfecto of his own. Girardi recalled the helpless feeling as he watched Wells get one out after another, anxious for his young protégé Posada as he called each pitch.

"It's actually more nerve-racking being in the dugout," Girardi said. "We all feel that when we have a piece in it or feel like we're in charge of the situation, it's not as nerve-racking as when you're sitting and watching. I wanted it so bad for David and Jorge, because I really felt that it would put a mark on Jorge's career. The hardest thing to prove when you're a young catcher is your defense. I knew he was good, but that was an 'I've arrived' moment."

Wells held a 2–0 lead at the seventh-inning stretch, so while the perfect game was at the forefront of everybody's minds at the stadium, the game was far from decided. Darryl Strawberry tripled in a run in the bottom of the seventh, then Chad Curtis drove Strawberry in, pushing the lead to 4–0.

When Wells went out for the eighth, he noticed the fans jeering home-plate umpire Tim McClelland with every ball call, no matter how far off the plate the pitch might have been. This worried Wells, who was concerned the hostile crowd might have a negative influence on McClelland, whom Wells believed "wasn't the nicest of umpires."

"He always had a chip on his shoulder," Wells said. "I was going out there trying to make pitches, going down and away and trying to get them to roll it over or staying in tight to jam them."

The approach worked. Marty Cordova grounded out to shortstop, then Ron Coomer hit a bullet to second base, where Chuck Knoblauch made the play. Alex Ochoa hit a pop up that Tino Martinez caught, leaving the man they called "Boomer" three outs from an accomplishment that seemed like a million-to-one shot only a few hours earlier.

"That line shot Ron Coomer hit to Knobby, that was a bullet," Wells said. "Knobby got it and he had time because Ron wasn't a good runner, but he was known to throw it away. That went through my mind. But he didn't. That was really the only ball that was remotely a threat."

The bottom of the Twins lineup was hardly Murderer's Row, but Wells knew that one bad pitch was all it would take to end his bid for perfection.

"In the ninth when I came out, I was like, 'Don't screw this up, man,'" Wells said. "I had come that far, I had to just bear down and play catch; focus, focus, focus. That's what I did."

Jon Shave hit a routine fly ball to Paul O'Neill in right field, then Wells struck out Javier Valentin. Pat Meares lifted Wells' 120th and final pitch to right field; all Wells could do was watch.

"When Meares hit it, I thought the ball was foul," Wells said. "I turned around and Paul was standing underneath it. I was like, 'This is going to happen.' I was just jumping a little bit and when I saw him squeeze it, I jumped up and started punching toward the ground.

"God damn, what just happened? It was kind of bizarre. I was looking for Jorge, but Sojo came and grabbed me. I was like, 'Get off me, man! Where's Jorge?' He was down the line behind first base. I got mobbed. Darryl and Willie Banks picked me up on their shoulders. Bernie was part of that, too. Straw said, 'Damn, he's heavy!' They carried me off and the place was going nuts."

O'Neill, who has been on the field for three perfect games—Wells and Cone in New York, Tom Browning in Cincinnati—was just thankful that the final out was a routine play.

"The last thing you want is a hard play," O'Neill said. "You don't think much about it at the time, but then you look back and it's really cool to be part of that. People talk to me about being the only guy to be a part of three perfect games, but all that tells you is that I was a part of some great teams with great pitching."

As Wells prepared to speak with reporters in the clubhouse, a familiar face appeared out of the throng of writers and cameras.

"I said, 'I'm sorry, I just got here. What happened?'" said actor/ director/comedian Billy Crystal, who was in New York shooting *Analyze This*. "He said, 'Where's your ticket? I'll sign it for you.'"

Crystal had come to the game with a couple friends, sitting in a luxury suite. Around the fourth inning, he realized Wells was nearly halfway to perfection.

"I thought, 'He's 12 up, 12 down,'" Crystal said. "Being the ex–high school baseball player I was—not to mention a superstitious actor—I had this Coke in my hand and every time I would put it down, I'd put it down in the same ring the humidity was making on the glass. I nursed that thing for nine innings."

When all the interviews were over and the crowds had dissipated, Wells went back to the dugout with Cone and cracked open a beer.

"Coney said, 'Look at the scoreboard. You'll never see that again.'" Wells said. "He was right. It's a lot of pressure to go through that kind of game. Your nerves are going. You're relieved when it's over, but you did it. To do it in Yankee Stadium, that's the biggest stage in baseball."

# David Cone Honors Yogi Berra and Don Larsen Perfectly

**P**erfect games don't come around very often, so after David Wells threw his gem in May 1998, Yankees fans probably didn't think they would see another for quite some time. After all, it had been 42 years since Don Larsen threw the first one in Yankees history, doing so in the 1956 World Series no less.

Sunday, July 18, 1999, was already going to be a memorable day. Only nobody knew quite how memorable it would be.

In January 1999, Yogi Berra had made peace with an apologetic George Steinbrenner following Berra's 14-year self-imposed exile. Berra had stayed away from Yankee Stadium—his baseball home for 18 seasons and all but four games of his Hall of Fame career— furious over his 1985 firing as manager after only 16 games, a message delivered by the Boss through an intermediary. Steinbrenner referred to his handling of Berra as "the worst mistake I ever made in baseball."

Six months after Steinbrenner's apology, the Yankees held Yogi Berra Day in the Bronx. His No. 8 had been retired 27 years earlier, while a plaque was hung in Monument Park in 1988, but this day marked Berra's official return to the Bronx, and the sellout crowd on hand at the Stadium was ready to shower the legend with affection.

"I remember warming up before the game, watching Yogi ride around the field in a convertible," said David Cone, who was slated to start the game against the Montreal Expos. "It made me pretty carefree; I was more interested in watching Yogi than even warming up. I wanted to enjoy the pageantry. The look on Yogi's face, he was just so happy."

The Yankees had brought in Larsen to throw the ceremonial first pitch to Berra, his catcher for the best game of his life, adding a nice touch to the day. As he arrived at the mound to throw his pitch, Larsen shook Cone's hand. Cone later referred to the "Yankee magic" that must have rubbed off, though he couldn't possibly have known what would happen a little more than two hours later.

Joe Girardi, who was set to catch Cone that day, looked for a little extra luck before the game.

"I asked Yogi to bless my glove that day when he went out to catch the first pitch," Girardi said. "I think it adds to the mystique of being a Yankee. Don Larsen was in attendance and threw out the first pitch. Strange things happen when you're a Yankee and you were at that Stadium."

In September 1996, Cone had taken a no-hitter through seven innings in Oakland, but he never had a chance to finish off his historic bid. Less than four months earlier, Cone underwent surgery to remove an aneurysm under his right armpit, leaving his pitching future in question. He returned on September 2 with seven no-hit innings against the Athletics, but manager Joe Torre removed him after 85 pitches, not wanting to push Cone too hard in his first game back.

"I could not let the no-hitter cloud what we set out to do," Torre told reporters. "If I leave him in and he throws 105 or 106 pitches and wakes up with a sore arm tomorrow, I'd never forgive myself for that."

Cone understood the decision.

"When you go through what I've gone through, you realize your mortality," Cone said after the game. "There's only so much tread left on the tire. I appreciate them taking me out. Getting to the World Series is more important."

The Yankees, of course, got to the World Series and won it all that season, their first title since 1978. Cone played an integral role in that championship, so the absence of a no-hitter on his résumé was just fine.

Cone had thrown three one-hitters and four two-hitters during his career, but a no-hitter remained elusive. Even after opening the game against the Expos with six strikeouts over four perfect innings, the idea of finally getting his no-hitter—or a perfect game, for that matter—hadn't even entered his mind yet.

That changed one inning later.

"It creeps in after five, then you realize it's too soon to think about it," Cone said. "But it's still on your mind. Then you get through six and the crowd starts to get into it. That was the first thing I noticed; the crowd picked up with every out. You get through seven innings and you're really starting to think, 'Wow, it's only six outs.'"

The eighth appeared to be Cone's biggest roadblock, with young slugger Vladimir Guerrero leading off the frame.

"The guy that I worried about most was Vlad Guerrero, because it didn't matter if you bounced it or threw it a foot outside, he could still hit it," Girardi said. "If we could get by him in the eighth, I really felt it was possible."

Guerrero swung at the first pitch in the eighth, popping it up to Girardi in foul territory. Five outs to go.

Jose Vidro grounded out to second base, where Chuck Knoblauch made a nice backhand play and a perfect throw to first. Cone then froze Brad Fullmer for a called third strike to end the inning.

He had been perfect through eight innings; 24 up, 24 down. The crowd was buzzing with excitement, almost in disbelief that it might witness a second perfect game in 14 months—and with Larsen in attendance on Berra's day just to add some more drama to it.

The Yankees held a 6–0 lead after eight innings, so Cone knew that a mistake wouldn't cost his team the game. It would just cost him what might have been his final shot at history.

"I was 36 years old; I had been close a few times in my career but had never gotten over the hump," Cone said. "I knew it was probably the last chance I'd ever have to do something like that."

Chris Widger, Shane Andrews, and Orlando Cabrera stood between Cone and perfection. He had thrown only 77 pitches through eight innings, so he was still pretty fresh for the ninth.

"What you go over in your head is how you got the guys out the last time—over and over and over," Girardi said. "You don't want to repeat the pattern and let them figure it out. I was excited for him. My thought was, 'If he does get it, protect him.' I've been on the bottom of those piles and we needed that guy."

All Cone had to do was control his emotions—and his nerves.

"Walking out for the ninth, the adrenaline rush was just unbelievable," Cone said. "It was so intense, I could feel my hair growing. It's like your head is on fire. I remember walking up into the clubhouse between innings to change undershirts and it was a ghost town. The vibe of the whole stadium was intense."

Cone struck out Widger to start the ninth, then pinch-hitter Ryan McGuire flied out to left field. That left Cabrera as the only remaining obstacle, but on Cone's third pitch of the at-bat, Cabrera hit a foul pop-up that landed in third baseman Scott Brosius' glove for the 27th and final out.

"He popped him up! He's going to get it! Brosuis down from third, Brosius makes the catch!" radio voice John Sterling said. "Ballgame over! A perfect game! A perfect game for David Cone!

"27 up, 27 down! David Cone has attained baseball immortality!"

"It was euphoric," Cone said. "To finally do it, being older, I could appreciate it."

During his six seasons with the Yankees, Cone went 64–40, winning 20 games in 1998. He made two All-Star teams and collected four World Series rings, but it's that magical day in the heat of summer that will forever stand out when it comes to the right-hander's place in Yankees lore.

"The further removed I get from it, the more I realize how lucky it is to have a signature moment like that," Cone said. "People will always remember that signature moment. A lot of people don't realize I was on all four championship teams, but they remember that game. I'm thankful for it."

While most people will remember July 18, 1999, as the day Cone threw a perfect game at Yankee Stadium, the pitcher himself continues to view himself as the second-biggest story of the day.

"It's still Yogi Berra Day," Cone said. "I threw a perfect game on his day. The fact that we're linked together is a tremendous gift."

# The Worst Loss in Yankees Postseason History

For all of the great moments in Yankees history, the franchise has had its share of disappointment as well.

No event exemplifies this more than the 2004 American League Championship Series, where the Yankees were on the wrong side of history in baseball's greatest rivalry.

The Yankees and Red Sox had engaged in some great battles over the years, the biggest coming in 1978 when Bucky Dent broke Boston's heart in a one-game playoff at Fenway Park.

But things changed in the mid-1990s once baseball introduced the wild-card format, allowing division rivals to meet in the postseason for the first time.

The Yankees got the better of the Red Sox in their first two postseason meetings, beating Boston in the ALCS in both 1999 and 2003. The latter featured Aaron Boone's Game 7 walk-off home run, putting yet another dagger in the heart of Red Sox Nation.

The following October, the Yankees dispatched the Minnesota Twins in the AL Division Series, while the Red Sox swept the Anaheim Angels, setting up another best-of-seven series between the two rivals with a trip to the World Series on the line.

The Yankees won the first two games in the Bronx, beating Curt Schilling and Pedro Martinez to take a commanding 2–0 lead. As the series shifted to Boston, the Yankees' bats busted out for 19 runs in Game 3, getting a pair of home runs from Hideki Matsui and long balls from Alex Rodriguez—who had nearly been traded to the Red Sox the previous winter before winding up with the Yankees—and Gary Sheffield, leaving them one win away from their seventh AL pennant in nine years.

"We feel like we have a lot of momentum," Rodriguez said after Game 3. "It doesn't matter who we're facing or who is pitching."

"No team had ever blown a 3–0 lead before," said Jack Curry of the YES Network, who covered the series for the *New York Times*. "They won Game 3 19–8, absolutely destroying the Red Sox. You believed it would just be a matter of time before they finished them off. Whether they won it in Game 4 or Game 5 was the only question."

The only teams in the four major North American sports that had ever overcome 3–0 deficits were the 1942 Toronto Maple Leafs and the 1975 New York Islanders. Of the 25 previous baseball teams to fall behind 3–0, 20 of them had been swept.

Despite the seemingly insurmountable lead, the Yankees weren't taking the Red Sox for granted.

"Right now, we're not even thinking about what we've done," Sheffield said after Game 3. "We have to win one more ballgame to get to where we want to get to."

With the Yankees holding a 4–3 lead in the ninth inning of Game 4 and Mariano Rivera on the mound, it looked like they were on their way to a sweep. But Kevin Millar led off with a walk, then pinch runner Dave Roberts stole second base, a moment many point to as the turning point in the entire series.

Bill Mueller singled in Roberts to tie the game, setting the stage for David Ortiz's walk-off home run against Paul Quantrill in the 12th. The Red Sox were down 3–1 in the series, but they were still alive.

"Once the Red Sox got one, well, now they had one and they only needed three more," Curry said. "Baseball players love the cliché— and reporters hate it—but it is one game at a time. If you get one, you only need three. If you get a second one, you only have to win two more. Suddenly you're putting pressure on the Yankees."

That second one came in Game 5 as the Red Sox mounted another late comeback. The Yankees held a 4–2 lead in the eighth, but Ortiz trimmed the lead to one with a leadoff home run against All-Star reliever Tom Gordon.

Gordon followed with a walk of Millar, who was replaced for pinch runner Roberts for a second straight night. Trot Nixon hit a single, advancing Roberts to third base representing the tying run.

Manager Joe Torre called on Rivera to put out the fire, but Jason Varitek hit a sacrifice fly that scored Roberts, tying the game and giving the Fenway Faithful another jolt of hope. The game remained tied into the $14^{th}$ inning as the teams battled in another late-night marathon.

Esteban Loaiza pitched a quick $13^{th}$ for the Yankees, but Johnny Damon drew a one-out walk in the $14^{th}$, then Manny Ramirez walked with two out, putting Damon in scoring position. Up stepped Ortiz, who delivered the game-winner for the second straight night, hitting the $471^{st}$ pitch of the game for an RBI single that scored Damon to extend Boston's season at least one more day.

"Ortiz was already a great hitter, but he became an October legend that week," Curry said. "He was such a clutch hitter. If you look at what Ortiz has done in his career, there's no doubt he's the guy the Red Sox wanted up in those situations."

Although the Yankees still led the series 3–2, Yankees broadcaster Michael Kay remembered thinking that the Red Sox had taken control of the series as it headed back to New York.

"When they lost that game, I thought they were done because of the way the pitching lined up," Kay said. "The Red Sox had some mojo and the Yankees had doubt in their eyes."

Schilling, who had dominated the Yankees in the 2001 World Series en route to winning co–Series MVP honors with the Diamondbacks, took the mound with three sutures in his right ankle to secure a dislocated tendon.

"I'm not sure I can think of any scenario more enjoyable than making 55,000 people from New York shut up," Schilling said before the series. Then he went out and backed up those words.

With blood seen seeping through his sock, Schilling grinded through seven innings of one-run ball, beating the Yankees 4–2 to send the series to a decisive Game 7. The "Bloody Sock Game" cemented Schilling's place as one of the best postseason pitchers of all time.

Game 7 was a disaster from the start for the Yankees, as Ortiz blasted a two-run homer in the first inning against starter Kevin Brown. Boston continued its onslaught in the second, loading the bases against Brown before Torre brought in Javier Vazquez.

Damon—who would sign with the Yankees as a free agent two years later and play a key role in their 2009 World Series run—belted a grand slam on Vazquez's first pitch, giving the Red Sox a stunning 6–0 lead before many fans had settled comfortably into their seats.

Derek Jeter got the Yankees on the board with an RBI single in the third, but Damon slugged his second homer of the night in the fourth, a two-run shot that gave Boston an 8–1 lead.

There would be no miraculous comeback for the Yankees, who dropped a 10–3 decision that sent the Red Sox to the World Series.

"All empires fall sooner or later," Red Sox president Larry Lucchino said.

"It was absolutely devastating for the Yankees," Curry said. "It was the most devastating postseason series the Yankees have ever had."

The Red Sox swept the St. Louis Cardinals, winning their first championship since 1918 to break the 86-year-old "Curse of the

Bambino." But the comeback against the Yankees remains the most memorable part of Boston's run, one that kicked off a 10-year stretch that saw the Red Sox win three World Series titles.

For the Yankees, the series loss was demoralizing, and while they would make the playoffs in each of the next three seasons under Torre, the memory of their 2004 collapse was impossible to forget.

"In the year 3050 when Joe Buck IX is doing the World Series, they're going to show a graphic of teams to blow a 3–0 lead and it's still going to say the Yankees," Kay said. "It's one of the worst moments for any team in baseball history. It's your archrival, your mortal enemies. Had it been against the Kansas City Royals, it would have been bad enough. But the Red Sox were riding this curse since 1918 and you owned them. For them to do that, it changed the narrative in baseball for a while as the Red Sox went on to win three World Series. That's hard to get over."

· · · · · · · · · · · · · · · · · · · · · · · · · · · · · ·

# "The King" Holds Court in the 1996 World Series

Some people don't believe in the concept of clutch. Those people have obviously never met Jim Leyritz.

Nobody will ever confuse Leyritz with the most prolific catchers of all time, but when it came to getting the big hit at the right moment, few could compare to the man known as "The King."

"Jimmy was one of those guys; that's what he did," Andy Pettitte said. "There was no moment too big for him. He had so much confidence and was so sure of what he could do if given the chance, he expected to play every day even if he didn't get a chance to. He felt like he deserved to be in there. That's the kind of guy you want at the plate."

Leyritz first gained postseason notoriety during the 1995 American League Division Series with his game-winning home run in the bottom of the 15th inning of Game 2 against the Mariners. Leyritz's blast ended the five-hour, 12-minute marathon, sending the Yankees to Seattle with a 2–0 lead in the best-of-five series.

"That was the first time I really saw the upper deck shake at the old stadium," David Cone said. "I really thought it was going to fall. I was like, 'Stop jumping!'"

The Mariners would win the next three games at the Kingdome to take the series, leaving the Yankees with a bitter taste in their mouths despite getting to the playoffs for the first time since 1981.

Though the Yankees went through several changes before the 1996 season—Joe Torre took over for Buck Showalter as manager, captain Don Mattingly retired, Tino Martinez was acquired from Seattle, and rookie Derek Jeter became the everyday shortstop—the disappointment of the previous fall helped drive them.

After capturing their first American League East title in 15 years, the Yankees beat the Texas Rangers in the ALDS, then sent the Baltimore Orioles packing in five games in the ALCS, advancing to the World Series for the first time since 1981. It had been 18 years since the Yankees' last title, but the Atlanta Braves—the defending world champions—came to the Bronx and won the first two games, leaving the shell-shocked Yankees simply hoping not to be swept.

"All of us were kind of overwhelmed; it was the first time for us in a World Series, including Joe Torre," Leyritz said. "To come into our park and take two from us the way they did, it seemed like a daunting task to beat them, especially with that pitching staff.

"On the plane ride out there, one of the things Joe emphasized was an article written in the paper where the Braves said they were so happy to get out of New York, they can't wait to win the series at home and not have to go back and deal with our fans and our crowd. It was bulletin board material; all we had to do was to get the series back to New York and we would have a chance to win this thing."

Cone and Bernie Williams led the Yankees to a Game 3 victory at Fulton County Stadium, but they needed one more win in Atlanta to guarantee that the series would return to the Bronx.

Kenny Rogers started Game 4 and put the Yankees in a quick hole, giving up five runs in two-plus innings.

"I remember a few guys in the dugout in about the fourth inning talking about, 'Thank God we didn't get swept,'" Leyritz said. "It didn't look good. If they won Game 4, we would have had to come back against [Tom] Glavine, [Greg] Maddux, and [John] Smoltz. There's no way."

The Braves took a 6–0 lead into the sixth inning when the Yankees rallied for three runs against starter Denny Neagle, cutting the lead in half.

"Joe was talking about just chipping away," Leyritz said. "We got the three runs in the sixth, but we still had two men on with nobody out, so we felt like this was our inning. [Mariano] Duncan struck out, then [Paul] O'Neill pinch hit and struck out, then Tino pinch hit and struck out. To me, that was our chance. It was going to be tough to rally against Mark Wohlers for three runs."

Wohlers, Atlanta's All-Star closer, entered the game in the top of the eighth with the three-run lead. Charlie Hayes and Darryl Strawberry opened the inning with a pair of singles, then Duncan hit a grounder that shortstop Rafael Belliard—who had entered the game as a defensive replacement the previous inning—bobbled, allowing him to get only the force at second base rather than turning a double play.

That brought Leyritz to the plate as the tying run.

"Before that inning started, Straw was at the bat rack and he had a brand new box of a dozen bats," Leyritz said. "I said, 'Hey, this guy throws 100 and I don't want to break my bat. Can I borrow one from you?' He said, 'Go ahead; take any one you want.'"

Leyritz grabbed one of Strawberry's bats, then checked in with bench coach Don Zimmer for a quick scouting report on Wohlers.

"I asked, 'What's this guy got?'" Leyritz said. "Zim said, 'Jimmy, this guy throws 100. Get ready.' That's all I knew. We all talk about sabermetrics, scouting reports, and all the video guys watch today, but if I knew Mark Wohlers had a split-fingered fastball, I might not have hit that slider out because I might have been looking for that. I thought he was only a fastball-slider pitcher, so my ignorance helped me in that particular at-bat."

Fox analyst Tim McCarver commented on the broadcast that Wohlers was going to his breaking ball too much, saying, "If you get beat, you want to get beat on your best pitch."

Leyritz got ahead 2–1, then fouled off two pitches. Expecting an inside fastball, Leyritz backed off the plate a half-step, thinking he would take any pitch inside because it would definitely be a ball.

"If he tried to go away with anything, I would already be out looking that way," Leyritz said. "Sure enough, he came with the slider and he hung it."

Leyritz took his typical big swing and sent the ball soaring toward left field.

"In the air to left field, back, at the track, at the wall, we are tied!" said play-by-play man Joe Buck, calling the shot for Fox.

As he headed toward first base, Leyritz saw Andruw Jones climbing the left-field wall, but the ball cleared it before bouncing back on to the field.

"As I rounded first base, all I could think was, 'We just tied this game up,'" Leyritz said. "As I rounded second, I thought, 'If we don't win, this is going to be just like the Seattle home run,' which I thought would be my biggest home run ever. It would just be another footnote if we didn't win the game and then win the Series."

The Yankees' dugout went crazy as Leyritz rounded the bases, maybe believing for the first time that they could win it all.

"When that happens, it's kind of like, 'OK, we're going to do this,'" Pettitte said. You really feel that way. We had a lot of confidence going in, but that was a huge home run for us, a big lift against Mark Wohlers, who was one of the most dominant closers in the game. You felt like when he came in, the game was over. To have that at-bat he had, that was the turning point of the series."

That it was Leyritz who delivered the big blow was hardly a surprise to his teammates.

"Jimmy did have a knack; he was fearless," Cone said. "He was supremely confident; he was the type that didn't understand why he wasn't playing every day. That can be a good quality to have; arrogance can help you sometimes as a pro athlete. It can hurt you, but it can be better to have some of that on your side—and he definitely had it."

Leyritz knew his reputation, and to some extent, it motivated him to step up in the biggest moments.

"The biggest knock on me was that I claimed I should have been an everyday player and that I would have been a Hall of Famer," Leyritz said. "That was the mindset that I had. In the situation I was in, the only way I was going to get a chance to play was if I performed every at-bat.

"That mindset wasn't different if it was the second game of the season or a World Series game. My mindset was, 'This might be the only chance that I have to do something special.' I wanted to be remembered for things. Every kid has a dream of hitting a home run in a World Series. I got to live it."

The Yankees went on to win the game in the 10<sup>th</sup> inning, scoring the go-ahead run on a bases-loaded walk by Wade Boggs before adding an insurance run on an error. That evened the series at two games apiece, giving Pettitte a chance for redemption following his disastrous 12–1 loss in Game 1.

Leyritz had caught Pettitte in the opener, which saw the left-hander allow seven runs in just 2⅓ innings. Torre initially informed Leyritz he was starting Joe Girardi in Game 5, but the manager changed his mind.

"He decided to catch me, but he said, 'Go by the game plan.'" Leyritz said. "Andy always had confidence that I was calling the right pitches, so he didn't shake me off. In Game 1, we got behind every hitter 2–0, he didn't have his good stuff and we got killed. Maybe Joe was nervous, maybe it was his psychology of getting me to concentrate harder because he thought I was lackadaisical behind the plate because I didn't read all the reports the way Joe Girardi did. I did it more by watching a hitter change in the box, watching what my pitcher had that day."

Pettitte and Leyritz teamed up on a 1–0 win against Smoltz, sending the series back to the Bronx, where they finished off the Braves in Game 6 to clinch the 23<sup>rd</sup> World Series title in franchise history.

"The home run was great; it switched the momentum and started a dynasty because it gave us a chance to win that series," Leyritz said. "But I still take more pride in catching that Game 5."

# Don Larsen Does the Unthinkable in the World Series

**P**erfection. Every athlete strives for it, but few ever achieve it.

On a sunny October afternoon at Yankee Stadium in 1956, Don Larsen was perfect.

The right-hander was probably the last person anybody expected to pitch the greatest game in World Series history. All-Stars Whitey Ford and Bob Turley were bigger names on the Yankees' staff; the Dodgers' rotation featured All-Stars Sal Maglie, Clem Labine, and Carl Erskine, while a rookie named Don Drysdale was pitching out of the bullpen in the first year of what would wind up a Hall of Fame career.

Larsen? The 27-year-old was 30–40 with a 3.82 ERA in his first four years in the majors, pitching for the St. Louis Browns and Baltimore Orioles in his first two seasons before landing with the Yankees in 1955.

The Yankees had staked Larsen to a quick 6–0 lead in Game 2 of the World Series, but the righty failed to get through the second inning. He allowed four unearned runs to score thanks to four walks, helping Brooklyn mount a 13–8 comeback victory to take a 2–0 series lead.

After the Yankees won the next two games at home to even the best-of-seven series, manager Casey Stengel opted not to take the ball away from Larsen in Game 5, trusting him to deliver a better performance than he had only three days earlier.

"It was as God intended it: a day World Series game on a beautiful weekday afternoon," said Marty Appel. "When the Yankees played

Brooklyn, that was a national conversation. All the stars on those two teams, it was amazing. New York was the center of the baseball universe."

Larsen opened his afternoon with two strikeouts, catching Pee Wee Reese looking at a 3–2 pitch for the second out. That would be Larsen's lone three-ball count of the game, though nobody—certainly not Larsen or his catcher, Yogi Berra—realized what would develop over the next two hours.

"The biggest part of pitching is control, and I never had such good control," Larsen told MLB Productions for its *Baseball's Best Moments* series. "Everything that Yogi called for, I threw it pretty close to where he wanted it."

Larsen and Maglie matched zeros into the fourth, when Mickey Mantle took Maglie deep down the right-field line, giving the Yankees a 1–0 lead.

Mantle not only gave his starting pitcher a lead; he also saved the perfect game in the next inning, chasing down Gil Hodges' deep fly ball to left-center field and making a backhand catch for the second out. Sandy Amoros nearly tied the game moments later, hitting a rocket down the right-field line that veered foul by mere inches. Amoros would ground out to second baseman Billy Martin instead, keeping Larsen perfect through five innings.

Hank Bauer added an RBI single in the sixth, giving the Yankees a 2–0 lead. Larsen was still nine outs away from completing his mission.

Actually, it wouldn't become Larsen's mission until he got through the seventh. As he returned to the dugout, he pointed out the zeros on the scoreboard to Mantle, his first mention of his flawless day to that point.

"In the bottom of the seventh inning, I came in the dugout and I told Mantle to look at the scoreboard," Larsen said. "I said, 'Wouldn't it be something? Two more innings to go.' I probably shouldn't have said anything because then nobody would talk with me."

Jackie Robinson had come closest to collecting a hit against Larsen, his second-inning line drive deflecting off third baseman Andy Carey's glove and right to shortstop Gil McDougald, whose throw to first beat Robinson to the bag.

Robinson was the first batter in the eighth, but Larsen got him to hit a comebacker to the mound—the pitcher's lone fielding play of the day—for the first out. Hodges lined out to third and Amoros flied out to center field, leaving Larsen three outs from perfection.

"I'm glad I didn't have a big lead, because I could have relaxed," Larsen said. "Just one pitch, with that lineup with the Dodgers, I could have blown it very easily."

With the game still very much in doubt, Larsen took the mound in the ninth trying to finish off his perfect game while also giving the Yankees a 3–2 edge in the series.

As Joe Trimble reported in the *Daily News* the next morning, "With the tension tearing at their nerves and sweat breaking out on the palms of the onlookers, Larsen seemed to be the calmest man in the place. He knew he had a perfect game and was determined to get it."

Carl Furillo flied out to right field, then Roy Campanella grounded out to Martin at second base. Pinch-hitter Dale Mitchell was all that stood in Larsen's way of immortality.

"Before he came to bat, I probably said a little prayer; 'Oh man, get me through one more,'" Larsen said. "I was shaking a little bit. Quite a bit."

His first pitch was a ball, but Larsen responded with two strikes, leaving him one strike away. Mitchell fouled off Larsen's fourth offering, then took a fastball, Larsen's 97th pitch of the game.

Home-plate umpire Babe Pinelli punched Mitchell out—Larsen's seventh and final strikeout victim—setting the 64,519 in attendance into a frenzy and Berra rushing out to leap into his pitcher's arms.

"Got him! The greatest game ever pitched in baseball history by Don Larsen, a no-hitter, a perfect game in a World Series," Vin Scully called on the broadcast according to *USA Today*. "Never in the history of the game has it ever happened in a World Series."

Larsen had made history in a mere two hours six minutes, leaving the Yankees one win from the sweetest revenge against the Dodgers, who had beaten them in seven games in the previous year's World Series.

Brooklyn came back to win Game 6 at Ebbets Field to force a decisive Game 7, but the Yankees routed the Dodgers in the finale, hitting four home runs—two of them by Berra—to cruise to a 9–0 win and the franchise's 17th championship.

Larsen won series MVP honors thanks to his Game 5 performance, one that has gone unmatched ever since.

"This game has been played over 100-something years and there's never been a no-hitter in the World Series," Berra said in the same MLB Productions special. "And he pitched a perfect one."

# Chapter 5

# That's Entertainment

Attending a game at Yankee Stadium is nice, but sometimes you just want to curl up on the couch with a good book, throw on some tunes, or grab a bag of popcorn and watch a movie or some television.

No problem. Here are some ways to enhance your fandom and knowledge of the Yankees that have nothing to do with the game on the field.

# Live from New York...it's the New York Yankees!

**S**aturday Night Live and the Yankees are two great New York institutions. So what would be more New York than putting them together?

Beginning with Billy Martin in 1986, the Yankees have left their own indelible mark on NBC's popular late-night show. Three members of the organization have hosted it—Martin, George Steinbrenner, and Derek Jeter—while many others have made cameo appearances. Some members of the 1998 Yankees interrupted host Ben Stiller's monologue, while David Wells and David Cone showed up on Jeter's episode as fellow Yankees wives. (We'll explain later.)

Martin cohosted the Season 11 finale with Anjelica Huston on May 24, 1986, and while his comedic timing left much to be desired, he had a couple of highlights.

The biggest came when Lorne Michaels fired him for being drunk and slurring his lines, prompting Martin to literally set the studio on fire.

"If I'm fired, then I'm taking the whole cast with me!" Martin exclaimed.

Michaels chose to save only one cast member—Jon Lovitz—setting up a cliffhanger as to which cast members would survive. Michaels rebooted the show the following season with a mostly new cast.

Four years after Martin's cohosting gig, George Steinbrenner gave it a whirl, hosting the show on October 20, 1990. As Peyton Manning (another sports figure to host the show) said during SNL's 40th anniversary special, being asked to host the show is essentially being asked to "totally humiliate yourself," something you wouldn't have expected Steinbrenner to do.

In his monologue, Steinbrenner informed that audience that there are traditionally two types of people that host the show, "entertainers—you know, actors and comedians—and then beloved figures from other walks of life."

Steinbrenner went on to list a variety of things he would not be doing on the show—"I'm not going to put on a dress and sing old Judy Garland songs" and "I'm not going to catch a bullet in my teeth—I hope," after which he declares, "The way I see it, if I'm not an entertainer, I must fall into that other category—beloved Americans from another walk of life."

The Boss poked plenty of fun at himself and appeared to be a great sport during his week on the show, never more so than during the "Ultra Slim-Fast" sketch in which the owner hawked the weight-loss product alongside Idi Amin (Chris Rock), Saddam Hussein (Kevin Nealon), and Pol Pot (Dana Carvey). As they begin to shoot the "commercial," Steinbrenner realizes something doesn't add up:

> George Steinbrenner: "Hold on a minute here....Lorne! I think something is very wrong here."

Lorne Michaels: "Come over and here and talk about it. What's the problem?"

Steinbrenner: "Lorne, What's the joke here? What's the point of this whole sketch?"

Michaels: "It's a parody of the Ultra Slim-Fast commercials."

Steinbrenner: "I know that, but why am I up here with these guys? They're ruthless dictators; I'm a baseball owner!"

Michaels: "I understand."

Steinbrenner: "I should not be up there; I should be with owners of baseball teams like Bud Selig and Jerry Reinsdorf."

Michaels: "But most people don't know Jerry Reinsdorf. They know Pol Pot."

Steinbrenner: "Sure they know Pol Pot. He killed a million people! Is that a joke? Linking me with these guys?"

Michaels: "No. No, absolutely not."

Steinbrenner: "I'm getting the feeling that this whole idea is just to humiliate me!"

Michaels: "Why would we do that? We're all Yankee fans!"

Michaels then brings out the sketch's writer—and future United States Senator—Al Franken, who convinces Steinbrenner he's there to represent the antithesis of the dictators, which seems to satisfy the owner. It's smart, funny stuff.

Three days after sweeping the San Diego Padres in the 1998 World Series to put an exclamation point on one of the greatest seasons ever, five members of that team showed up on *SNL* during Stiller's monologue.

*David Wells, David Cone, and Derek Jeter had a memorable turn in Saturday Night Live's "Yankee Wives" sketch in 2001.* (NBC/Photofest)

As Stiller spoke to the audience about his résumé and his latest projects, Tino Martinez walked on the stage and waved to the crowd. Stiller, unaware of Martinez's arrival, thought the applause was for him. It only got louder as Chili Davis, Graeme Lloyd, Cone, and Wells joined them on stage, getting a rise out of the crowd.

"It was cool; Ben was talking and we came out behind him, but he had no idea we were there," Wells said. "It was fun for us. That's when I really got to know Lorne Michaels. He rolls out the red carpet for Coney and I; we pretty much have carte blanche whenever we go there. He's become a really good friend of mine over these last 20 years. He's such a positive guy, it's fun to be around him. He's got great stories and he gives you positive influence on life."

Cone and Wells would have a much more memorable appearance on SNL three years later, showing up on December 1, 2001, the night Jeter hosted the show.

According to Wells, he was actually in line to host the show until the producers were able to get Jeter to agree to the gig. Wells was "a little bitter" as a result, so when coproducer Marci Klein called him about doing a cameo on the episode, Wells resisted.

"I was in New Jersey doing a signing with Coney and Don Larsen, and Marci called me to do a cameo; I said no at first, then my phone rings and it's Lorne," Wells said. "He said, 'David, this is Lorne. Are you coming to do the show?' I told him I was a little bitter and he said, 'I'll make sure you get on.' I said the only way I was going to do it was if Coney could do it with me. He said, 'Done. Here's Marci.'"

The two pitchers headed into Manhattan for the show, arriving to find out that they would be dressing in drag as "Skank No. 1" and "Skank No. 2" for a "Yankee Wives" sketch in which Jeter plays "Candy Soriano," wife of Alfonso Soriano.

"As we were driving in for dress rehearsal, they were putting the skit together," Wells said. "They had us dressing in drag and they wanted me to shave. I said, 'I ain't fuckin' shaving. The season's over; I've got my goatee and I don't have to shave anymore.' So I didn't do it."

Once Cone and Wells arrived at Studio 8H, they were ushered into the wardrobe area to get fitted for their "skank" clothes.

"I remember trying to find an outfit that worked," Cone said. "I had a little easier time than Boomer did; nothing fit him. I slipped into a little miniskirt and it was fine. They found a huge black thing that fit over him and they went with it. I did it all: nails, makeup, wig, the full Monty. I looked a little too good, I think."

Wells, goatee and all, finally found the right outfit with the help of the show's wardrobe department.

"They had to find the XXL size for me. They found a long black dress and gave me some big old boobs; during dress rehearsal, Derek started playing with them. We were cracking up. Lorne said, 'Is this going to be a problem when it's live?' We pulled it off."

Jeter's episode featured several other hilarious sketches, including his monologue, during which he injured fans as he hit baseballs into the crowd; "Derek Jeter's Taco Hole;" and of course, his point-counterpoint segment with Seth Meyers on Weekend Update, "Derek Jeter Sucks/No I Don't."

Jeter appeared on the 40th-anniversary show with Manning, introducing a segment featuring some of the most memorable athlete segments in the show's history.

Cone's take on his experiences on *SNL*? It makes a baseball clubhouse seem tame by comparison.

"It's chaotic behind the stage," Cone said. "Behind the scenes at *SNL*, there's unbelievable chaos because for every skit, there's actors running around changing wardrobe, makeup. Everyone there is unbelievably talented."

To see some of the most famous Yankees-related sketches, visit www.nbc.com/saturday-night-live.

· · · · · · · · · · · · · · · · · · · · · · · · · · · · ·

# Yada, Yada, Yada... Watch the Yankees on Seinfeld

It was the greatest sitcom in television history. So when the producers of *Seinfeld* decided to incorporate a baseball team into the fabric of the show, who else but the greatest franchise in baseball history would suffice?

With all due respect to Keith Hernandez and the "magic loogie," the Yankees' involvement with the show went far beyond George

*In the Seinfeld episode "The Wink," Kramer tries to convince an incredulous
Paul O'Neill that he must hit two home runs for the benefit of a sick child.*
(NBC/Photofest)

Costanza's fictitious job as the assistant to the traveling secretary. (No, that job does not exist.)

From Elaine Benes and her Orioles cap to Cosmo Kramer getting into a brawl with Mickey Mantle at fantasy camp after drilling one of his teammates ("Joe Pepitone or not, I own the inside of that plate!") or spotting Joe DiMaggio dunking at Dinky Donuts, *Seinfeld* used the Yankees to conjure up the absurd and insane. (As insane as trading Jay Buhner for Ken Phelps? Don't ask Frank Costanza.)

But the producers took things one step further, putting George to work for the Yankees, opening the door for some of the most memorable pinstriped cameos in TV history.

"The only reason I was even approached to do it is because I was one of the New York Yankees," said Paul O'Neill, who appeared on "The Wink" episode in 1995. "It was special. I didn't know anything about the show. The first time I was asked, I was so into the game, I didn't want to do anything outside. The year after that, my mom and dad were huge fans and I became a huge fan of the show."

In O'Neill's appearance, Kramer sneaks into the clubhouse (warning: don't try this yourself) and informs the right fielder that he has promised a sick boy that O'Neill would hit two home runs for him that night, leading to this exchange.

O'Neill: "That's ridiculous. I'm not a home run hitter."

Kramer: "Babe Ruth did it."

O'Neill: "He did not."

Kramer: "You're saying Babe Ruth was a liar?"

O'Neill: "I'm not calling him a liar...but he wasn't stupid enough to promise two."

The show sent a car to Anaheim to pick up O'Neill, who was in town to play the Angels. He wasn't sure what to expect when he got to the studio, but once he met Michael Richards, who played Kramer, he knew it was going to be an interesting day.

"I remember being in makeup and Kramer walked in," O'Neill said. "He was talking to me and I thought, 'Is this dude in character?' It was bizarre. We did it in two takes. It was fun. To be a part of that show, even today, you'll meet a couple and the guy will say, 'I remember when you won the 1998 World Series,' and his wife will say, 'You were on *Seinfeld*!'"

Buck Showalter wasn't very familiar with the show at all when he was approached to make an appearance, but at the urging of his wife and kids, he agreed to tape a scene in the auxiliary clubhouse at Anaheim Stadium early one morning in 1994.

The episode, titled "The Chaperone," was the Season 6 premiere. One storyline had George working to change the Yankees' traditional uniforms from polyester to cotton in an effort to make the players cooler throughout the summer.

He takes the idea to Showalter, who likes it. As you would expect, it does not go well. The uniforms shrink after their first washing, leading to an announcer declaring, "Oh my God! Mattingly just split his pants!"

Showalter did his six lines without incident, filming the scene with George (Jason Alexander) in one take. Danny Tartabull, who would have a hilarious appearance two episodes later ("The Pledge Drive"), also had a scene in "The Chaperone."

"It was fun," Showalter said. "I know they are used to having a lot of takes with Kramer and all those other guys. They cracked each other up. You could really tell they enjoyed being around each other and had a great rapport. I was trying to get out of there and not make many mistakes."

Derek Jeter and Bernie Williams show up in the ninth episode of Season 8, "The Abstinence." George's abstinence turns him into a

# THE BOSS—REAL AND IMAGINED

**P**utting George Costanza to work for the Yankees was a stroke of genius. Having an unseen Larry David portray George Steinbrenner? Comedic gold.

The Yankees' legendary owner "appeared" in 13 *Seinfeld* episodes between 1994 and 1998 according to IMDB.com, though the face of the actor playing him was never seen. David, the show's executive producer, provided the voice for Steinbrenner, though he never received a mention in the credits.

"After we wrote the [Steinbrenner] character, I was just talking about it with Jerry. And he said, 'Well, what is this character? What does this character sound like?' And I did the voice that I did on the show, and Jerry goes, 'Well, you should do it,'" David told *Rolling Stone* in a 2014 interview. "And I said, 'OK.' You know, it was no big deal. But we always knew that we would only see him from the back. In fact, I think we changed the guy who did it—I don't think anybody knows that."

David's portrayal of Steinbrenner took on a cartoonish quality, mocking the Boss' bombastic tone and infamous temper by taking it to another level.

"It was an actor's portrayal, but it was so perfectly done, it was funny," Paul O'Neill said.

Bernie Williams called David's Steinbrenner "one-dimensional," and while the real Steinbrenner had much more depth to him, Williams couldn't help but laugh at the portrayal on the show.

"I know that Mr. Steinbrenner had a lot more facets to his personality than what was portrayed on *Seinfeld*, but it was still hilarious," Williams said. "I was fortunate enough to meet him in many different settings and saw a lot of his sides: his compassionate side, his intense side, his emotional side, his fierce, competitive side. He was great. But seeing one of his sides portrayed on TV, it was very funny."

Buck Showalter didn't watch much television when he agreed to appear on *Seinfeld*, so he had no idea how much the show poked fun at Steinbrenner. When he discovered that his boss was being used a punch line, Showalter made a decision.

"You notice I didn't do a follow-up episode," Showalter said. "Later on, he kind of embraced the whole thing and took part in it. I wasn't told not to do it again, but it was strongly implied that it wasn't casting our owner in a really good light. I didn't know that."

The real Steinbrenner did indeed embrace the show after a few years, even filming a cameo of his own. It was set to appear in the Season 7 finale, "The Invitations."

In his first scene, Steinbrenner enters George's office while Elaine is telling him she won't attend his wedding because she doesn't have a date and won't sit at the singles table. Steinbrenner begins to lecture Elaine:

"Wait a minute, young lady. What's this about singles tables?" Steinbrenner says. "I don't sit at singles tables; singles tables are for losers! The Yankees have won 33 pennants and 22 world championships. We're winners. We don't sit with losers!"

Steinbrenner then declares that Elaine will be his date for the wedding.

"You dance, don't you? Lose a little weight, get yourself in shape, and when they throw the bridal bouquet, you'll maybe get it."

Elaine and Steinbrenner wind up on a dinner date in a second scene, where the Boss complains about not being an usher in George's wedding. Steinbrenner is in the familiar spot of having his back to the camera, but he offers to switch seats with Elaine. Once her back is to the audience, she morphs into a David-esque impression of Steinbrenner, prompting the Boss to make up a dental emergency to escape.

Sadly, both Steinbrenner scenes were cut before the show aired, but the clips are available on YouTube. I highly recommend checking them out.

genius, compelling him to offer hitting advice to the two players, fresh off their 1996 World Series victory.

> George: "Guys, hitting is not about muscle. It's simple physics. Calculate the velocity, V, in relation to the trajectory, T, in which G, gravity, of course, remains a constant. It's not complicated."

> Jeter: "Now who are you again?"

> George: "George Costanza, assistant to the traveling secretary."

> Williams: "Are you the guy who put us in that Ramada in Milwaukee?"

> George: "Do you want to talk about hotels, or do you want to win some ballgames?"

> Jeter: "We won the World Series."

> George: "In six games."

Williams and Jeter were flown to Los Angeles to film the scene, which first aired less than four weeks after the Yankees beat the Braves in the World Series.

"We spent a few hours taping the show," Williams said. "I had my goatee, because it was the offseason, so I didn't have to follow the no-facial-hair policy. It was one of the most fun things I've ever done outside of baseball, having an opportunity to be a part of that iconic show. The relationship that show had with the Yankees, it was such a fun thing to be a part of."

Williams said he doesn't get a lot of people talking about his cameo, calling it "one of the lesser-known" appearances by a player.

"I think they show my episode on reruns every once in a while, but I do see a lot of photos of me, Derek, Jason Alexander, and Jerry Seinfeld at trade shows," Williams said. "I sign a lot of those."

Considering his episode aired more than 20 years ago and the show ended its NBC run in 1998 (it lives on in syndication, of course), O'Neill is constantly amazed at how often somebody mentions his *Seinfeld* appearance to him even to this day.

"I go into the weight room in Cincinnati or New York and at least two or three times a month, someone will say, 'I saw your *Seinfeld* episode last night!'" O'Neill said. "I always laugh and think, 'Well, I have $52 coming for my residual check.' It's an iconic show that was on for a long time. To be part of it is special. It's hilarious."

Those residual checks aren't as welcome for Showalter, who joked that he has probably lost more money than he's made by appearing on the show.

"It still costs me," said Showalter, tongue firmly planted in cheek. "You had to join the actors' guild. Every time someone said, 'I saw your episode,' I go, 'Gosh, there's another income tax return I've got to file.' Because I get like $19 per episode and then you've got to pay taxes. So I end up losing money every time they show the episode by the time you pay your accountant and everything. So when someone is like, 'Hey, I saw the episode today,' I go, 'Oh geez.' I'm losing money every time they show it. I hope it goes out of syndication."

(*Seinfeld* remains in syndication everywhere, and is also available on Hulu.)

# Read Bill Madden's Two Great Yankees Books

**A**s a baseball writer for the *Daily News* for more than 35 years, Bill Madden had a front-row seat for pretty much everything that happened with the Yankees from the late 1970s through 2015.

That included a half-dozen World Series championships, countless controversies on and off the field, and, of course, nearly all of George Steinbrenner's tenure as the Yankees' principal owner.

"He was obviously a larger-than-life character," said Madden, who was honored with the Hall of Fame's J.G. Taylor Spink Award in 2010 for his meritorious contributions to baseball writing. "He was a man of many mood swings and many dimensions. He was a very complex personality."

Madden tackled the enormous task of chronicling the Boss' life in his terrific biography, *Steinbrenner: The Last Lion of Baseball*. Published in May 2010—two months before Steinbrenner's death—the book looks at Steinbrenner's ownership of the Yankees beginning with his initial 1973 purchase from CBS all the way through 2009, when the Yankees won their final World Series title under his watch.

"George was probably one of the most important figures not just in sports, but in America, during that period of the mid-1970s through the late 1990s," Madden said. "His bigger-than-life status, all the things he did. If he ever goes into the Hall of Fame, it won't be just for the championships he won, but for what he did for franchise values, television contracts and all these things in the business side of the game.

"When you look at some of the owners in the Hall of Fame, I mean, Tom Yawkey is in the Hall of Fame and George isn't'? He was the most influential and transformative owner of his time. The only guy that can even compare to him was O'Malley. What Walter O'Malley was to the '40s and '50s, George Steinbrenner was to the '70s, '80s and '90s."

Madden's book is not only a well-reported look at Steinbrenner's reign, but he had the benefit of notes and audio tapes made by former Yankees team president and general manager Gabe Paul.

Paul, who died in 1998, had kept a notebook with detailed information about Steinbrenner's purchase of the Yankees, which proved to be crucial for Madden, who did not begin covering the team until Steinbrenner had already been in charge for a few years.

"This was manna from heaven," Madden said. "[CBS chairman William S.] Paley was dead, [former Yankees president Mike] Burke was dead, and Gabe was dead, but the whole thing was written down, day by day. This was huge."

Paul had also recorded hours of audio tape during his time working for Steinbrenner, which was uncovered by one of Paul's children after his death. Madden cites the tapes in the book, making it feel like he had interviewed the late executive from the afterlife.

Steinbrenner's battles with Billy Martin, Reggie Jackson, Dave Winfield, and even Derek Jeter are chronicled in the book, which looks at Steinbrenner's banishment from baseball, his return, and the moves that helped make the Yankees a $1 billion franchise.

On the flip side from the Steinbrenner book, Madden's *Pride of October: What It Was to Be Young and a Yankee* looks at the organization's legendary history through the eyes of 18 men who helped create it.

"I wanted to tell the history of the Yankees, but not in my own narrative," Madden said. "I figured the unique way to do this would be to find Yankees from all different eras to tell the history of the

Yankees themselves. I had a relationship with almost every guy I selected. They all opened to me in a way they had never opened up before."

Among the more poignant subjects is Jerry Coleman, who played his entire nine-year career with the Yankees before moving on to a successful broadcasting career.

Coleman had also flown in both World War II and the Korean War, making him the rare baseball player to serve in two wars. As the conversation between Madden and Coleman turned toward his time in the Marines, Coleman spoke of his best friend and roommate, Max Harper, who was shot down over Korea while the two were flying next to each other.

"There was nothing I could do but follow it all the way down to mark the spot where it crashed," Coleman told Madden.

Shortly after Coleman returned home, the Yankees held a day in his honor. What should have been the greatest day of his baseball career, he said, turned into the worst when Harper's widow showed up, refusing to believe her husband was dead until she heard it from Coleman.

"He broke down and started crying," Madden said. "Here's this vibrant, virile war hero crying at our breakfast table and he said, 'I'm sorry, Billy. I don't mean to do this, but I haven't talked about this in 40 years.' I told my wife that day, 'If the rest of these guys were going to be like this guy was, this is going to be one hell of a book.'"

Madden tells equally moving stories from others including Mel Stottlemyre, who spoke in detail about the death of his youngest son, Jason, who lost a five-year battle with leukemia. Phil Rizzuto spoke of his sadness following the 9/11 terrorist attacks, telling Madden, "I'm an old man and I've seen a lot. But this...this has really got to me. I thought I lost my innocence when I went into the navy. I never thought I'd lose it again."

Don Mattingly talks about the difficulty of watching the Yankees become a dynasty immediately after his retirement, and the back injury that likely cost him a shot at the Hall of Fame. The captain tells of a sign he once saw in the stands that got him thinking about his career. It said DON MATTINGLY—THE CHOSEN ONE.

"I thought to myself, 'What does that mean, anyway? What am I chosen for?'" Mattingly said. "Now that it's done, maybe it means I was chosen to be the guy right in the middle of it all who doesn't get his shot at it."

Other Yankees profiled in *Pride of October* include Yogi Berra, Whitey Ford, Ralph Houk, Marius Russo, Tommy Byrne, Bobby Richardson, Joe Pepitone, Charlie Silvera, Ron Blomberg, Bobby Murcer, Lou Piniella, Reggie Jackson, and Paul O'Neill. Madden also dedicates a chapter to Arlene Howard, widow of Elston Howard.

"This was the human emotion," Madden said. "You're going to learn a lot more than just the history of the Yankees with this book. You'll see the human emotion of these guys, what they were really like. It all came out in this book."

· · · · · · · · · · · · · · · · · · · · · · · · · · · · · · · ·

# Delve Inside Derek Jeter's Mind with The Life You Imagine

Despite his second life as a publishing magnate, Derek Jeter isn't likely to write any tell-all books any time soon. But a book he wrote (with Jack Curry, then of the *New York Times*) in 2000 looked at 10 lessons that guided him through his first 25 years of

# STOCK YOUR LIBRARY WITH THESE YANKEES CLASSICS

There have been literally hundreds and hundreds of books written about the Yankees over the years, including the one you're reading right now.

It would take far too long to read them all, so here's a quick guide to a half-dozen to get you started.

*The Yankee Years* by Joe Torre and Tom Verducci: The Hall of Fame manager of the late-1990s/early-2000s championship teams joined with noted baseball writer/broadcaster Verducci on this 2009 book that dives into Torre's 12-year run with the Yankees. From the triumphs to the tough times, Torre takes readers inside the dugout, the clubhouse, and the front office as he and Verducci relive the glory and agony of the Yankees' most recent dynasty.

*Joe DiMaggio: The Hero's Life* by Richard Ben Cramer: Few athletes in America achieve the type of celebrity that Joe DiMaggio did, but how well did anyone really know the Yankee Clipper? Cramer spent five years reporting on this 515-page masterpiece, digging into sides of DiMaggio few people had ever seen. "Joe had been hiding his life away for more than fifty years before I ever came on the scene," Cramer told CNN in 2000.

*A Pitcher's Story: Innings with David Cone* by Roger Angell: I'm not recommending this one because Cone wrote the foreword for this book (though I do appreciate that he did), but rather because Angell is one of our greatest baseball writers, earning the Hall of Fame's J.G. Taylor Spink Award in 2014 despite never having been a member of the Baseball Writers Association of America. Angell had intended to chronicle Cone's 2000 season, which proved to be the worst of his career. Instead, the book covers Cone's entire life and career, providing plenty of great stories along the way.

*Pinstripe Empire* **by Marty Appel:** Frank Graham wrote an informal narrative history of the Yankees in 1943, but not since then had anyone tackled such a task. Appel, a former Yankees public relations executive during the 1970s, provides an in-depth look at the franchise's storied history "from before the Babe to after the Boss" in a book released in 2012.

*Driving Mr. Yogi* **by Harvey Araton:** For years, one of the great joys I had during my annual trips to spring training was watching the special friendship that Ron Guidry and Yogi Berra shared. Araton's sweet, touching story of their relationship and two lifetimes in baseball is a must-read. One of my favorite Yankees books.

*Ball Four* **by Jim Bouton:** When it was published in 1970, Bouton's inside look at the game was considered to be incredibly controversial—and is widely viewed as the most important baseball book ever written. Written in diary form, *Ball Four* follows the pitcher's 1969 season with the expansion Seattle Pilots and the Houston Astros, though Bouton chimes in about many of his former Yankees teammates along the way. In 1995, the New York Public Library included *Ball Four* on its "Books of the Century" list.

*There are literally hundreds of Yankees-related books out there, but here are some of our suggestions to polish up on pinstriped history.*
(Mark Feinsand)

life, helping him achieve his lifelong goal of playing shortstop for the Yankees.

"We all have this belief that Jeter's life and career was a magic carpet ride," Curry said. "Don't get me wrong; I'm not going to say there weren't parts of his career that were magical, but this book will take you back to when he's a teenager and he's dealing with some of the obstacles every teenager deals with.

"Dealing with being a biracial kid growing up in Michigan, many people not being tolerant of that; stories about his parents getting shut out of getting a particular apartment because his mom was white and his dad was African-American...it reminds you that everyone, no matter how great they end up becoming, has to overcome some obstacles along the way.

"That's probably the biggest selling point. It takes you back in time to remind you that he could have been a few missteps away from not becoming Derek Jeter. He could have done some dumb things along the way that cost him from getting where he eventually got."

At a young age, Jeter and his parents, Charles and Dorothy, devised a plan to help him achieve his dream. Among the rules Jeter maps out are setting your goals high, finding the right role models, thinking before you act, surrounding yourself with a strong supporting cast, and, perhaps the one he's spoken of most often throughout his career, challenging yourself and not being afraid to fail.

Curry believes that "anybody that likes Derek Jeter will get something out of the book," though *The Life You Imagine* was marketed toward younger readers.

"This was for kids who hadn't really made those life choices yet and still had life in front of them," Curry said. "Maybe Jeter telling them a story about not being afraid to fail—if you don't try to succeed and do something, you're never going to have the chance to fail—will make a difference.

"That was one chapter that always stood out for me. Jeter could be 0-for-20 with 19 strikeouts, down 0–2 against Pedro Martinez, and he believed he was getting a hit. He had that mental strength. This book points out some of where that came from. From a young age, he wasn't afraid to fail and he had a lot of confidence in his abilities. A 50-year-old could read this book and still get something out of it."

# See Bernie Williams in Concert

Since he was eight years old, Bernie Williams has been consumed by two loves: baseball and music.

The Puerto Rico native was exposed to sports, music, and arts by his mother, Rufina, an educator for 40 years.

"They were staples in my life," Williams said.

Attending a performing arts high school, Williams was a well-rounded child, one his mother figured would go on to a professional career as a doctor, lawyer, architect, or engineer. But as his baseball skills flourished, it became obvious that Williams was destined for something else.

Williams signed with the Yankees on his 17th birthday, launching what would be a glorious 16-year major league career that saw him hit .297 with 287 home runs and 1,257 RBI, earn five All-Star selections, and win four World Series titles.

"I was able to make sports the way that I made my living for a long time," Williams said. "When it came to music, that was something I always did."

Williams brought his love of music into the Yankees clubhouse, often sitting in his corner locker at the old Yankee Stadium with nothing but his guitar and his thoughts.

"He'd sit in his locker and play," teammate Joe Girardi said. "That's what brought him peace and got him ready to go every day."

Williams would sometimes play with teammate Paul O'Neill, a drummer in his spare time. The two even filmed a television commercial for MSG Network, jamming together in the team's locker room.

"I knew he was good, but I didn't realize he was as good as he was," O'Neill said. "He was a little more skilled than I was."

In 2003, Williams released his first album, *The Journey Within*, personally composing seven of the 13 tracks. The album also included his takes on Kansas' "Dust in the Wind" and Billy Joel's "And So It Goes," among others. His debut effort was widely praised, reaching No. 3 on Billboard's Contemporary Jazz chart.

During the 2003 All-Star break, I had a chance to see Williams play a concert at the House of Blues in Chicago. If you didn't know he was the center fielder for the Yankees, it would have been easy to assume he had been performing on stage his entire life.

Williams' final season with the Yankees was 2006, though he didn't officially announce his retirement for nearly a decade.

Three years after his final game, Williams released his second album, appropriately titled *Moving Forward*. The recording featured guest appearances by Bruce Springsteen, Jon Secada, and others, debuting at No. 2 on the Billboard Contemporary Jazz chart. Two singles from the record, "Go for It" and "Ritmo de Otono," reached No. 1 and the album was nominated for a Latin Grammy Award in the Best Instrumental Album category.

"Once I was done with baseball, I started really focusing more on music," Williams said. "It got me away from thinking that I could still play baseball, and it gave me an outlet that I could still be challenged.

"One of the biggest challenges for a person in my line of work is finding something as challenging as baseball was for me as far as being engaged, getting that rush and feeling like I have a purpose. Waking up every morning thinking about facing a guy with a 95 mph fastball, being in a pennant race, going through slumps, things like that; there aren't a lot of things in normal life that compare to those things, especially for the amount of time that I did it.

"You get used to all of that excitement, those emotions and intensity and a life full of those things. For me, it was important to find something that mentally and intellectually kept me challenged and pushed me outside of my comfort zone that I could become better and better at every day. I found that in music."

Having already studied guitar and composition for a year at the State University of New York at Purchase, Williams continued his education in 2013 after being accepted into the Manhattan School of Music to begin as a sophomore.

"In many ways, I considered it starting over again," Williams said. "That definitely kept me up; studying, doing projects and interacting with many young, talented people, it kept me in that mode. I had played professional baseball up to the highest level, winning championships with one of the best franchises in sports, but here I was, a virtually unknown musician trying to make it. It required a lot of work."

That work paid off three years later, as Williams graduated with a Bachelor of Music degree in jazz guitar. At 47 years old, Williams was ready to start the next phase of his career.

His baseball career helped him when it came to discipline and perseverance, but that's where the comparison between the two trades ended for Williams.

"Playing music has a different dimension than playing professional sports," Williams said. "Playing music touches my spirit more. I'm able to reach my soul better than I was doing playing baseball. The competition is more for me, in myself, then competing against a pitcher or a team. Music has provided a soulfulness and spirituality that is really refreshing.

"The better I get, the more I understand music, the more I'm humbled to the fact that anything I could ever think of, somebody else probably thought of it or did it 600 years earlier—and they were better and more efficient. It's about finding a personal journey for me in music as opposed to being a flat-out competition to see who is the best."

Williams has kept a connection to the Yankees, who retired his No. 51 in 2015. The previous September, he took the field at Fenway Park and played "Take Me Out to the Ballgame" prior to the final game of Derek Jeter's career.

The work ethic he displayed during two decades of professional baseball has carried over to his music career. Williams works tirelessly at his trade, though most of the time playing guitar doesn't feel like work for him.

"The highest compliment that I could ever get would be that I'm a musician that happened to be a baseball player at some point in their life," Williams said. "Once I started thinking about all this stuff in the grand scheme of things, I figured that I was approaching baseball the same way I would approach art. Paying attention to detail, working really hard on my craft, just finding a way to make it more art as opposed to just mechanical. It just kind of fits in with what I'm doing with music."

Just as he did with his teammates in the Bronx, Williams views his work with his "All-Star Band" as a group effort, even if he happens to be the headline name people are coming to see.

"When you collaborate with people in music, it's all about the sum of the parts, not necessarily being a soloist or the center of attention," Williams said. "It's about being a team player, trying to be a contributor to the sum of the parts so the music itself sounds as good as it can possibly sound."

While Williams routinely headlines concerts in the tri-state area, he can often be found in one of Westchester's small music clubs, making an impromptu appearance during one of their open mic nights. He's not doing it to keep himself sharp, but simply to feel the rush of sharing a musical experience with a live audience.

"As a musician, you kind of savor those moments when you are able to play in front of an audience," Williams said. "It's gratifying to have people relate to what you're doing, and actually feeling the same emotions that you're feeling when you're in that moment of time, grooving to whatever you're playing. It's exhilarating. It's part of my DNA right now; I just want to play as much as I can."

While Williams' early shows were heavily attended by Yankees fans, he has seen a change in the crowd's demographics in recent years. He is always happy to see his baseball fans in attendance, though he hopes they leave with an appreciation for his new career and feel inspired to come back for another show.

"I think I'm making the transition with the Yankees fans in the sense of having then coming to the concerts because they want to support a former Yankee and they're curious to see if I can really play," Williams said. "What has been happening over the course of time is that people stay because they actually do like the music for what it is. It has nothing to do with baseball.

"As a player, as an artist, I can never divorce myself from the fact that I'm a former Yankee—and I will always be a Yankee, which has helped me tremendously with opening doors. For the avid music listener, I know for a fact it has nothing to do with anything. They come and pay money to see a show; to be entertained. I can sprinkle a couple Yankees stories in there, but the bread and butter of the show is the music."

For more information on Williams' tour dates, visit bernie51.com or follow Bernie at facebook.com/berniewilliamsofficial or on Twitter at @bw51official.

# Watch Nine Innings From Ground Zero

New York was a strange place to be in the days and weeks after the terrorist attacks of 9/11. While rescue and recovery efforts continued at Ground Zero, New Yorkers did their best to return to their everyday lives, but in reality, life would never be quite the same again.

The city's baseball teams returned to work a week after the attacks, though many players wondered whether it was appropriate to be playing games while the city tried to recover from the worst event in New York's history.

But as both the Mets and Yankees would quickly learn, they were a vital part of the city's healing.

HBO's 2004 documentary *Nine Innings From Ground Zero* looks at the impact that baseball had on the city during this difficult time, and if you didn't live there at the time, its influence might surprise you.

"It kept my mind off of everything else that was happening," said Stacey Gotsulias, a former Yankees ticketholder who was interviewed for the film. "For those few hours a night, either at home watching the games or being in the stadium, although being in the stadium was nerve-racking because of the increased police presence and wondering if, who knows, maybe someone might blow Yankee Stadium up. It was an uneasy time. I felt better watching the games at home, but I felt defiant being at the stadium for a game."

Several Yankees fans who lost family members in the attacks are interviewed in the documentary, recounting their personal tales while discussing how baseball—the Yankees' run to the World Series, in particular—helped them get through the toughest period in their lives.

*Newsday* sportswriter Shaun Powell, whose brother, Scott, was killed in the Pentagon attack, is particularly moving as he discusses his personal story of covering the Yankees while dealing with his own grief.

"I liked the diversity of the people that they interviewed; they interviewed firefighters, they interviewed people who lost someone, and they interviewed regular shmoes like me," Gotsulias said. "They interviewed players that were involved in the series. They did a good job of weaving it all together."

The documentary begins with footage of the final at-bat of the 2001 World Series, followed by sights of workers at Ground Zero. While the city dealt with the aftershock, the Yankees and Mets did their part to help out any way they could.

With Shea Stadium's parking lot transformed into a staging area, manager Bobby Valentine and his players helped load trucks with water and supplies. The Yankees traveled downtown to the Armory, where families were awaiting word—and holding out hope—on the fate of their missing loved ones.

"We didn't really know if we should be there," manager Joe Torre said in the film. "This is where families were all gathered to wait on word if their loved ones were alive. If they weren't alive, evidence that they weren't alive, so they were doing DNA samplings.

"I remember one very poignant moment when Bernie Williams went up to this woman and he was sort of fumbling and he said, 'I don't know what to say, but you look like you need a hug,' and he put his arms around her. I think it sort of broke the ice to see that these people needed this. At that point in time, I realized that there was a role for us."

Scott Brosius recalled thinking to himself, *What am I doing here? What do I have to offer these people?* It wouldn't take long for him to realize that he and his Yankees teammates had plenty to offer a city in need of something to smile about.

After play resumed on September 18, the Yankees—who had a sizeable lead in the American League East—cruised into the postseason. They dropped the first two games against the Athletics in the AL Division Series, but with the help of Derek Jeter's famed "Flip play," they won both games in Oakland before winning Game 5 in the Bronx to advance to the AL Championship Series.

"It was amazing to see the transformation because for the rest of that year, anyway, we weren't the hated Yankees," Brosius said in the film. "It was kind of like we were the symbol for these people in New York going through this."

The Yankees trounced the 116-win Seattle Mariners in five games to advance to the World Series. As New York tried to heal, the Yankees were giving the city something to cheer for.

"Watching the games kept my mind off the fact that anthrax was being found in the building where I worked or that they started bombing in Afghanistan," Gotsulias said. "It was definitely an escape. There was a feeling of, 'Should this really be happening?' But it definitely helped."

"It was almost like the city needed something to try to get away from it just for a few hours," Paul O'Neill said in the film. "It gave people something to look forward to the next day, all the way into the World Series."

The World Series began in Arizona, where the Diamondbacks won the first two games. As the series shifted back to New York—where the New York City Marathon was also set to be run that week—the mayor's office was dealing with the potential for further attacks as the city was put on high alert.

The decision was made to allow the games to take place.

"There was something about baseball, which is the American sport," Mayor Rudy Giuliani said in the film. "And it's outdoors, and it's in the fall, and it was right in the city that had been brutally attacked. It had a wonderful impact on the morale of the people of the city. It was exactly what they needed to get their eyes up off the ground, looking into the future."

The Yankees closed the gap in the series with a Game 3 victory, though the game was only the second most memorable event of the night. It was October 30, only seven weeks after the attacks, that President George W. Bush took the field to throw out the ceremonial first pitch, and whether you leaned Democrat or Republican, you likely felt pride in your country's leader that night.

Bush, dressed in a bulletproof vest, warmed up in the underground batting cages, wanting to make a good, strong impression on the country with his effort.

"I wanted to make sure that if I was going to throw out the ball, I was able to do so with a little zip," Bush said in the film. "I didn't want people to think that their president was incapable of finding the plate."

Jeter even offered some advice to Bush: throw from the mound—and make sure it crosses the plate.

"He's walking out and he looks over his shoulder and he says, 'Don't bounce it. They'll boo you,'" Bush said.

Bush delivered a perfect pitch to Yankees catcher Todd Greene, causing the stadium to erupt with chants of "USA! USA!"

"I'd never felt what I felt before when I walked out of that dugout," Bush said. "I felt the raw emotion of the Yankee fans."

The Yankees would win Games 4 and 5 thanks to two of the most amazing feats ever, as Tino Martinez and Brosius each hit two-out, two-run home runs in the ninth inning to tie the game against Arizona closer Byung-Hyun Kim. Jeter's "Mr. November" home run won Game 4, while Alfonso Soriano's 12th-inning hit sent the Yankees back to Arizona only one win from a title the entire country (outside of Phoenix) seemed to be pulling for.

"Those two games were absolutely like miracles," Giuliani said in the film. "They just lifted the spirits of New York. The Yankees, whether they could accept this or not through humility or whatever, really had the city on their shoulders."

The Diamondbacks won Game 6, forcing a winner-take-all Game 7.

"Few events in sports can compare to a seventh game of a World Series," narrator Liev Schreiber said in the film. "This one would be the culmination of a series that, in its own humble way, had served a grander purpose. And no one wanted to see it end. On this night, fans of a wounded nation would have one last chance to lose themselves in a baseball game."

The Yankees took a one-run lead into the ninth before Arizona stunned the world with its comeback win against Mariano Rivera. The Yankees may not have won the World Series, but as *Nine Innings From Ground Zero* recounts during a memorable one-hour documentary, "You're this close to just having something really cool; not just for us and not just winning, but for the city," Brosius said in the film. "Life is not fair. If there's ever a fair time for the Yankees to win the World Series, that was the year."

(*Nine Innings From Ground Zero* is available on Amazon.com and can also be seen on YouTube.)

# Make a Playlist of Famous Yankees' Walk-Up/Entrance/Warm-Up Music

It's unclear when major league players began personalizing music for their at-bats, warm-ups or, in the case of relief pitchers, entrances into the game, but is there any fan out there that doesn't think of Mariano Rivera every time they hear Metallica's "Enter Sandman" on the radio?

Players' music has become as much a part of the ballpark experience as hot dogs and Cracker Jack, blaring over the PA system as each player steps to the plate or jogs in from the bullpen.

But how did this tradition start? It wasn't until the early 1990s that teams began to play specific songs for players, though it was common back then for the teams, not the players, to select the music.

Personalized entrance music for relievers became a trend after Charlie Sheen's character in the 1989 movie *Major League* entered games to "Wild Thing" by the Troggs, though Yankees reliever Sparky Lyle is believed to be the first pitcher to ever have his own custom music played as he made his way in from the bullpen.

"There was something so dramatic, such a great flair, almost like WWF, of Sparky coming into a game," said Marty Appel, who was a Yankees public relations executive while Lyle pitched for the team. "I asked a friend of mine who was a musician to give me some music that would go with such an entrance. He said, 'Pomp and Circumstance' is like a culmination—the end.' It was perfect.

"Toby Wright was our organist and the whole drill was I'd watch with binoculars to see if Sparky was getting into the car and then I'd pick up the direct phone to Toby and I'd say, 'It's Lyle.' The music would start and the place would go crazy. After all those Horace Clarke years, it was such drama at Yankee Stadium, it was a monumental thing. From that came all the entrance music and walk-up music you hear today."

As it turned out, Lyle wasn't a fan of the music, telling Appel and Wright to knock it off at some point, though the trend picked up again years later and hasn't faded.

"Sparky wanted the music to stop," Appel said. "He said it added extra pressure and he didn't need it."

As walk-up music became the norm in the mid-1990s, players were beginning to customize it themselves. Some would change it up weekly or monthly, while others chose a song or two (or three or four) and stuck with it for years.

"Jeet and those guys would change it weekly, but once I picked it, that was it forever," said Paul O'Neill. "Every time I hear 'Baba O'Riley' or Mellencamp, it brings me back to coming up to the plate."

The first few notes of The Who's "Baba O'Riley" still evoke memories of O'Neill walking to the plate, though he also used Bon Jovi's "Keep the Faith" and John Cougar Mellencamp's "Crumblin' Down" for his at-bats. O'Neill remembered one specific at-bat during the 2000 World Series against the Mets during which he got to hear far more of "Baba O'Riley" than he ever had before.

"I was going to hit off Mike Hampton and they started my music," O'Neill said. "Usually you only hear like 30 seconds of it, but as I started to go out, Bobby Valentine was going to the mound. I got to sit there and listen to that for like a minute and a half, which was so awesome."

To this day, those three songs have the ability to get O'Neill focused the moment he hears them.

"When I'm in the weight room and it comes on, it's like I'm getting ready to hit again," he said. "It never leaves. Some things are just ingrained in you."

That's how CC Sabathia feels when he hears the Notorious B.I.G.'s "Big Poppa," which he's used as his warm-up track since his first season with the Yankees in 2009.

"I started off the first half of the season looking for something iconic, something New York," Sabathia said. "I'm a big rap fan. That year, [his wife] Amber and I went on vacation during the All-Star break and that song was playing. She said, 'Why don't you just come out to this?' I've always been a huge Biggie fan, so it just kind of fit. It works for me."

Although he's heard plenty of songs that would work for him, Sabathia has stuck with the song for his entire run in pinstripes.

"It gets me fired up," Sabathia said. "That's my song. I've had it for so long now; nobody else uses it in the league."

Sabathia may not have changed his own music, but that didn't mean he didn't have input in new tunes at the Stadium. Derek Jeter used to change his walk-up music frequently, often relying on suggestions from friends including Sabathia and Jorge Posada.

"Jeet was very superstitious, obviously," Sabathia said. "It would take something happening for him to want to change. It was always fun to be able to help him come up with the song he was going to play. I felt good to be in that council."

For every player like Sabathia who puts time and effort into choosing their music, there's a guy like Brett Gardner, who simply picks whatever is his favorite country song at the start of the season and sticks with it until the following year.

"I'm not really a big music guy," Gardner said. "I don't really have a favorite artist, but I'll just find a song that I like. Country music doesn't really pump you up that much, but maybe it takes my mind to a good place."

Some players have their music chosen for them, then choose to stick with what's working. Rivera had no role in selecting "Enter Sandman" for himself, but after a stadium scoreboard employee began playing it for the closer, it just stuck.

Same with Didi Gregorius, who walks to the plate to the Notorious B.I.G.'s "Notorious B.I.G" track. You see, "Notorious" kind of rhymes with "Gregorius," something a minor league scoreboard employee in Billings, Montana, took note of in 2009.

"Every time I got a hit, they would play that song," Gregorius said. "It was one of the best years I had in the minors, so people were like, 'You have to stick with the song!' That's how I got stuck with 'Notorious' as my music. I decided to stay with it. It's close enough to my name, and it's Biggie, so I like it."

In the spirit of an old mix tape combined with a baseball roster, here's my favorite lineup of Yankees walk-up/entrance/warm-up music from the past 20 years:

## Lineup

Derek Jeter: "Otis" by Jay Z and Kanye West

Paul O'Neill: "Baba O'Riley" by The Who

Nick Swisher: "Buzzin'" by Mann

Mark Teixeira: "Alive" by Pearl Jam

Jason Giambi: "Rock Star" by N.E.R.D.

Alex Rodriguez: "Run This Town" by Jay Z

Brett Gardner: "Guitar Slinger" by Crossin Dixon

Tino Martinez: "You Shook Me All Night Long" by AC/DC

Chase Headley: "Here I Go Again" by Whitesnake

**Starting Rotation**

CC Sabathia: "Big Poppa" by the Notorious B.I.G.

Phil Hughes: "For Whom the Bell Tolls" by Metallica

Mike Mussina: "The Zoo" by The Scorpions

Andy Pettitte: "The Boys of Summer" by The Ataris

A.J. Burnett: "Returns a King" from the *300* soundtrack

**Bullpen**

Gabe White: "Seven Nation Army" by The White Stripes

Mike Stanton: "Fantasy" by Aldo Nova

Steve Karsay: "Down with the Sickness" by Disturbed

Joba Chamberlain: "Shout at the Devil" by Mötley Crüe

Andrew Miller: "God's Gonna Cut You Down" by Johnny Cash

Mariano Rivera: "Enter Sandman" by Metallica

· · · · · · · · · · · · · · · · · · · · · · · · · · · · · · ·

# Relive the Summer of '61 with 61*

**W**hen Billy Crystal was 13, he was always Mickey Mantle. It didn't matter who else was playing in the stickball game; Crystal was No. 7.

He never imagined years later that he would become a friend of Mantle's—or that he would direct a movie about the most exciting sports summer of his childhood, watching Mantle and teammate Roger Maris go head-to-head as they tried to chase down Babe Ruth's single-season home run record.

"I was so fortunate to become a really good friend of Mickey's, and he started telling me stories about that summer that I didn't think people were aware of," Crystal said. "They grew to be such friends even though they were in such a fierce competition—albeit on the same team and at different points in their career."

HBO was working on a film about Mantle and Maris, but when the script made its way to Crystal, he realized he knew more about the story than what was in the script. He began working with writer Hank Steinberg and HBO executive Ross Greenburg, trying to make the project as accurate as possible.

"I knew so much about that season; it was so indelibly set in my mind, I remembered all of these things," Crystal said. "It wasn't so much the way the stadium looked, because you can do that from photographs; it was the feeling in the ballpark, the plays that Maris made in right field, the great series against Detroit when Mantle pulls a forearm muscle and basically hits a home run one-handed. I remember all of those things. I tried to give it the authenticity that so many baseball movies don't have.

"I wanted to make an accurate movie about two amazing athletes who shared a summer together that was just extraordinary."

Crystal had signed on as a producer, but it wasn't until he went on a scouting trip to old Tiger Stadium in Detroit that he agreed to direct the film.

"Ross said, 'You've got to do this.' I said, 'Where are you going to find a Maris and Mantle? Where are you going to find a ballpark? The stadium didn't look like it did; it's going to look phony,'" Crystal said. "Then we flew to Detroit because the Tigers had abandoned the great old stadium for Comerica, and it was two days before Thanksgiving, so it was freezing. The almost winter light on the ballpark was so gorgeous, and when we walked around, the clubhouse, they were there. Those low-roof dugouts, they were there. It looked like the stadium.

"It was one of those last old decked ballparks that had the same vertical majesty that the original stadium had. I started thinking of shots, looking at shots; 'I could do this, I could do that; boy, we can really make this look real.' Before I got on the plane to go back to California, I said, 'OK, let's do this.' Once I knew I could tell the story right, that's what really made we want to do it because I knew I could."

Crystal's friendship with Mantle gave him insight into the Hall of Famer that few others had, but when he met with Mantle's widow, Merlyn, and their sons, Danny and David, the family gave him their blessing to tell the story the way it happened.

"I couldn't sugarcoat it; to a degree, he did womanize, he did drink. I think we did it with an honesty that wasn't rubbing it in anyone's face, especially the family," Crystal said. "They said, 'You have to tell the truth. It wouldn't be right if you didn't tell the truth.' They respected that I did it the right way.

"The same with Roger and his surliness, his moodiness. Telling it without being salacious about it, but yet truthfully presenting who they were, that was a goal. I wouldn't have done the movie if I couldn't do that."

With the script polished to his liking, Crystal had another tall task: He needed his Mantle and Maris.

Finding his Maris proved to be easier than expected. Crystal went to see *Saving Private Ryan* in the theater, where Barry Pepper's face jumped off the screen.

"I said, 'Oh my god, that's Roger Maris! Look at him!'" Crystal said. "And he was left-handed."

Once Crystal convinced Pepper to take the role, he still needed his Mantle. He met with actor Thomas Jane, who flew up from Mexico to discuss the part with Crystal. HBO executives weren't excited by the choice, but Crystal seemed convinced that he had his man.

"Tom is a wonderfully gifted actor, but he has certain quirky oddities that are very endearing and also very strange," Crystal said. "He told me he was a football player and that yes, he had played baseball—but he was also barefoot in the meeting. His hair was down to his shoulders for the movie and he's smoking."

Crystal showed Jane a sizzle reel he had put together of Mantle, a compilation of his great moments on the field and footage of him at other events, even some of him telling inappropriate jokes.

"I watched him sort of move his neck around while he watched him; he almost got bigger during the meeting because he was so enthralled," Crystal said. "I fought for him to be cast."

Crystal got a No. 7 jersey for Jane, pinned his hair up and taught him not only how to do Mantle's Oklahoma accent, but also what kind of answers he would often give to reporters.

"I interviewed him a place where it looked like he was at batting practice," Crystal said. "It was a three-minute screen test and I brought it to HBO, who didn't want him originally. I said, 'I've got this guy. Take a look at this guy.' They didn't recognize him and they said, 'Wow, who is this?' I said, 'That's Thomas Jane, the guy you don't want.' They said, 'Well, now we do.'"

With his leads cast, Crystal ran into one significant problem: Pepper was a natural ballplayer, but Jane had no idea what he was doing.

"That was a nice little surprise after I cast him," Crystal said.

Reggie Smith, a 17-year veteran with 314 career home runs, had been hired as a technical advisor for the film. Crystal brought Jane to Smith's academy in the valley—again, barefoot and smoking a cigarette—to have him meet with Smith.

"Here's Reggie Smith, one of the best switch-hitters of all time and a terrific outfielder, who had played against both Mickey and Roger," Crystal said. "The first thing I hear Tom say is, 'How do I hold the ball?' I looked up and said, 'You told me you played.' He just looked at me and smiled. At which point I reached up, took the cigarette out of his mouth and said 'OK, you're going to become a baseball player.'"

Smith told Crystal to give him two weeks with Jane. Don't call, don't check in, just let them work. And trust him.

Two weeks later, Crystal drove out to Smith's academy to see if Jane had learned to play.

"I said, 'Where's Tom?' Reggie said, 'Tom's not here.'" Crystal said. "I see in the outfield, a guy shagging balls. Reggie yells, 'Mickey!' and Mantle catches a ball—it's Tom—and he runs in with that limp that looks like it's painful. Then he says a greeting to me the way Mickey always greeted me: 'Hey, you little son of a bitch, how you doing?' I was like, 'Oh my god.'

"He had taught him Mantle's swing from both sides of the plate; how the knee caved in a little bit when he would swing. There it was."

The chore of casting the rest of the Yankees—as well as many of their opponents—was one Crystal embraced. Since most of the baseball scenes were being shot in Detroit, they held a tryout for "players" there, with about a thousand actors/players showing up.

"My memory of the players they played against was crazy; I was like Rain Main," Crystal said. "I'd say, 'That guy's a lefty first baseman—he could be Norm Cash. This guy, he's a Frank Lary. This guy could be Hank Aguirre.' On and on and on until we had cast great lookalikes for everybody, especially the Yankees. Great Bobby Richardson, terrific Moose Skowron, Yogi, Elston Howard. It was so much fun. I don't think I've ever had as much passion doing anything except my Broadway show in making something."

Crystal relied on Academy Award–winning cinematographer Haskell Wexler for many details, such as right-handed Anthony Michael Hall playing lefty ace Whitey Ford.

"We flipped the film to make him look lefty; he actually wore the number 61 on his back so it would be 16," Crystal said. "We had done vast research on the teams that they would play, how to change the ballparks around so it looked like we were on the road at Fenway, Griffith Stadium in Washington, Baltimore."

The day before shooting was set to start at Tiger Stadium–turned–Yankee Stadium, Crystal organized a practice for his Yankees team, uniforms and all. As a special surprise, Yogi Berra attended the practice, quickly pointing out to Crystal that the monuments in the outfield needed to be shifted about six feet to the right.

"Yogi walks out, greets me, and tears come to his eyes," Crystal said. "He said, 'Oh my god, look at the ballpark.' Then he looks at me and says, 'You know I hit one on the roof here, kid. I told Mel (Allen) I was gonna do it, too. I pointed up to him, waved to him in the press box and said, 'I'm going out.' It's not only Ruth—I called a shot, too.'"

Also at the practice were Danny, David, and Merlyn Mantle, who got their first look at Jane as the late Mick.

"The way the sun was hitting the 7 and the 9 was just ridiculous; the sound of batting practice, people shagging, Merlyn took one look at Tom and just gasped," Crystal said. "She said, 'Oh my god.' I waved to him, he came running in with that same limp, meets the family and they all hugged him. It was like Mickey had come to life for a few minutes in what would be probably the greatest year of his career. It was amazing to be able to witness all this stuff."

Marty Appel, the former Yankees public relations executive, served as a consultant for the film, helping Crystal make sure every nugget was as accurate as it could be.

"The attention to detail was very important to Billy," Appel said. "We had to make sure we got everything just right. It captured the fact that you would wake up in the morning and want to know if Mickey or Roger hit one. It was important."

The film follows Mantle and Maris through the entire 1961 season as they each slugged home runs at a prodigious pace. We all know how the race turned out—and the controversy that accompanied Maris' pursuit of the record, which he finally broke in the 162<sup>nd</sup> game of the season—but Crystal's film takes fans so much deeper inside the season, it almost feels like a documentary.

"This was just the perfect thing for me to do at that point in my life," Crystal said. "I reveled in it because everyone seemed real. They all seemed real to me. When we were shooting a restaurant scene with Mantle, Maris, Ellie Howard, Yogi, and Whitey, and they're talking about how DiMaggio was coming to throw out the first pitch and Mickey gets cranky, I was able to feed Anthony the right way to say it because I had spoken to Whitey about it.

"My research was beyond books and looking at tapes because I've had the fortune of knowing a lot of these guys and having conversations with them. I didn't want to let them down; I wanted it to be as accurate as I could. It was beyond fun. It was perfect. It was a perfect thing for me to be a part of."

Since it debuted on HBO in 2001, *61\** has been screened in Maris' hometown of Fargo, North Dakota, to commemorate the 50<sup>th</sup> anniversary of Maris' 61<sup>st</sup> home run, as well as in Cooperstown, where the script and several of the movie's artifacts were admitted to the Baseball Hall of Fame.

How realistic was *61\**?

"When Bryce Harper was breaking into the majors, they asked him who his favorite baseball player was and he said Mickey Mantle," Crystal said. "They asked him if he's ever seen him play and he said, 'No, but I saw the movie *61\**.' I wanted to tell him, 'Tom Jane is your favorite baseball player.'"

# Sources

## Articles

Araton, Harvey. "A Yankee's Forgiveness Won't Be Forgotten." *The New York Times*. Sept. 23, 2015.

Associated Press. "Cone Is Sharp in Return." *Los Angeles Times*. Sept. 3, 1996.

Associated Press. "Middle of Order Powers Yankees." *ESPN.com*. Oct. 17, 2004.

Associated Press. "Yankees' Bullpen Comes Apart in 14th." *ESPN.com*. Oct. 19, 2004.

Associated Press. "Boston's Blow Out Caps Unequaled Comeback." *ESPN.com*. Oct. 21, 2004.

Botte, Peter. "Memories of Maier as Yanks Take on O's." *Daily News*. Oct. 7, 2012.

Coffey, Wayne. "When Lightning Struck; Ron Guidry Reflects on His Brilliant Season of 1978." *Daily News*. June 21, 1998.

Doherty, Rosaleen. "Lou Gehrig Retires from Yankees as 'the Luckiest Man' in 1939." *Daily News*. July 5, 1939.

Feinsand, Mark. "Jeter's new nickname a perfect fit." MLB.com. Nov. 1, 2001.

Feinsand, Mark. "A-Rod Powers Yanks to Victory." *Yankees.com*. April 27, 2005.

Feinsand, Mark. "A-Rod's Historic Night in the Bronx." *Yankees.com*. April 27, 2005.

Feinsand, Mark. "CAREER CAP-ER! Derek Jeter Delivers Game-winning Hit in Final Yankee Stadium At-bat." *Daily News*. Sept. 26, 2014.

Feinsand, Mark. "Thurman Munson Legacy Lives on in Awards Dinner." *Daily News*. Jan. 24, 2015.

Fenn, Lisa. "Chris Chambliss Remembers His Walk-off HR." *ESPN.com*. Oct. 21, 2010.

Greenhouse, Pat. "Ted's Williams Blasts Longest Home Run in Fenway Park." *The Boston Globe*. June 10, 1946.

Maier, Jeffrey. "How a Home Run Changed My Life." *Bleacher Report*. Apr 6, 2014.

McCarron, Anthony. "Storming History: Yanks Belt 3 Slams, Top A's 22–9." *Daily News*. Aug. 25, 2011.

McCarron, Anthony. "Derek Jeter Moments: The Game That Made Him Mr. November." *Daily News*. Sept. 25, 2014.

Muskat, Carrie. " Martinez, Jeter stun D-Backs to even series." MLB.com. Nov. 1, 2001.

Pepe, Phil. "Chris Chambliss Home Run Ends 12-year Drought in 1976." *Daily News*. Oct. 13, 2015.

Sandomir, Richard. "Mel Allen Is Dead at 83; Golden Voice of Yankees." *The New York Times*. June 16, 1996.

Smith, Claire. "Allie Reynolds, Star Pitcher For Yankees, Is Dead at 79." *The New York Times*. Dec. 27, 1994.

Trimble, Joe. "Yankees' Don Larsen Pitches World Series Perfect Game in '56." *Daily News*. Oct. 9, 1956.

Wenner, Gus. "Yada, Yada, Yada: Larry David Looks Back at 25 Years of *Seinfeld*." *Rolling Stone*. July 7, 2014.

### Websites

Baseball-Reference.com

BaseballHall.org

Yankees.com

RedSox.com

Orioles.com

Mets.com

NBC.com

*YesNetwork.com*

http://sabr.org

YouTube.com

MLB.com

CNN.com

USAToday.com

IMDB.com

## Books

Appel, Marty. *Pinstripe Empire: The New York Yankees from before the Babe to after the Boss.* New York: Bloomsbury, 2012.

Berkow, Ira. *The Gospel According to Casey.* New York: St. Martin's Press, 1992.

Madden, Bill. *Pride of October: What It Was to Be Young and a Yankee.* New York: Warner, 2003.

# About the Author

Mark Feinsand has covered the Yankees and Major League Baseball since 2001 for the New York *Daily News* and MLB.com. He appears regularly on multiple television and radio outlets including MLB Network, YES Network, and WFAN.